# Sport and International Politics

# Sport and International Politics

*Edited by*

# Pierre Arnaud and James Riordan

**E & FN SPON**
An imprint of Routledge
London and New York

First published 1998
by E & FN Spon, an imprint of Routledge
11 New Fetter Lane, London EC4P 4EE

Simultaneously published in the USA and Canada
by Routledge
29 West 35th Street, New York, NY 10001

Selection and editorial matter © 1998 James Riordan and Pierre Arnaud;
individual chapters © their contributors

Typeset in Baskerville by M Rules
Printed and bound in Great Britain by St Edmundsbury Press

*British Library Cataloguing in Publication Data*
A catalogue record for this book is available from the British Library

*Library of Congress Cataloguing in Publication Data*
A catalogue record for this book has been requested

ISBN 0–419–21440–2

*Sport and International Politics* is the story of how, between 1918 and 1939, sport spilled over the boundaries of national states and became truly international.

To create national strength through sports training, and international harmony through sporting competition.

(Pierre de Coubertin, Revue des sports, Brussels, 1920)

# Contents

**11  Between revolutionary demands and diplomatic necessity: the uneasy relationship between Soviet sport and worker and bourgeois sport in Europe from 1920 to 1937**          **184**
ANDRÉ GOUNOT

**12  Interwar sport and interwar relations: some conclusions          210**
RICHARD HOLT

# Contributors

**Teresa Gonzalez Aja** is Director of the Instituto Nacional de Educacion Fisica, Madrid, Spain.

**Pierre Arnaud** is Director of the Centre de Recherche et d'Innovation sur le Sport, Université Claude Bernard, Lyon, 1, France.

**André Gounot** is Lecturer at the Institut für Sportwissenschaften der Frei Universität Berlin, Germany.

**Allen Guttmann** is Head of the Department of English at Amherst College, MA, USA.

**Richard Holt** is Visiting Professor at the Faculteit Lichamelijke Opvoeding en Kinesitherapie, Katholieke Universiteit Leuven, Belgium.

**Arnd Krüger** is Director of the Institut für Sportwissenschaften, Georg-August Universität, Göttingen, Germany

**James Riordan** is Academic Head of the Department of Linguistic and International Studies, University of Surrey, Guildford, UK.

**Angela Teja** is Lecturer at the Instituto Superiore di Educazione, Rome, Italy.

**Jan Tolleneer** is Chief Librarian, Katholieke Universiteit Leuven, Campus Kortrijk, Belgium.

# Acknowledgements

Thanks are due to James Riordan, Josh Ord-Hume, Richard Holt and Alessandra Fazio for their work in the translation and editing of this book.

# Introduction

*James Riordan*

Sport became truly international only after the First World War. It was then that politicians began to appreciate its potential as a vehicle of national values and policies – even for demonstrating and advertising the potency of a political ideology. During the 1920s and 1930s, therefore, sport was inextricably bound up with international relations. Further, in countries where the State had direct control over sport – the 'authoritarian' states of the Soviet Union, Germany, Italy and Spain – sport grew to be an adjunct of foreign policy.

Sporting competition was thus circumscribed by political considerations that often transformed purely sporting contests into other rivalries: communism v. capitalism, fascism v. liberal democracy, communism v. social democracy.

Yet there were other socio-political contenders for attention and influence that impinged upon sport – religion, especially the Roman Catholic Church, and the workers cultural movement. All the same, each had to contend with its own internal struggles, such as Catholicism v. Protestantism v. Judaism, on the one hand, and communism v. social democracy, on the other.

The whole area of sport and international relations has been largely neglected by sports scholars and general historians. And yet it involved more players, spectators and officials than any other social movement. It was also in the first part of the 20th century that sport first became internationalized, thereby setting a pattern for the latter part of the century.

This book brings together eminent sports scholars from Europe and North America; they each examine the development of foreign sports relations at a significant period of history for their country of origin. We start with two studies by Pierre Arnaud: the first on the emergence of sport as a vehicle of national representation, the second on the situation prior to the First World War when, with certain notable exceptions, sport was confined to national boundaries.

Allen Guttmann writes of the dilemma of a liberal democratic state, the USA, when confronted with the problem of its athletes competing in a blatantly politicized event – the Olympic Games of 1936, staged in Berlin in the presence of Hitler. Similarly, Richard Holt describes the quandary of the British government: should it dictate to British sports associations about their relations with fascist and communist states?

For a communist perspective on a hostile capitalist world, James Riordan makes reference to the Soviet authorities of the period 1917–41, as they faced a dilemma of whether to ignore all 'bourgeois' sport, including the Olympic Games, and concentrate only on worker sport. The issue was further complicated in that worker sport was split into two warring camps: communist and social-democratic.

Three authors shed light on the emerging sports policies of fascist regimes – each of which differed in significant ways: Arnd Krüger on Nazi Germany, Angela Teja on Fascist Italy and Teresa Gonzalez Aja on Fascist Spain. Meanwhile, Pierre Arnaud describes ambivalent French policy towards those three countries, as well as the Soviet Union, in the interwar years.

Finally, two scholars, Jan Tolleneer of Belgium, and André Gounot of Germany, provide insights into wider socio-political movements and their entanglement with sport in the international arena: the Roman Catholic Church and the worker sports movement.

Richard Holt draws all the threads together in his concluding chapter.

While the book lays no claim on any original thesis on sport and international relations, what our material does reveal is that many accepted notions of the role of sport in international relations may be called into question, including that of sport as 'peacemaker'. As Pierre Arnaud makes clear in his first chapter,

> it seems that the initial boycott operations, often attributed to authoritarian regimes in the 1930s, were actually implemented from 1919 by democratic states, on the initiative of England, and then relayed effectively by Belgium and France.

Here, then, are insights into the role played by sport in Europe and North America when athletes first started to represent their country abroad.

# Chapter 1

# Sport – a means of national representation

*Pierre Arnaud*

When and in what circumstances did sport become a matter of prestige among nations, a propaganda medium, an indicator of national vitality or the showcase of a political regime? When was the boycott (the voluntary cessation of all relations with a country) first used to put pressure on or to take reprisals against a state? And what were the motives for such action? Sporting? Political? Economic? The questionnaire might well be extended. This is our justification for publishing this work: sports historians have, with a few notable exceptions, tended to ignore this area of research. [1, 2, 3]

It is in the interwar period that the internationalization of sport and its audience began to attract the interest of politicians and to destroy the myth of sport as peacemaker, an idea so dear to the heart of Pierre de Coubertin. This fact, that is nowadays so banal, was much less so in the first decades of the 20th century.

## Sport and gymnastics: a cultural problem, a political alternative

The foundation of modern sport is not linked to the intervention, interference or control of the State. It differs profoundly from gymnastics in that respect. [4, 5] In Europe, as in the United States, modern sport was born of the will of individuals and private groups. In that sense it is a social innovation that has its roots in the emergence of new forms of sociability. Sport and modernity are connected and inscribed in the industrial change and economic evolution of the age.

True, the State can, here or there, hamper or restrain freedom of association. But each time that happened – as was the case in Victorian Britain, in France of the liberal Empire or at the outset of the Third Republic, in post-Bismarck Germany – the new social strata born of industrialization and urbanization found in sport the instrument of an associative life. Engendered by private initiative, the sports associations and clubs possessed a resolve that was essentially commercial and hedonistic. In every European country the State displayed a total lack of interest.

The belated emergence of modern sport, in its institutionalized and competitive form (the creation of national and international federations, the organization of international competition between national representative teams, the renovation of the Olympic Games), barely permits one to envisage it being used for political ends. The defenders and promoters of sport could hardly have imagined, in the final third of the 19th century, that sporting competition could have an impact on public opinion and become an instrument of international policy. It was the same for ministers of 'foreign affairs'. Sport, sportsmen, sports associations and clubs were never perceived as potential actors in social and cultural life, economics and politics.

What is more, in Continental Europe, for historical reasons relating to the constitution of the nation-state, it was not sport but gymnastics, shooting and military instruction that were at the heart of national battles. The French Revolution, then the Napoleonic Wars paved the way for associations concerned with military fitness and training, as well as patriotic fervour. This produced the first gymnastics societies in a number of states.

The gymnastics societies were the pedagogical and political instruments for constructing a national identity. To learn to put one's body at the service of one's country stems from a strategy of acculturation and nationalization of the masses in the same way as was the learning of language and national culture. The Turnen of Jahn and the Sokol movement of Myroslav Tyrs provide the prime examples. In France, the defeat in the Franco-Prussian War of 1870 led Republicans to favour the development of conscriptive societies and the creation of scholarly battalions.

Further, this nationalism began to merge with patriotism in so far as it had primarily an 'internal' significance (giving the idea of belonging to the same nation). But why only internal? The reason was quite simple: gymnastics competitions did not yet bring together national teams (the European Gymnastics Federation and the International Gymnastics Federation were only set up in the early 20th century) and the process of the 'sportization' of gymnastics only began in earnest after 1930. [6] Such gatherings therefore could not have a bearing on foreign policy or national prestige.

In England, however, gymnastics did not have the same impact: other factors determined the construction of a national identity. First, its insularity had saved it from the troubles of Continental Europe. Secondly, the English had rarely had to defend their territory, their language or their culture against a foreign invader. Thirdly, the Industrial Revolution and economic liberalism were born there: rich, powerful, boasting the largest Navy in the world, England had built the world's greatest colonial empire in just a few decades. Military and disciplined gymnastics were therefore never an instrument for shaping and integrating the masses. On the other hand, it was England that gave birth to modern sport. [7, 8, 9] And it was precisely from England that it began to be diffused throughout the world. [10, 11]

As a consequence, if there does exist a political usage for bodily exercise by national governments, it probably rests on different choices made on both sides of the Channel. Does the concept 'sport' need enlarging? Should we designate by sport all forms of physical exercise? Or only big international competitions, sport as spectacle (football and rugby matches, track and field meetings, the Tour de

France, Tour d'Italie, etc.). Ought we to integrate in our analysis the mass demon-strations that testify to a mobilization of clearly symbolic aspects?

We adhere here to the classical approach to sport. We shall therefore not be studying mass manifestations like, for example, the Ballilas festivals in Italy, those of the Hitler Youth in Germany, those of the Sokol in Czechoslovakia or, in a cer-tain measure and perhaps with different significance, the youth festivals in France. These grandiose events had a single major function: to reinforce national cohesion, the identity and solidarity of members of the same nation and, eventually, a second function in playing a deterrent role in respect of potential enemies. They were unable in any event to be the object of manoeuvres to which a foreign country could retaliate.

We must therefore distinguish grand international sporting gatherings, whose results may reinforce or weaken the image of a nation or political regime in the eyes of foreigners, from mass manifestations that are an educational and stimulat-ing enterprise for internal usage – which do not exclude intimidatory designs in regard to foreign states.

At the centre of our study is sports competition between national representative teams – 'official' sport, so to speak, that makes the newspaper headlines, that mobilizes crowds and excites passions, that lends itself to innumerable 'autho-rized' commentaries or dominates discussions in 'commercial parlours'. Whether one is impassioned or not about sport, actor or spectator, everyone comments on the results of international sports competitions, has something to say about them – whether England should have met Germany at football on the eve of the Second World War, whether democracies should have sent their national teams to the Berlin Olympics, or, finally, whether sport and athletes should be 'above politics', ignoring political tensions between states.

We must therefore identify the factors which, at a given moment in history, have justified the use of sport for foreign policy ends. Is sport dependent on or inde-pendent of historical political events whether national or international? Can we insidiously question the mythical 'neutrality' of athletes (sport's apolitical role) towards political events.

## Effects of context, effects of circumstance

A fairly banal observation guides our questions: since 1918 we have been witness, particularly on the European continent, to an extraordinary upsurge in the sports phenomenon and, more especially, to a constant rise in the number of interna-tional meetings. Europeanization and universalization of sport are the remarkable traits of the post-1918 world. This is a new situation by its sheer amplitude and impact on the public. Major press coverage helps expand sport and sporting spec-tacle into a universal phenomenon. On the other hand, the geopolitical upheavals which followed in the wake of the First World War seemed to weigh on the orga-nization of international competitions: not all national teams meet and certain 'absences' have an evident significance. We might therefore put forward the hypothesis that the First World War exacerbated sports nationalism and that the stadium became an arena of 'revenge'.

It is true that the German question dominated international political debates: the Treaty of Versailles, the problem of reparations and occupation of Ruhr were all subjects that precipitated crises and tensions, and fostered hatred. Were the Allies, through their sporting surrogates, following up the war against the vanquished? And for what motives?

There remained the barely foreseeable situation of the coming to power of authoritarian regimes (communism from 1917, fascism from 1922, Nazism from 1933, Francoism from 1936) that put the international sports movement (international federations, the International Olympic Committee) on the horns of a dilemma. We may well imagine that national and international sports federations did not enjoy much liberty in taking decisions. Political relations with authoritarian regimes were likely to risk modifying sports relations between states. Besides, the policies pursued by Germany, the USSR and Italy gave considerable weight to sport, initially for different motives. Which of the democratic and authoritarian regimes used sport as a means of exclusion or propaganda?

During the 1920s sport began to attract a national and international audience, particularly in Europe. However, the relationship between sports events and geopolitical events was posing an autonomy problem for the national and international sports movement, because of its capacity to override petty hatreds and divergent ideologies. Did not the big sports meetings and showdowns risk, in those circumstances, becoming hostage to international politics?

## What stakes?

When France met England, Belgium or Germany in an official football or track and field match, was it a competition between states or between nations? This distinction is not purely a semantic one.

If the competition is between states, we are dealing with 'state athletes' mandated by their government to represent their political regime or to be agents of its cultural, industrial or economic influence, in the same way as were novelists, artists, successful fashion designers or chiefs of the automobile and aeronautical industries. The selected athletes were the 'ambassadors', the 'official representatives' of a political regime or of their 'national culture'. It is useful to analyse the effects of sports results on the political world, the press or public opinion, or the influence of crises (or tensions) in international politics on the organization of national and international sports meetings (for example, the use of sport for propaganda purposes).

On the other hand, where competition is between nations, the 'nation' implies a sort of solidarity between a people and its national representatives. This invites the question about the state of public opinion, the 'national' mentality or 'national character', the picture that a people itself creates and what it creates from others in terms of its influence, its prestige and its vitality. [12] As Girault and Frank write, 'public opinion becomes a mass phenomenon for those concerned and not simply a problem of elites'. [13] States have, in effect, the obligation of preserving and reinforcing their international cohesion, and retaining their external prestige. And sport plays this role for the majority of great political powers.

The specialized press may therefore reinforce (or contend with) the most hackneyed stereotypes. The results of big international meetings orient our perception on the idea that each one has a powerful relationship between nations and states and probably accentuates the collective representations connoted in a pejorative manner. One may think, in the domain of football, for example, of the collective discipline of the Germans, as opposed to the imaginative, creative and individual play of the Latins. Sports chauvinism may be encouraged by its reputation for exciting violence and xenophobia whenever tensions exist between peoples. Mob aggression against US rugby football players during the 1924 Olympic Games served not only German propaganda, but also illustrated perfectly the consequences of international politics on public opinion.

Finally, sports nationalism is nothing but the exacerbation of a chauvinism, of a xenophobia or, in a euphemistic way, of a 'marked preference' for one's country. It is vying for its 'honour', its 'reputation', its 'identity'. It is simply a problem of arrogance on the part of all those who pretend to 'be born somewhere' and, in so doing, to be the inheritors of a singular history. One has only to examine the representations, i.e. the pictures which a society gives itself in regard to sports results by its representative teams at the time of big international competitions (World Cup in football, Olympic Games, European Championships, etc.) to detect, depending on the epoch, a certain national pride or, on the contrary, a certain malaise in respect of foreign nations.

Faced with this alternative, the option we take is not without risk. The first may remove, if we are not careful, all historical dynamism from our contribution, to the extent that our research could limit investigations in certain very precise periods, inasmuch as the international policy of states, just like public opinion, does not act simply as a function of international crises or tensions. That the one determines the other at a given moment is undeniable.

The second may lead us to underestimate the weight of circumstances and to give greater importance to that of mentalities. This is yet another reason to take account of the historical dynamism which affects international relations across changes in political regimes, and crises between states or empires. The question to ask is: If sport is effectively integrated into the project of international politics, can it be an instrument of pressure or dissuasion?

## Independence of sports powers and political powers

The history of international relations traditionally is a study of dealings between governments and hence the political interests of states. [14] What is the relationship between the foreign policy of governments and international sports meetings, and under what conditions is that relationship formed? Is there not a contradiction between the desire to use sport for political ends and the concern to affirm sport's 'neutrality'? What relations are established, then, between political power and sporting power? Does this carry some responsibility in utilizing sport as a means of political pressure? Should we be defending sport as something 'neutral' and 'pure', or is it a 'natural' medium for politicization?

A few remarks may clarify the proposition. While Great Britain hardly sought actively to diffuse sports practice, it certainly played a role as 'policeman' for preserving an international sporting order. Those who ran British sports federations did not exert any pressure after 1918 to force a split between the victorious Allies and the vanquished and neutral. Their directives were not, however, always followed by the various national and international federations. This poses the problem of how much real power was held by the national federations, international federations and that supranational private and aristocratic organization, the International Olympic Committee (IOC).

This logic of exclusion rests equally on the intervention of political power which lies with the initiative of national governments and, in one instance, supranationally, the League of Nations. Governments of the victorious Allies seemed to settle fairly easily in the years following the end of the First World War on a 'hard-line' position, according to which, any international meeting with vanquished and neutral states could only be authorized by countries belonging to the League of Nations.

What relations did these two sets of powers finally establish? Which is the defender of the interests of athletes and of their ethics? Should we oppose the apparent unity and cohesion of the positions taken by the national and international political powers in regard to the division of national and international sports powers? To that we must add the conflicts or tensions resulting from their respective prerogatives, which may lead to lack of respect by certain national or international sports federations for directives issued by political powers. On the one hand, the sports movement was claiming its autonomy, its independence, in relation to politics (according to the formula 'sport has nothing to do with politics'). On the other hand, it was a direct tributary of orientations in national and international politics (evidently a more frequent occurrence). Two hypotheses are possible.

1.  Sport may be very easily integrated into the political projects of governments. There was therefore a 'sports policy' inspired and put into action by foreign affairs ministries with or without recourse to national sports representatives. A government may thus give instructions to its representative(s) (for example a sports minister), even to the leaders of national federations. This poses the problem of independence of the national sports movement in regard to governmental policy or that of the meddling of politics in sports affairs.

2.  It is only on the occasion of grave political crises that a government may judge it opportune to use sport for the purpose of exerting pressure or making some retaliation with or without the consent of sports powers. Such political crises are particularly numerous from 1919 onwards. Nonetheless,

there is no proof that there was a cause and effect relationship between them and the tensions affecting international sports meetings. The former do not necessarily follow from the latter. There may even exist sports crises outside of any political crisis between states or nations. That was, for example, the case with rugby when, during the 1930s, the conflict that separated France and England led to frosty relations in matches played within the Five Nations Tournament.

But these questions become inextricably complex if we integrate into each of these schemas the role which international sports bodies (international federations or the IOC) can play. A national sports federation may receive contradictory directives from its government and from its international federation. The issue of autonomy of sports power is therefore also simultaneously political and sporting.

The divisions and rancours born during the First World War, to which we may add the effects of geopolitical repercussions of the Treaty of Versailles and those of the Bolshevik Revolution in Russia, give some idea of the complexity of the problems that political and sports leaders had to resolve, as well as for the athletes themselves and public opinion. Could one envisage during the 1920s, for example, a renewal of sports meetings between France and Germany, Britain and Germany, Belgium and Germany? Should Soviet athletes have been invited to Western Europe? And should, a few years later, the national teams of democratic states have met their counterparts from fascist Italy? And then from Nazi Germany? Political power and sporting power had to respond to these challenges also by taking public opinion into account.

To the German question (which affected the organization of sports meeting with Germany from 1920, and then after 1933, even more so after 1937) was added that of the coming to power of authoritarian regimes which posed an invariable problem to respective governments and national and international sports organizations. What was, for instance, the impact of the Bolshevik Revolution on the organization of national and international sport? Irrespective of the consequences for the organization of national sport (internal splits), political power seemed to favour the exclusion of athletes (and of their representative organizations) affiliated to socialist and communist sports organizations. Was the exclusion of the USSR (at least where the country did not exclude itself) from all international sports competitions the expression of the will of political powers or of sports powers? After all, Russia took part in Olympic events from the London Games of 1908. Finally, did the arrival of fascism not force governments very early (in reality from 1922) to take a more or less coherent stance on events marking their relations with Italy?

## Divisions in sports organizations and the problem of citizenship

International tensions and crises, and the changing of political regimes, can split national and international sports organizations. From this standpoint, one may not ignore the splits that occurred in certain sports federations in most European states after 1919, under the impact of the new authoritarian regimes (USSR, Italy, Germany, etc.) and which tended to result in, for example, the autonomization of worker sports organizations, if not to their actual banning.

These problems are bound to be studied uniquely through a political prism. The true history of national sports organizations shows that the splits between the 'official' sports federations and the 'corporative' or 'related' sports organizations had existed long before their respective international sports federations came into being or before political crises caught up with them. [15] The question posed is that of 'winning over' these 'non-official' (socialist, communist, Catholic, school, university, etc.) national sports federations to the national and international sports organizations recognized as such by national and international political powers.

A hypothesis equally meriting verification is this: Were the internal divisions in the national, then international, sports movement in the interwar period the expression of marginalization of their representative bodies by the official sports federations since the end of the 19th century? Did these divisions generate contradictory positions taken as much by the sports as by the political authorities when big international political crises occurred.

Should the State take a neutral or interventionist attitude in regard to national and international sports organizations? When a government refused access to its territory of certain categories of athlete, to what extent was it targeting the athlete or the citizen of a certain state? The question can only be put correctly from the moment when sports meetings become inscribed in a global strategy aiming at normalizing international relations. In becoming a major social factor in modern times, sport cannot escape the high stakes involved in international politics, in so far as it is already at the heart of tensions and conflicts that split its own national organizations. Is one a citizen before being an athlete? Or is one an athlete before being a citizen? Ought an athlete to be the ambassador of a new citizenship founded on internationalism and pacifism, and a propaganda agent for peace among the peoples?

From this viewpoint, international political crises can be 'interpreted' differently according to whether one is an athlete on the 'Left' or on the 'Right', whether one belongs to an 'official' sports federation or, on the contrary, whether one subscribes to a militant perspective. French athletes, for example (and especially their leaders) of the Worker Sports Federation and of the Socialist Sports and Worker Gymnastics Union from 1923 onwards, and the Sports and Worker Gymnastics Federation from 1934, did not have the same perception of international political crises as those of the 'official' sports federations affiliated to the National Sports Committee or the IOC. [16] In such circumstances, it is important to examine the influence that ideologies can exercise on the internal (national) development of sports groupings.

It is equally worth noting, moreover, that supranational political and sports powers have been able at times to join forces to protect sport from the influence of the foreign policies of governments. In 1920, for example, some statesmen discussed

the possibility of the League of Nations replacing the IOC as the body for organizing international sport because they perceived that the two institutions
subscribed to the same value system: pacifism and internationalism. It is equally
probable that the majority of leaders of French sport (with the exception, of course,
of the leaders of worker sport, particularly the communists) were agreed that the
hazards of political tensions should be removed from national sport and conflicts
among nations. Did not sport, as a vehicle of pacifism and entente between the peoples, become after 1918 one of the powerful symbols of apoliticism for its fiercest
defenders?

## Sporting events and forms of political action

If political crises and tensions are fairly easily identifiable, inasmuch as they are
known and listed by historians of international relations, it remains to identify the
nature and extent of the means used in what one might call the political usage of
sport (sporting meetings). Thus, a political crisis between two states, when it is
adjudged to be serious, may be translated into the domain of international sports
relations by the following.

1.  Propaganda. Here, sports victories by a national team contribute to reinforc-
    ing the image of respect in the world, strength and vitality, and even the
    legitimacy of a political regime. During the 1930s the fascination of a fraction
    of the French public with authoritarian regimes was fostered on the success of
    Italian and German athletes in demonstrating that political will could make a
    contribution to national redress and the improvement of the race.
2.  The freezing or banning of sports competitions between national teams. A
    government may ban its representative team from meeting such and such an
    adversary for strictly political reasons. This would be political usage of sport
    for the purposes of reprisal. Thus, Vidal was in favour of boycotting the coun-
    tries of the 'centre' up to the moment when they were admitted into the
    League of Nations. In September 1919, the French football team, yielding to
    the injunction of British sports federations, refused to meet the Swiss team –
    because it had played a match against the Germans. The objective was to put
    pressure on public opinion so that it helped to change the foreign policy of its
    government. Boycott operations, well known in our own day and age, were uti-
    lized by all governments (and not only those of authoritarian regimes) during
    the interwar period. That was the case with the Italian cycling team in 1936
    which, after the Ethiopian affair and the League of Nations sanctions, did not
    participate in the Tour de France by order of Mussolini. A few months later,
    a football match between Holland and Germany was cancelled a few days
    before the marriage of Princess Juliana, successor to the Netherlands throne,
    to the German Prince Bernard de Lippe, for fear of anti-German demon-
    strations. It was this incident which decided the Reich to break off all sports
    relations with the Netherlands. In the same manner, the French government

banned its national football team from meeting Italy and Portugal in 1937, then Germany in 1938, for fear of provoking popular protest, although in the German case the Reichsführer for sport stated that French footballers coming to Germany would be protected against all nationalist and xenophobic feelings! Thus, the stance taken by the major European powers towards competitive sport between nations was political, determined by policy, and usually manifested by persuading national sports federations to 'toe the party line'. On the other hand, the sports event may be a pretext for a hardening of foreign policy, as is testified to by incidents, relatively frequent, that accompanied the playing of national anthems after 1925. A sports federation may equally ban all international competition for its nationals for strictly sporting motives. This is quite rare, although it happened in 1910 when the Union of French Societies of Athletic Sports (USFSA) broke off relations with the international football body FIFA, and banned its members from meeting those affiliated to FIFA. It happened again in 1931 when England suspended relations with France in the Five Nations Tournament. The alleged motives were: combating violence and resisting professionalism. So international sports crises are not always fed by political tensions between states and their governments.

3.  Popular discontent expressed in protest can lead to disorder and even violence either at the sports event itself or in the town/city where it is taking place, or both. Through word and action, it can result in a sort of nationalism and xenophobia, and the 'anti'-sentiments expressed can be political or sporting. Thus, during the Italy–France match in Naples in 1938, the *tifosi* demonstrated how aggressively patriotic they were when unleashing violence against French players. Such sentiments express a picture often caricatured and pejorative of the people incriminated and manifests itself by a vocabulary or expressions of a certain type. We should identify such manifestations of hostility, as well as the argumentary themes on which the discourse rests.

It is still too early for all the documentation brought together in this book to provide material for an original 'thesis'. Nonetheless, some ideas on the place of sport in international relations and on its pacifist function may be called into question. In particular, it seems that the initial boycott operations, often attributed to authoritarian regimes from the 1930s, were actually implemented from 1919 by democratic states, on the initiative of England, and then relayed effectively by Belgium and France.

All the same, it was certainly the political tensions between states and their governments that were at the source, in an almost general fashion, of sport being used for the purposes of propaganda, exclusion or retaliation. The upsurge in fascism in the 1920s, then the emergence of Nazism after 1933, were to turn 'the international sports order' upside down. If the facts are reasonably well known, it remains to discover how these intimidatory manoeuvres by contending athletes were put into operation, which countries they affected and, above all, the effect that such events were able to have on public opinion. If sport has any claim to be outside of time, or above politics, athletes, actors, spectators or simply witnesses are also citizens who do not always perceive the contradictions of this double standard.

# References

1. *Relations internationales*, no. 38, summer 1984, Paris.
2. Arnaud, P. and Wahl A. (1994) *Sports et relations internationales*, Centre de recherche Histoire et civilisation, Metz.
3. Actes du colloque *Géopolitique du sport*, Besançon, UFR-STAPS et laboratoire de géographie humaine, 1990.
4. During, Bertrand (1981) *Des jeux au sport*, Vigot, Paris.
5. Clément, J. P., Defrance, J. and Pociello, C. (1994) *Sport et pouvoirs*, Presses Universitaires de Grenoble, Grenoble.
6. Barrul, R. (1984) *Les étapes de la gymnastique au sol et aux agrès en France et dans le monde*, Paris.
7. Elias, N. and Dunning, E. (1970) *La violence maitrisée*, Fayard, Paris.
8. Holt, Richard (1989) *Sport and the British, A Modern History*, OUP, Oxford.
9. Arnaud, Pierre (1995) 'La méthod des modèles en histoire, in J. P. Augustin and J. P. Callède, *Le sport, lieux et liens*, Maison des Science de L'Homme d'Aquitaine, Bordeaux.
10. Pivato, Stefano (1994) *Les enjeux du sport*, Casterman-Giunti, Paris and Florence.
11. Arnaud, Pierre (1995) *Une histoire du sport*, La Documentation Photographique, La Documentation Francaise, Paris.
12. Milza, P. (1987) *Le fascisme italien et la presse francaise*, Edit. Complexe, Paris.
13. Girault, R. and Frank, R. (1988) *Turbulente Europe et nouveaux mondes, 1914–1941*, Masson, Paris, p. 88.
14. Renouvin, P. (1968–9) *Histoire des relations internationales*, vols 7 and 8, Hachette, Paris.
15. *Revue de droit et d'économie du sport*, editions Lamy et CNOSF, Paris (1994, 1995, 1996).
16. Arnaud, Pierre (1994) *Les origines du sport ouvrier en Europe*, L'Harmattan, Paris.

# Chapter 2

# Sport and international relations before 1918

*Pierre Arnaud*

The relationship between sport and international politics is integral to the inter-nationalization of sport itself. However, although essentially accurate, such a statement requires comment, if only to recount briefly the stages through which the internationalization of the sporting phenomenon and sporting event have passed.

## Beginnings

The modern sport era began in England early in the 19th century. By the end of the century its whole ethos had spread throughout Europe and many countries in the rest of the world, and this was due in no small measure to the English. Their first sports clubs were set up in 1812 and were located along the trade routes lead-ing to India, and in particular on Mauritius, which they had taken possession of two years previously. From about 1850 onwards the number of clubs and associa-tions increased as more and more people left England to live and work in many of the world's large industrial or commercial centres, or ports (i.e. in places where the English had business interests). Between 1855 and 1892 English traders or English engineers responsible for railway construction founded sports clubs (including Rugby football clubs) in Belgium, Czechoslovakia, France, Holland, Russia and Switzerland, and also in South America. This acted as a catalyst, and by the mid-1890s clubs were being formed by local inhabitants and not just by the English. This was particularly the case in Argentina, Brazil, Italy, Portugal and Spain after 1895.

In 1872 the Le Havre Athletic Club in France was founded by the British. It was headed by F. F. Langstaff, manager of the South Western Railway, which had arrived in France complete with its workforce to undertake railway construc-tion. The Paris Football Club in 1879, again was founded by the English, and in Lyon the formation of the cricket club owes a great deal to the help given by English silk traders who were located there. In Lisbon, Barcelona, Rio Tinto, Marseilles, Anvers and Hamburg, the first clubs were founded by the British who were there to put up telegraph lines. In Warsaw the English had virtually a monopoly founding rowing clubs (1878), football and athletics clubs (1889) and later ice-skating and cycling clubs (1893) and it was only after 1903 that the numbers of clubs (i.e. university and civil clubs) formed by the local population started to increase. These included la Slava, la Cracovia, la Vista and le Club sportif de Lodz.

However, not all English sports spread across the world with the same speed: the fastest sports to catch on were rowing, running, cycling and Rugby football. It is generally believed that by the end of the 19th century, all the countries which had commercial links with England had their own sports teams. English engineers, traders, business travellers as well as young, inexperienced men were largely responsible for this wave of enthusiasm. However, the influence of colonization on the growth of sports world-wide, especially after 1920, cannot be ignored. The same applies to the French colonization of Madagascar, equatorial and western Africa, Algeria, Tunisia, Morocco, Indochina, etc.

If British influence was so strong [1], it was because the bourgeois and aristocratic members of high society were infatuated with the public school system of education which favoured athletic sports, such as racing, running and later on Rugby football. Also highly influential was the change in mentality that resulted from changes in society, such as increased urbanization, industrialization and the growth of capitalism in a free economy. It is equally probable that the political changes at the end of the 19th century and the progressive democratization of teaching played a decisive part in motivating people to want to play by rules. As During points out,

> Traditional games are associated with weakly centralised societies, where most of the power lies within the community itself. Disciplined and rational gymnastics are associated with the age of enlightened despotism, along with the development of strong central powers and nation states. Sport, however, transcends such associations: it does not have the elitist aspects of traditional games, and everybody has the right to participate. If modern centralised states want to last, they must evolve away from despotism. Their people must be urged to become active members of something, their membership being committed and constructive. The rules of these sports must then be assimilated by individuals in such a way as to enable them to apply these rules to all aspects of their lives. [2]

However, the English do not seem to have consciously endeavoured to spread 'their' sport throughout the world, and so other reasons must be found to explain its rapid diffusion: in Italy, for example, it was the Swiss or the Italians who, having studied in England, founded the first sports clubs on their return (in Milan, for example). The English were therefore not always the founders of the first sports clubs in the larger European towns: for example, out of the 58 football clubs founded in Italy between 1892 and 1914, only 4 were of English origin. Nevertheless, as far as clubs' names are concerned, the anglomania of the period remains quite apparent. The oldest Italian football club was called Genoa Cricket and Football Club (1892). If the English language forced itself into the field of sport, it was simply because it was the fashion for it to do so: 'running-footmen', 'jockey', 'gentleman-reader', 'turf', 'sportsman', 'riding-coat', and 'dead- heat' are all terms borrowed from horse-racing. It is also worth bearing in mind that the first foot races were organized in England at the end of the 18th century on race-courses, which explains the similar vocabulary and why bets were placed on the competitors. [3] The first rowing races (*le rowing* in French) which were held between 1840 and 1850 also borrowed terms from the same sources. In all cases lamarckism and positivism justified the notion of competition: its aim was to improve the equine race, the human race or simply boat technology.

The spread of English sports is also linked to the anglomania that prevailed among the schoolchildren of the day. In Italy, La Juventus de Torino was founded in 1897 by pupils from the Massimo d'Azeglio school thanks to the influence of a shop owner who had lived briefly in Switzerland. In France, pupils from the Lycée Condorcet in Paris performed send-ups of horse-races in 'la salle des pas perdus' (the room of lost steps) in the Gare Saint-Lazare. Dressed as jockeys, complete with helmets and riding whips, they would give themselves horses' names before competing before an audience composed largely of young girls; members of the public would bet on these 'horses', the bets being taken by *un bookmaker*. Chiefly designed to shock upright passers-by, such comic adolescent pastimes were far from serious.

However, one peculiar case stands out: the United States remained somehow resistant to the influences of football and rugby, preferring to develop its own sports which did not spread throughout the world so easily. These included the very violent American football (around 1870) and baseball (1864), which was later to become the most popular American sport. Although a number of 'European' sports enjoyed brief success, such as track cycling at the end of the 19th century, they were soon to surrender their place to more violent and spectacular sports, such as boxing and car racing.

Historians seem agreed nowadays that the birth and development of sport can be essentially explained by the phenomenon of urbanization and industrialization which was affecting modern societies. In France, the supposed efficiency of the English models of education and economic and social development which the more cultivated and financially comfortable members of society were keen to promote was also of considerable importance. The same can be said for Italy, Spain, England and Germany.

> Modern sports are closely linked to the development of large democracies. Sport, which is an organised and ordered pastime, and consequently part of a consumer culture, evolves in the same way as industrialisation, education and the ever-growing involvement of an increasingly large number of citizens in politics and economics. These are the major elements of modernisation. The creation, and above all the spread of modern sports shares many of the characteristics of a bourgeois life-style. [4]

Such was the way in which those who were trying to inject new life into the French education system praised the spirit of competition which, in their eyes, could somehow encourage economic growth and further France's influence throughout the world. At least, these were the arguments they used when they wanted to fight against an education system which was judged to be 'too disciplinarian: athletic sports seemed to be the most appropriate when it came to cultivating the spirit of adventure or enterprise of the colonizers', as well as of 'men of action, with swift determination and daring initiative. Athletic sports seem to be exactly what is needed to revive our men. The bouts of fatigue from which our sportsmen suffer during a game of football or during a race are excellent physical training for colonial life.' [5] Similarly, in his speech at the Congrès Olympique du Havre in 1897, Père Didon spoke of 'the educational force and the moral value of open-air physical exercise on young people together with the forming of their character and the development of their personality [. . .] their fighting spirit [. . .] sports clubs are schools of democracy, of freedom, places where people have chosen to live freely in discipline . . .' [6]

The first 'athletic sports clubs' in France were founded after 1880: these were the Racing Club de France in 1882 and Stade Français in 1883. As in England, Ireland and Scotland, it was schoolchildren (in the large university towns) who were a deciding factor in their creation. [7, 8] However, their intent was not in any way to do away with the idea of traditional education. Bourdon talks of these schoolchildren, and of their

> childish experiments. They had no future. Deprived of any guiding force in their lives, left entirely to their own devices, totally bereft of all, including theoretical, knowledge of the new territory through which they were venturing, in all likelihood with very little encouragement from their families, given to considering their games as mere diversions and becoming alarmed at exercise of a harsher nature, it was natural that these people should fail [. . .] Indeed, these young people seemed to have scarcely any concern for their education, and even less awareness of the moral or physical nature of the task they were undertaking . . . [9]

In 1888, through the impetus of Pierre de Coubertin and G. Saint-Clair, the school athletics sports clubs started to prosper. Their initial success was in Paris; however, they later spread to the provinces, rapidly challenged after 1889 by the proliferation of 'civil' clubs. Despite the hostility shown by a few doctors and educationalists who were anxious to protect the young from excesses of sport or to preserve France from Anglo-Saxon imperialism, sport began to expand rapidly with the founding of the Union des Sociétés Françaises de Sports Athlétiques (the Union of French Athletic Sports Clubs) on 1 January 1889. The first sporting events of the period could therefore only be between Paris civil clubs and the school clubs.

## Moving from a local to a national level

Sporting competitions were most often organized by local initiatives or by the sports press, especially in cycling, swimming, athletics, and of course, in boules. However, in order for competitions to take place, there had to be a sufficient number of sports clubs to participate, a set of uniform rules and regulations had to be adopted, and the clubs had to have access to the necessary transport and communications. How did these competitions which, when all is said and done, were quite discreet, become the first national competitions?

The founding of the British sports federations provides an example. In the second half of the 19th century, a substantial number of organizations were founded: these included the Football Association in 1863, the Rugby Football Union in 1873, the Swimming Association of Great Britain in 1874, the Amateur Athletic Association in 1880, the Amateur Rowing Association in 1888, and the Northern Rugby Union (which was professional) in 1895. These were the federations who fixed the rules and regulations of the sporting competitions, the same rules and regulations which were to be used a few years later by the national sports federations. The British, particularly the English, established themselves as strict enforcers of the regulations that they had invented.

In other countries, the first national sports federations were created some time after, which probably explains why competitions between national teams took so long to evolve. In Italy, the Federazione Italiana Gioco Calcio was not founded until 1898. In France, the Union des Sociétés Françaises de Course à Pied (the organization of French foot racing clubs) was created in 1887, later to be replaced by L'Union des Sociétés Françaises de Sports Athlétiques (the USFSA – the organization of French athletics clubs – in 1889): however, it was still a 'multisport' federation whose somewhat authoritarian aims hindered the development of sport in France until 1920. In Germany, the Deutscher Fussball-Bund (DFB) was founded in 1900. Generally speaking, it was foot racing, in its codified and competitive form, which appeared before Rugby football. [10, 11]

Nevertheless, there was the Union des Sociétés Gymnastique de France (USGF) – organization of gymnastics clubs of France – founded in 1873, which organized a major national competition in a different town each year in order to publicize gymnastics. The founding of a number of regional federations affiliated to the USGF guaranteed its spread all the more easily since all the federations benefited from the help and encouragement of the republican government. However, the same could not be said for the first sports federations. The founding of the USFSA was not helped in any way by politics: it was a strictly private initiative, supported by a passionate few, many of whom had a considerable personal fortune. If sport spread in France, it did so as a result of factors that were independent of politics.

Let us first consider a simple established fact: at each international sporting event, each country would be represented by a national team. Each 'French' team was required to be made up of the best athletes or players, and it was only possible to ascertain who these were if a national championship or similar such event was held beforehand. In France, the first rowing championships were held in 1876. For athletics and Rugby, they were held in 1888 and 1876 respectively. The Rugby team was made up of the best players (mainly secondary schoolchildren) from the capital's three teams. The prize was the famous Bouclier de Brennus, awarded by Pierre de Coubertin. The first selection was made up of players from the Racing Club de France and Stade Français who were to face England in 1893. This took place in Richmond on 13 February 1893 against the Civil Service; then again in Blackheath on 14 February 1893 against Park House FC. It should be noted that Blackheath FC, created in 1858 by schoolchildren, was the oldest of the English Rugby football clubs. France's first football championships in 1890 were little more than an inter-schools event that brought together three of Paris's school clubs. [12] The inter-club championships (or 'civil' club championships) started in 1890 (they are therefore considered as being distinct from the inter-schools championships). From this period onwards, France's championships concerned not only football but steeplechasing, cross-country, sprinting, long-distance running and hurdling. [13] The USFSA even organized a Coupe de France de football, which was held for the first time in 1897. [14] The distinction between inter-club competition, inter-schools competitions and national competitions was officially made by the USFSA at the general meeting in February 1892. It was also declared necessary to harmonize the rules of the sports events throughout the country and in all fields. [15] All of France's other championships started after 1890: professional track cycling in 1890, road cycling in 1899, then amateur cycling in 1910; fencing in 1896; and boxing in 1903. However, basketball and horse-riding had to wait until 1921 and 1931 respectively before any kind of championship was organized for them. These dates illustrate that, between 1880 and 1895, sport remained a relatively confidential practice, mainly restricted to the Paris region. It would therefore be incorrect to speak of the 'French team', since it only represented the best clubs of the capital, not the rest of the country. By way of proof, it is worth bearing in mind that the USFSA membership figures at the time were still low. With only 69 sports clubs in 1892, growing to 142 in 1894 and eventually 155 in 1895, the national championships had little substance, and the reserve of athletes from which the selectors could draw in order to make up the French team was quite limited. Moreover, the Comités régionaux de l'USFSA (the regional committees) were not created until 1894, which gives an indication that the growth of French sport was relatively slow. [16]

## The initial stages of the internationalization of sport

The spread of sport on an international scale seems to have resulted from three major developments:

1.  The spread of sport throughout the world. The English, who were omni-present at the time, increased the number of their sports clubs, first in their

colonies (New Zealand, Australia, South Africa, the Indian Ocean), and then later in Europe, Latin America, Asia and Africa. Eventually, the native inhabitants of these countries increased the numbers of *their* clubs. Although the English never actively sought to impose their sports on other countries, it must be admitted that England's economic growth and colonial conquests played an important part in the world-wide development of sports. The upper classes, who suffered from having little, apart from money, to distinguish them from the rest of society were inspired by their way of life. Anglomania or anglophilia are both phenomena very much linked with changing fashion. They spread quite widely, even to the point of touching the 'women of sport' who were depicted in France by Baron de Vaux in 1885. In this way sport became associated with the more refined forms of world cultural life.

2.    The setting up of international federations which guaranteed that the rules would be consistent and respected the world over. Until 1914 there were only 13 of these, which is evidence of how weak the growth of sport world-wide had been up to this point. After 1918, the number increased to 21, eight new federations being created between 1924 and 1932 (see Table 2.1). However, very often these were created without the knowledge or against the will of the British. It would not be over nationalistic to mention that a number of these federations were created through French initiative. This is how the Fédération Internationale de Gymnastique was founded, with the support of Charles Cazalet, chairman of the Union des Sociétés de Gymnastique de France. Similarly, the Fédération Internationale de Ski was created through the initiative of the Club Alpin Français, and the Fédération Internationale de Football Amateur in 1904 by Robert Guérin, even though England was opposed to it. Fencing and horse-riding could also be mentioned, both of which have their international headquarters in France. [17]

3.    The founding of major international competitions which put sport in the public eye. A number of these competitions were the result of French enterprise, in particular the modern Olympic Games, revived in 1892 by Pierre de Coubertin, which took place for the first time in Athens in 1896, and later the Coupe du monde de football (football world cup), which was founded by Jules Rimet in 1928, the first competition taking place in 1930 in Uruguay [18, 19] Jules Rimet was chairman of the International Federation of Football at the time. Furthermore, the World Cup was founded during the Amsterdam Olympic Games, where football featured among the events for the second time. It is true that in football, like in most other sports, granting autonomy to a Coupe du monde resulted from a visible desire to escape the restrictive protection of the Olympic Games. The Olympic Games were reserved for amateurs, whereas the Coupes du Monde allowed amateurs to compete against professionals. Nevertheless, most of the world championships were created before 1939: ice-skating in 1896, shooting in 1897, tennis in 1900, gymnastics in 1903; then after the First World War: fencing and cycling in

*Table 2.1* Founding of the French Federations and of the international Federations (by year and by sport)

| Sport | French Federation | International Federation |
|---|---|---|
| Gymnastics | 1873 | 1881 |
| Cycling | 1881 | 1900 |
| Fencing | 1882 | 1913 |
| Shooting | 1886 | 1887 |
| Rowing | 1890 | 1892 |
| Swimming | 1899 | 1908 |
| Archery | 1899 | 1931 |
| Field hockey | 1901 | 1924 |
| Boxing | 1903 | 1946 |
| Yachting | 1912 | 1907 |
| Wrestling | 1913 | 1912 |
| Weightlifting | 1914 | 1920 |
| Football | 1919 | 1904 |
| Rugby | 1920 | 1954 |
| Skating | 1920 | 1892 |
| Bobsleigh | 1920 | 1908 |
| Ice-hockey | 1920 | 1908 |
| Athletics | 1920 | 1912 |
| Tennis | 1920 | 1948 |
| Horse-riding | 1921 | 1921 |
| Skiing | 1924 | 1924 |
| Table tennis | 1927 | 1924 |
| Canoeing | 1931 | 1924 |
| Basketball | 1932 | 1932 |
| Volleyball | 1936 | 1947 |

1921, bobsleigh and ice-hockey in 1924, table tennis in 1927, wrestling in 1929, football in 1930 and skiing in 1937. The swimming and athletics world championships were not inaugurated until after the Second World War, and were for a long time considered unnecessary because of the Olympic Games. It is also worth mentioning the major national competitions whose participants came from all over the world. Many of these events were sponsored by the press, and included such events as the Tour de France, which was founded in 1903 by the French newspaper *L'Auto*, and the Tour d'Italie (the 'Giro'), which was founded in 1909 by the Italian *Gazetta dello sport*, and was very much based on the Tour de France.

However, the spread of sport internationally did not automatically lead to events organized between national teams: the very first events were organized between clubs. And the French clubs were obviously in a hurry to do battle with their English masters. The first Rugby football match between Paris FC and the Civil Service took place in 1885 in Dulwich, England, at the same time as English and French sailors were competing in Belgium. The 5 March 1892 edition of the magazine *Sports athlétiques* announced the match between Stade Français and Rosslyn Park Football Club at the Levallois stadium. The following year, a football match between the Civil Service Football Club and a team selected from the USFSA was held in England. This was probably the first French attempt to create a team made up of players from different clubs, which the newspaper editors pompously referred to as the 'France team'. [20] Six thousand spectators attended the match, which the French lost 2–0. Events involving German clubs seemed to have begun in 1900 with the Exposition universelle (the world fair): university teams from Heidelberg and Frankfurt played against the English club Moseley FC, and then against a 'French team' in a triangular tournament.

It would, however, be incorrect to say that the English had originated all these competitions. The example provided by cycling is quite revealing in this respect: all the 'classic' major cycling events were French, Belgian or Italian initiatives: the Bordeaux–Paris and the Paris –Brest–Paris in 1891, the Paris–Brusselles in 1893, the Liège–Bastogne–Liège in 1894, the Paris–Roubaix and the Paris–Tours in 1896 and the Milan–San Remo in 1907.

## The first national teams and the first international matches

The idea of making up a team which is representative of a whole country could only come to fruition if there was a sufficient number of clubs and sports associations for each event. This is essential if both playing and watching sport are to become mass phenomena. In this respect once again, the British were ahead. The very first international event had been between the England Rugby team and its Scottish counterpart on 27 March 1871. The match took place in front of between two and three thousand spectators. In 1877 it was Ireland's turn to play against England, and in 1881 England took on the Welsh.

By the early 1900s national teams were competing against each other on a regular basis. In Rugby, France played Canada and lost on 23 October 1902. On 1 January 1906 they played against the New Zealand's All Blacks in front of more than 5000 spectators. Three months later, on 23 March 1906, the French were beaten by the English at their first official meeting. The following year France played against South Africa before returning to England for a second match, and in 1909 they confronted Ireland for the first time. The sheer frequency of these matches led to the creation of the Tournoi des cinq nations (the Five Nations) on 22 January 1910. For the French this was a supreme honour because they considered the standard of their Rugby to be at least equal to that of the other members. The first match between France and Belgium also took place in 1906 (Table 2.2). Leaving aside the exceptional case of the Olympic Games, events organized between nations seemed generally to have become institutionalized after 1900. Dr Bellin du Coteau noted in 1920 that the first 'France team' was created in 1896 expressly for the Olympic Games of that year which were held in Athens. [21]

Table 2.2  The first national teams to play against France in official matches

| Year | Country | Sport |
|------|---------|-------|
| 1893 | The First European Rowing Championships | |
| 1902 | Canada | Rugby |
| 1906 | Belgium | Football |
| 1906 | England | Rugby |
| 1906 | New Zealand | Rugby |
| 1907 | South Africa | Rugby |
| 1908 | Wales | Rugby |
| 1909 | Ireland | Rugby |
| 1910 | Scotland | Rugby |
| 1910 | Creation of the Five Nations (Rugby) | |
| 1912 | Belgium | Athletics |
| 1919 | Belgium | Athletics |
| 1920 | England | Football |
| 1920 | Belgium | Swimming |
| 1920 | England | Football |
| 1921 | Ireland | Football |
| 1921 | England | Athletics |
| 1921 | Switzerland | Athletics |
| 1921 | Sweden | Athletics |
| 1921 | Italy | Football |
| 1921 | Belgium | Football |
| 1921 | Holland | Football |
| 1922 | Spain | Football |
| 1922 | Norway | Football |
| 1922 | Finland | Athletics |
| 1923 | Switzerland | Football |
| 1924 | Romania | Rugby |
| 1925 | Brazil | Football |
| 1925 | Uruguay | Football |
| 1925 | Austria | Football |
| 1926 | Portugal | Football |
| 1926 | Germany | Athletics |
| 1926 | Yugoslavia | Football |
| 1927 | South Africa | Football |
| 1927 | Germany | Rugby |
| 1928 | Czechoslovakia | Football |
| 1928 | Italy | Athletics |
| 1930 | Scotland | Football |
| 1930 | Hungary | Athletics |
| 1931 | Germany | Football |
| 1936 | Japan | Athletics |
| 1937 | Italy | Rugby |
| 1938 | Poland | Athletics |
| 1939 | Poland | Football |
| 1939 | Holland | Athletics |

*The Olympic Games and international events between clubs or unofficial sports Federations are not counted here.

The internationalization of sports events is therefore a recent phenomenon, dating back only as far as the beginning of this century. The number of participating countries in the Olympic Games, for example, show that 13 entered the Athens Games of 1896 and this had increased to only 29 at the Anvers Games of 1920. However, the Paris Games of 1924 saw a significant boom in their popularity: 44 countries competed that year, and by the Berlin Games of 1936 this figure had risen to 49 (Table 2.3). By 1920, the Comité International Olympique (the International Olympic Committee), which had been founded in 1894, represented 35 different nationalities. [22]

However, many other factors hindered the organization of sports events or championships, of which one was the means of transport available. The success of the national and then international championships was very much dependent on the expansion of communications links, most notably those of the rail system. [23] For example, the regional committees of the Fédération Française des Sports d'Aviron (The French federation of rowing sports) were organized according to the railway layout. For a long time, a sporting event or even a regional or national championship in a particular town was dependent on whether or not it had a railway station! This explains why sports clubs were created so late in isolated rural areas. Similarly, the lack of sports facilities severely hampered the development of playing and watching sports, especially in France. If sport became an ever-expanding social phenomenon, it was at least partly due to the efforts of a few towns which had stadiums, swimming pools, and velodromes that could house both athletes and spectators. [24] However, this policy really took effect only after 1925.

The rapid growth of sporting competitions also owes much to the advertising and business improvement opportunities that they presented to builders,

*Table 2.3* The Olympic Games (1896–1936)

| Year | Place | Number of countries | Number of athletes |
|------|-------|---------------------|--------------------|
| 1896 | Athens | 13 | 295 |
| 1900 | Paris | 20 | 1077 |
| 1904 | St Louis | 11 | 22 |
| 1908 | London | 22 | 2034 |
| 1912 | Stockholm | 28 | 2504 |
| 1916 | Berlin | did not take place | |
| 1920 | Anvers | 29 | 2591 |
| 1924 | Paris | 44 | 3075 |
|      | Chamonix* | 16 | 293 |
| 1928 | Amsterdam | 46 | 3292 |
|      | St Moritz* | 25 | 363 |
| 1932 | Los Angeles | 38 | 1429 |
|      | Lake Placid* | 17 | 300 |
| 1936 | Berlin | 49 | 4793 |
|      | Garmisch-Partenkirchen* | 28 | 756 |

* Winter Olympics

manufacturers and salespeople. This, at least, was the case for 'merchandized' sports, such as cycling and car racing, as well as sports which required material accessories, such as tennis. The French newspaper *L'Auto* had also seen the promotional possibilities when it founded the Tour de France in 1903, and now other sporting newspapers followed suit. Bitter rivalries ensued as both French and foreign newspapers tried to gain maximum publicity through organizing competitions, meetings and international events. The best-known example is, of course, Le Tour de France, but swimming competitions – such as those which involved swimming the length of a river from one side of a town to the other, were also becoming increasingly popular in the larger towns at the beginning of the century. These were usually instigated by local newspapers. [25, 26, 27]

In short, from what has been said so far, it is difficult to pinpoint the factors which contributed to the internationalization of sport and the rapid growth of international competitions. So far, the history of sport has only been considered from local, regional and national points of view. It must now be considered on a more international basis.

## Sport and international relations: teething problems

The first international crisis in French sport had nothing to do with politics. On 1 January 1913, the spectators in the stadium in Colombes refused to acknowledge France's 21–3 defeat against Scotland, which led to an attack on the referee and the police had to intervene. The International Board issued the French team with a reprimand, while the Scottish Football Union blamed the French players and organizers, eventually deciding to suspend relations between the two countries. Official Rugby matches did not start again until 1920.

However, victories in international competitions were not yet meticulously recorded. At the very most, a country's supremacy in a certain sport was seen by chroniclers to be an indication of its strength, or of the efficiency of its education system, or of the enlightened nature of its training methods. The lucidity of somebody like Charles Maurras in 1896 was needed to predict how international sport would be used to nationalistic and fanatically patriotic ends (see Appendix, p. 28).

Before 1914, however, sport was not yet a vehicle of nationalism. [28, 29] This at least was the case in France, even though *La Marseillaise* was played at the beginning of each sporting event that involved the French team. The practice seems to have started in 1889 during the athletics competitions that were organized during the Great Exhibition. The French national anthem was played at the nouveau-Cirque in Paris during a Swedish gymnastics demonstration held on 14 July in honour of Octave Gréard by the Count of Löwenhaupt, the Swedish ambassador. The affair might well have created a diplomatic incident had the members of the Swedish monarchy been present. [30]

The 1912 Olympic Games in Stockholm are considered by some to be the first major sporting event where nationalism and sport became inextricably linked. [31]

With Japan and Russia (at war as recently as 1905) participating for the first time there was added tension, and some newspaper reports suggested that the competitors and athletes from a number of countries were displaying rather excessive xenophobic and nationalist feelings during the competition. In fact, some journalists even questioned the decision to hold the next Games in Berlin and endeavoured to paint the bleakest picture possible of what this would lead to, [32, 33, 34] although among intellectuals and athletes this did not give rise to an inordinate amount of concern.

The Stockholm Games were also the first to allow women to compete in swimming events. [35] They had competed in the tennis, archery and figure-skating competitions at the London Games in 1908, and were invited to compete again in the tennis competition at Stockholm, but to be invited to compete in swimming events was an 'innovation'. However, this was more an indication of the success of the Olympic Games than any wider political statement by the organizers.

On the contrary, the sports press seemed rather delighted by the French athletes' overall performance, and even the defeat of France's best hope for a gold medal, Jean Bouin, in the 5000 metres, did not seem to dampen its enthusiasm. L. Maertens wrote that their sole aim in taking part had been to put on a good show. If France had finished sixth out of twenty-eight countries (after America, Sweden, England, Finland and Germany), the only disappointment had been in finishing behind Germany. [36] But any bitterness gave way to pride when a newspaper editor remarked: 'Even if a country prides itself on excelling in athletic sports, when it can line up four men capable of running the 400 metres in 50 seconds, it is definitely among the very best.' [37]

If there was any dissatisfaction, it was concerned with exposing the bias of the Swedish judges: 'To avoid any suspicion of bias, the Olympic juries should be international, and consist of only one delegate per nation.' [38]

Perhaps the journalist who declared, alluding to the gold medal won by French horsemen at riding competitions, what a 'rousing thrill' it had been 'to see the French flag rise and wave above the German flag', can be accused of fanatical patriotism? [39] Certainly the political tension between France and Germany was giving rise to fears, and the same journalist later hinted at the possibility that French athletes would not attend the Berlin Olympics in 1916 – putting France in an ideal position to demand a change in the rules which governed how the juries were made up.

It is worth noting, however, that the tension which had built up between France and Germany following the war in 1870 had not sullied the sports relationship between the two countries. Admittedly there had been no Germans at the Sorbonne in 1894 when de Coubertin had announced his intention to revive the Olympic Games, but German athletes had later participated in the first Olympic Games in Athens in 1896, and then again in Paris, St Louis and London. The German members of the International Olympic Committee had even tried to organize the Games in 1908 and 1912, going so far as to obtain the support of the Kaiser. [40]

In truth, before 1914, any great international political crisis could not really have had any serious impact on sporting events between countries, because sport was still struggling to gain a foothold, and so little importance was attached to it by Europe and the rest of the world. As far as France is concerned, several fundamental reasons deserve mention.

- If the State was totally disinterested in sport, it was because it was more anxious to offer subsidies and support to the gymnastics, shooting and military preparation clubs; sport had not yet been recognized as an efficient means of preparing men for war. [41] What remained, therefore, were the private initiatives, which were placed under the protection of federations. With the exception of gymnastics and shooting clubs these federations had no official link with the State. This situation was not peculiar to France: a similar system was in operation in Italy, Germany and Spain. Furthermore, it is probable, although such a hypothesis would need to be verified, that the commercialization and the economic gambles taken in sport owe much to these federations, as the history of Italian, Spanish and South American football clubs shows. [42]
- Sport had not yet become a widespread social and political phenomenon. The important competitions of the day scarcely succeeded in attracting the crowds – contrary to the competitions which were taking place in England. France did not have large stadiums to seat tens of thousands of spectators, whereas the English Football League championship, founded in 1893, had been attracting more than 100 000 spectators for some matches since the early 1900s. Holt affirms that English Football League matches attracted more than six million spectators during the 1905–6 season. [43, 44]
- The revival of the Olympic Games was initially justified by their being a means to bring people and countries together. As such, the right to hold them was granted to cities and not to states or governments. But de Coubertin's message was scarcely heard. Participation in the various Olympic Games held after 1896 showed that, once again, very few countries had a sufficient number of athletes, and that above all people had not yet embraced the idea of international sporting events. If de Coubertin had cast himself in the role of the bard of pacifism and sports internationalism, the great cataclysm of 1914 put an end to his Utopia.

As the numbers of international sports competitions increased and became established, countries became aware of the extraordinary social, cultural, economic and political scope of sport. The phenomenon only took on real importance after 1918. It is difficult to tell whether its success was due to the advent of the authoritarian regimes which were a consequence of the geopolitical upheavals of the First World War, or to the popularization of sport itself. In any case, it was not until 1925 that journalists started keeping records of each country's total number of victories or medals so as to compare their respective national sports policies.

From that time onwards, it was no longer the Scandinavians, the English, or the Americans who were considered to be the paragons of vitality, but the Italians and then later the Germans, for whom sport was to become a reflection of their political regime.

## Appendix: Prophecies . . . ?

'And now let us consider these 'revived Olympic Games' which are being held for the first time in Athens [. . .] and which will take place every four years henceforth in Europe's capital cities.

'When the idea was aired for the first time, I confess that I condemned it with all my strength. I disliked this new sports internationale, seeing in it the desecration of what was once something splendid. It was anachronistic. Greek olympiads were possible when Greece existed. There is no Europe, or rather there is no longer any Europe: how would we envisage European olympiads? To my mind, bringing together such a mixture of races ran the risk of leading, not to an intelligent and rational ranking of modern countries, but to the most disorderly aspects of cosmopolitanism. I ask myself who reaps the benefits of this cosmopolitanism, and the answer is – that least heterogeneous of peoples, that most nationalist of races – the Anglo-Saxons. The era that is about to commence in Athens will only serve to breathe new life and prosperity into our eternal enemies, and the vocabulary associated with sport will add to the propagation of a language with which the entire planet is already infested.

[. . .] 'It was not that my initial reasons were without foundation: they were simply incomplete. I had failed to consider two major traits. As far as cosmopolitanism was concerned, I had anticipated problems for the simple reason that, when a number of different nationalities are brought together and forced to interact, instead of being united by their affinities, a hatred arises between them and they fight more and more the better they think they know each other [. . .] As regards the preponderance of Anglo-Saxon influence, I had forgotten that the only reason it was so widespread was because it had evolved with such a scholarly slowness. Its spread had been a mystery, a carefully guarded silence. Its progression had not been instantaneous, like that of Prussian influence [. . .]

[Maurras continues, discussing the success of the Greek athletes and the joy that they brought to the masses]

'I know this people well; I have seen them in the amphitheatre of Arles and playing in the naval battle scenes re-enacted in the arenas in Martigues [. . .] I do not intend to laugh at this great joy amongst the masses, nor do I wonder at it; I simply note its very national quality. One grieves to see a Greek hit the bar when pole-vaulting or turn in a less than perfect performance on the rings. One frowns when an American or a German has more dexterity and good fortune. In no way do such sentiments have an adverse effect on the fairness of the competition. People admire what deserves to be admired; however, they admire it more or less willingly according to the honour at stake [. . .] Far from stifling patriotic passion, all this false cosmopolitanism in the stadium serves only to aggravate it. I am most certainly not going to complain about that.

[. . .] 'The fatherlands have not yet been destroyed. Neither is war dead. In days gone past, races dealt with each other through Ambassadors. These people were solemn, poised, restrained, circumspect and abounding with wisdom [. . .] Nowadays peoples confront each other in the flesh, insulting each other face to face and disputing with all their hearts. The wind which brought them together will only serve to render international incidents easier. The Bismarcks of tomorrow still have a rosy future.'

Charles Maurras, Le Voyage d'Athènes: le stade panathénaïque in *La Gazette de France*, 19 April 1896.

# References

1. Wahl, A. (1993) *Les Archives du football*, Gallimard, Paris.
2. During, B. (1984) *Des jeux aux sports, repères et documents en histoire des activities physiques*, Vigot, Paris.
3. Radford, P. (1994) Women's foot-races in the 18th and 19th centuries: a popular and widespread practice. *Canadian Journal of History of Sport*, XXV (no. 1), May.
4. Markovits, A. S. (1990) Pourquoi n'y-a-t-il pas de football aux Etats-Unis? *Vingtième siècle, revue d'histoire*, April – June, 23.
5. Sport et colonisation. *Tous les sports* (1897–1917), **44** (27) August 1897, (Author not specified). This journal is a continuation of the USFSA bulletin, *Les Sports athlétiques*.
6. Didon (Père) (1897) Influence morale des sports athlétiques. Speech made at the Havre Athletics Congress in Paris, 29 July.
7. Holt, R. (1989) *Sport and the British, a modern history*, Clarendon Press, Oxford.
8. Mangan, J. A. (1981) *Athleticism in the Victorian and Edwardian Public School*, Cambridge.
9. Bourdon, G. (1924) La Renaissance athlétique, in *Encyclopédie des sports*, vol. 1, Librairie de France, Paris.
10. Mangan, J. A. (ed.), *International Journal of History of Sport*, Frank Cass, London. This journal gives some information, but no in-depth study has been made of these developments.
11. Dunning, E. G., Maguire, J. A. and Pearton, R. E. (1993) *The Sports process, a comparative and developmental approach*, Human Kinetics Publishers, Champaign.
12. *Les Sports athlétiques*, (94), 16 January 1892. There were to be 8 teams in 1891, 13 in 1892. But for the 1894 championships, the journal noted that only 11 teams participated, all of which were Parisian, meaning that football had not yet caught on in provincial academic establishments.
13. *La Revue athlétiques* (6), 25 June 1890.
14. *Les Sports athlétiques* (357), 31 January 1897.
15. *Les Sports athlétiques* (100), 27 February 1892 and (101) 5 March 1892.
16. *Les Sports athlétiques* (238), 20 October 1894.
17. Ben Larbi, M. and Leblanc, P. (1898) Les Fédérations sportives internationales: centres de décision et stratégies du pouvoir. Mappemonde (2). This was gathered from a file provided by the *Association Générale des Fédérations Internationales de Sports* (AGFIS), which

consisted of 57 International Federations in 1990, of which eight were governed or had their headquarters in France.

18. Wahl, A. (1993) *Les Archives du football*, Gallimard, Paris.

19. Vigarello, G. (1990) Les premières coupes du monde ou l'installation du sport modern, *Vingtième siècle, revue d'Histoire*, April–June.

20. *Les Sports athlétiques* (15), 18 February 1893. The photograph of this particular 'French team' was in issue no. 153 on 4 March 1893.

21. La Vie au grand air, 20 January 1920: an article about the preparations for the Olympic Games.

22. From a letter from Pierre Coubertin of 15 November 1920 addressed to Paul Hymans, the chairman of the *Société des Nations*. Taken from the archives of the *Société des Nations*.

23. see Arnaud P. (1987) Sport et Transport. *Science et Motricité*. (4).

24. *Spirales* 5, Les Politiques municipales d'équipements sportifs, XIX–XX siècles, Centre de Recherche et d'Innovation sur le Sport, Université Lyon I, 1993.

25. Arnaud, P. (1995) *Une Histoire du sport*, La Documentation photographique, La Documentation française, Paris.

26. Terret, T. *Naissance et diffusion de la natation sportive*, L'Harmattan, Paris.

27. Pivato, S. (1994) *Les Enjeux du sport*, Casterman-Guinti, Paris and Florence,

28. Arnaud, P. (1989) Sport et nationalismes in *Sport Histoire, revue internationale d'histoire des jeux et du sport*, 4th edn, Privat, Toulouse.

29. Arnaud, P. (1991) Dividing and Uniting, sports societies and nationalism, 1870–1914, in Tombs, R., *Nationhood and Nationalism, from Boulangism to the Great War*, HarperCollins Academic, London.

30. de Coubertin, P. (1909) *Une campagne de vingt et un ans (1887–1908)*, Paris, p. 37. It should nevertheless be noted that the custom of playing *La Marseillaise* by a military band was instigated by gymnastics clubs.

31. Spivak, M. (1988) Education physique, sport et nationalisme en France, du second Empire au Front populaire: un aspect original de la défense nationale, doctoral thesis presented at Université Paris I Sorbonne.

32. Thibault, J. (1973) *Sport et éducation physique*, Vrin, Paris.

33. Pierrefeu, J. de (1927) *Paterne ou l'ennemi du sport*, Ferenczi, Paris.

34. Arnaud, P. (1989) Diviser et unir: sociétés spotives et nationalismes en France, in *Revue Sport-Histoire*, 4th edn, Privat, Toulouse.

35. Hache, F. (1992) *Jeux Olympiques, la flamme de l'exploit*, Gallimard, Découvertes, Paris.

36. From *L'Auto*, after the Stockholm Olympic Games on 20 July 1912.

37. Ibid. The French relay team finished second after the Americans, but in front of the Germans.

38. From an article written by Paul Champ in *L'Auto*, 22 July 1912.

39. Ibid. The national flag of the Olympic medallists was hoisted up and their national anthem was played for the first time at the Los Angeles Olympics of 1932.

40. Hache, F. (1992) *op. cit.*, p. 52 ssq, for further details.

41. Spivak, M. (1987) *op. cit.* for the debate behind this belief.

42. Reports entitled *Le football et ses publics*, published par L'Institut Universitaire Européen de Florence on the Pierre Lanfranchi's initiative in 1990.

43. Fishwick, N. (1990) *English Football and Society, 1910–1950*, Manchester University Press, Manchester and New York.

44. Mason, T. (1980) *Association Football and English Society, 1863–1915*, Harvester Press, Brighton.

# Chapter 3

# The 'Nazi Olympics' and the American boycott controversy*

## Allen Guttmann

At their twenty-ninth session, which took place in Barcelona in April 1931, the members of the International Olympic Committee (IOC) were unable to agree upon the site for the 1936 Games, but a subsequent mail ballot produced 43 votes for Berlin and only 16 for Barcelona (with 8 abstentions). [1] The choice of Berlin ratified the full reintegration of postwar Germany, no longer a pariah nation, into the world of international sport. When the IOC's decision was announced on 13 May 1931, Heinrich Brüning was Chancellor of the Weimar Republic and a shaky centrist coalition was in power. When the Games were actually held, the National Socialists were in power and Adolf Hitler was Chancellor. In fact, Hitler's rule began only six days after the creation, on 24 January 1933, of Berlin's Olympic Organizing Committee. This state of affairs was certainly not what the IOC had expected when Berlin was chosen to host the Games.

Quite apart from any general concern they might have had about Nazism, there was reason for the IOC members to be worried. Although Hitler thought that German boys should learn to box, in order to steel themselves for the rigour of their role as natural rulers, neither he nor his cohorts were advocates of modern sport. Sports were almost unmentioned in *Mein Kampf* and in the pages of the party's newspaper *Der völkische Beobachter*. [2, 3] The problem as the Nazis saw it was that modern sports had developed in Britain rather than in Germany and they were, at least in principle, universalistic rather than particularistic. Among the most important characteristics of modern sports – in theory if not in practice – is equality; neither race nor religion nor ideology should be a factor in the determination of sporting excellence. Such a notion of equality was, of course, anathema to Nazis dedicated to a primitive belief in the racial supremacy of the 'Aryan' people. Accordingly, Nazi spokesmen like Bruno Malitz condemned modern sports because they were international, 'infested' with 'Frenchmen, Belgians, Pollacks, and Jew-Niggers'. [4] On 19 August 1932 *Der völkische Beobachter* demanded that the Olympic Games be restricted to white athletes.

---

* This essay revises and expands upon previous work published in *The Games Must Go On: Avery Brundage and the Olympic Movement* (New York: Columbia University Press, 1984), pp. 62–81; and *The Olympics: A History of the Modern Games* (Urbana: University of Illinois Press, 1992), pp. 53–71.

*Turner*

The Nazi conception of modern sports was only a little more demented than the attitudes of some of the traditional *Turner*, who were proponents of a vehemently nationalistic German version of gymnastic exercises. [5, 6] While the British and the Americans were inventing games like soccer, Rugby, basketball and volleyball, games that quickly spread throughout the world, most *Turner* remained devoted to gymnastics as their nation's sole authentic form of physical exercise. These believers in German gymnastics condemned competition, which is an inherent aspect of sports, and they were appalled by the specialization, rationalization and quantification characteristic of modern sports. The *Deutsche Turnerschaft*, the largest and most important gymnastics organization, had shunned the first Olympics and been quite ambivalent about participation in subsequent Games. The Nazis were ideologically close to the *Deutsche Turnerschaft*, whose last leader, Edmund Neuendorff, invited Hitler in 1933 to be the guest of honour at a grand *Turnfest* in Stuttgart. [7] Hitler accepted the invitation and was received by Neuendorff with hysterical declarations of fealty. Massed displays of Teutonic vigour and parades to martial music seemed much more in tune with Nazi ideology than an international sports festival open to African-Americans, to Asians; and to Jews. The IOC and the Games Organizing Committee braced themselves in anticipation for Hitler's announcement that he wanted another authentic German *Turnfest* in 1936 – not some international celebration of human solidarity.

Among the most worried were the President and the Secretary of the Organizing Committee, Theodor Lewald and Carl Diem. The former was the son of a Berlin lawyer and civil servant. A member of the IOC since 1924, Lewald had also served as President of Germany's National Olympic Committee (and as Chairman of the *Deutscher Reichsausschuss für Leibesübungen*, the closest German equivalent to the Amateur Athletic Association). Although Lewald seemed to typify the austere Prussian tradition of public service, he had good reason to be anxious about his personal safety as well as about the future of the Olympic Games. His father had converted from Judaism to Christianity and *Der völkische Beobachter* had already begun screaming for his dismissal. [8] Diem, the Secretary of the Organizing Committee, was a self-made man who had achieved considerable success in the fields of sports journalism and sports administration. At the age of 30 he was captain of the German team that competed in Stockholm. Despite his lack of formal education, he eventually developed into a remarkable scholar, still known for his comprehensive history of sports (published in 1960) and for many monographs in sports history. In 1920, with support from Lewald, he founded the *Deutsche Hochschule für Leibesübungen* (German Sports University). Although Diem was sufficiently a child of his times to have been an ardent nationalist throughout the 1920s, he was a believer in modern sports and was able to acknowledge the achievements of athletes from foreign nations. For the German tradition of *Turnen* he had less sympathy. Diem also had the problem that his wife had Jewish ancestors, and it was held against him that the *Deutsche Hochschule für Leibesübungen* had several Jews in its faculty. For these sins, Diem was denounced in the Nazi press as a 'white Jew'. [9, 10]

Given their endangered personal positions and the shrill hostility of many Nazis to sport in general and the Olympics in particular, neither Lewald nor Diem was optimistic about the 1936 Games and both were apprehensive when they were summoned, on 16 March 1933, to meet Hitler at the *Reichskanzlerei*. To their astonishment and relief Hitler did not order an immediate cessation of preparations. Instead, he gave them his tentative approval. This was not because he had suddenly changed his mind and become a convert to 'Olympism'. It was rather that his propaganda minister, Josef Goebbels, had realized that the Games were a splendid opportunity to demonstrate German vitality and organizational expertise. Lewald was forced to resign from his post with the *Deutsche Reichsausschuss für Leibesübungen* and Diem had to give up his position at the *Deutsche Hochschule für Leibesübungen*, but pressure from the IOC prevented the Nazis from expelling Lewald and Diem from the Organizing Committee. Lewald, Diem and Hitler became uneasy collaborators. In April, Lewald was optimistic (or dishonest) enough to write to Avery Brundage, President of the American Olympic Association, that 'there will not be the slightest discrimination made in the Berlin Games because of religion or race and furthermore . . . every participant has the fullest assurance of a kind, hearty and courteous reception'. [11] On 5 October 1933, Hitler toured the site of the Games, inspected the progress of the construction, and became positively lyrical about the prospects for the grandest Olympics ever. Five days later, at the chancellery, he promised the startled Lewald the full financial support of his regime, a sum later set at 20 million Reichsmarks. Lewald and Diem were stunned by their unexpected good fortune. [12]

Hitler's willingness to act as host allayed one set of anxieties and aroused another. The IOC was quite naturally worried by the glaringly obvious contradiction between the Olympic Charter and the racist principles of the new regime. In April and May of 1933 the *New York Times* questioned the appropriateness of Berlin as a venue. Was the Nazi regime ready to accept the terms of the Olympic Charter? American Jews were especially sceptical and their fears were only partly allayed when General Charles Sherrill, one of the three American members of the IOC, wrote to the American Jewish Congress, 'Rest assured that I will stoutly maintain the American principle that all citizens are equal under all laws.' [13] As Sherrill and twenty-eight other members of the IOC assembled in Vienna on 7 June 1933, the discrepancy between Nazi doctrine and the Olympic rulebook was a central issue. Belgium's Comte Henri de Baillet-Latour, elected to a second eight-year term as President (by a vote of 48–1), joined Sherrill and William May Garland to question the three German IOC members – Lewald, Karl Ritter von Halt and Adolf Friedrich von Mecklenburg – about Jewish participation. The crux of the matter was not the acceptance of Jewish athletes in foreign teams but rather the right of *German* Jews to take part in trials for *their* national team. Although von Halt, a Nazi party member, resisted the idea, the IOC insisted upon a written guarantee from Berlin to the effect that German Jews did, indeed, have this right. Lewald and von Halt were able somehow to secure the necessary written guarantee: 'All the laws regulating the Olympic Games shall be observed. As a principle, German Jews shall not be excluded from German teams at the Games of the XIth Olympiad.' [14, 15] The guarantee seems to have been given by Hans Pfundtner, an official in the Interior Ministry; Hitler, when he realized what had been done, was apparently outraged.

Sherrill was surprised at his own unexpected success. He told Amateur Athletic Union official Frederick W. Rubien all about it on 11 June. It had been the hardest fight he had ever been through. The Germans had yielded slowly and had initially offered merely to publish the Olympic rules, but Sherrill had pushed them until they telephoned the Ministry of the Interior and obtained a formal written statement of acceptance for Jewish athletes. Sherrill informed Rubien that he had had to persuade his British colleague, Lord Aberdare, that the IOC was indeed within its rights to demand that the composition of the German team conform to the rules. Victory, thought the triumphant Sherrill, was complete. [16]

Unfortunately, the reliability of Nazi guarantees, written or oral, was immediately called into question by reports of widespread discrimination against Jewish athletes. For the moment they were allowed to use public sports facilities, but they were expelled from the private clubs that were the main institutional form of German sports. Bernard S. Deutsch, an official of the American Jewish Congress, addressed an open letter to Brundage to alert him to violations of the spirit if not of the letter of the guarantees offered by the German government. [17] Even before Brundage received this letter, which he did not answer, he had confided his worries to a fellow sports administrator, Gustavus Kirby; Brundage was concerned that the 'very foundation of the modern Olympic revival will be undermined if individual countries are allowed to restrict participation by reason of class, creed or race'. [18] Kirby was far more upset than Brundage by the threat to Olympic principles. In his 40 years as an advocate of amateur sports, he was an unusually eloquent defender of the principle of equal access. [19] To a colleague in the American Olympic Committee he wrote: 'I am and have been always very serious in my conclusion that sport is the only true democracy . . .'. It doesn't matter, he asserted, 'whether you are as rich as Croesus or as poor as Job's turkey'. [20] To Kirby, religious discrimination was even worse than economic disadvantage. For the convention of the American Olympic Committee, on 22 November 1933, he prepared a resolution which threatened an American boycott unless German Jews were allowed in fact as well as in theory to 'train, prepare for and participate in the Olympic Games of 1936'. [21] Brundage expressed reservations about the confrontational tone of the resolution, but Kirby was ready for a confrontation: 'Undoubtedly it is generally wiser to "let sleeping dogs lie", but unfortunately these dogs are not sleeping, they are growling and snarling and snipping and all but biting'. [22] The American Olympic Association passed a slightly modified version of Kirby's strong resolution.

Hans von Tschammer und Osten, [23] whom Hitler had named *Reichssportführer* and placed in charge of German sports, tried to meet American concerns by issuing a statement that Jews were not barred from sports clubs by any *official* decree. [24] Brundage was not much reassured by this kind of double-talk. He wrote to Baillet-Latour: 'The German authorities have displayed a singular lack of astuteness in all of their publicity. On this subject, every news dispatch that has come from Germany seems to indicate that the Hitlerites do not intend to live up to the pledges given to the IOC at Vienna'. [25] Brundage kept his worries private because he did not wish to cause trouble for his German friends Lewald, Diem and von Halt. Kirby, however, refused to remain quiet in the face of newspaper reports of discrimination against Jewish athletes. He was among the Madison Square Garden speakers at an anti-Nazi rally held by the American Jewish Committee, on 6 March 1934.

When the IOC convened in Athens on 15 May 1934, Britain's Lord Aberdare, who had earlier been ready to accept Nazi assurances at face value, now expressed concern about reports from Germany. He asked his German colleagues point blank if their government's pledges were trustworthy. Garland asked the same uncomfortable question and Lewald and von Halt responded:

> It goes without saying that the pledges given by Germany in Vienna in 1933 to admit to the German Olympic team German sportsmen of non-Aryan [i.e. Jewish] origin, provided they have the necessary capability, will be strictly observed and facilities for preparation will be given to all sportsmen. [26]

For that purpose the *Deutscher Leichtathletik-Verband* (German Athletics Association) had invited Jewish sports organizations to submit the names of potential Olympic team members.

The IOC was satisfied. The American Olympic Association was not. When it met on 14 June, it postponed acceptance of the official invitation to the Games until an on-the-spot inspection by Brundage had been carried out. The German consul in Chicago (Brundage's home town) breathed a sigh of relief because he assumed, quite rightly, that Brundage's loyalty to his German friends and his fanatical commitment to the survival of the Olympic Games all but guaranteed a positive report. [27] IOC members Garland and Sherrill both urged Brundage to dismiss what they considered to be exaggerated reports of discrimination against Jewish athletes. [28]

A letter from Sweden's Sigfrid Edström, whom Brundage knew well because both men were leaders in the International Amateur Athletic Federation, gave Brundage some additional unsound advice:

> As regards the persecution of the Jews in Germany I am not at all in favor of said action, but I fully understand that an alteration had to take place. As it was in Germany, a great part of the German nation was led by the Jews and not by the Germans themselves. Even in the USA the day may come when you will have to stop the activities of the Jews. They are intelligent and unscrupulous. Many of my friends are Jews so you must not think that I am against them, but they must be kept within certain limits. [29]

With Edström's letter in his pocket, metaphorically if not physically, Brundage set off for his 'impartial' investigation of German conditions. He arrived at the port of

Cuxhaven on 3 August. On the 16th, German legislation outlawed all contact between Nazis and Jews. [30]

Before conducting his investigation, Brundage travelled to Stockholm to attend a meeting of the International Amateur Athletic Federation (and to confer with Edstrøm). Since Diem, von Halt and Justus W. Meyerhof, a Jewish member of the Berliner Sport-Club, were also present, Brundage asked the three of them about the German situation. Had German Jews been expelled from clubs and denied the right to use public facilities? Their account was reassuring. Things were not as bad as they had been painted. True athletes were not about to turn their backs on men and women with whom they had worked and played for decades. Diem made notes of the discussion for his journals:

> We showed Brundage documents indicating that the Jews are able to partici-pate freely in sports and to train for the Olympic team. Meyerhof told us that he had offered to resign from the Berliner Sport-Club but that the resignation had not been accepted. I was seldom as proud of my club as at that moment. Brundage was visibly impressed. He plans to speak with leaders of Jewish sports when he visits Berlin. [31]

The visit to Berlin was postponed for a month while Brundage and his wife hol-idayed in Italy and Yugoslavia. The on-the-spot investigation began on 13 September, when Brundage arrived in East Prussia. Since he did not speak German well, he was forced to rely on interpreters. (It was an additional drawback that he was never allowed to talk alone with representatives of the Jewish sports clubs. Nazi officials monitored his conversations.) Brundage told his oldest German friend, Karl Ritter von Halt, that he had met *Reichssportführer* von Tschammer und Osten and 'liked him very much' [32] and seems to have believed *Reichssportführer*'s claim that there was no discrimination against Jews who sought to become mem-bers of the German team. In short, Brundage believed what he was predisposed to believe. He returned to the United States and urged the American Olympic Association to accept the invitation to Berlin. To the press he announced: 'I was given positive assurance in writing by Tschammer (und) Osten, Germany's official Olympic representative, [it was of course an error to refer to Tschammer und Osten as 'Germany's official Olympic representative'] that there will be no dis-crimination against Jews. You can't ask more than that and I think the guarantee will be fulfilled.' [33]

Brundage's assurances persuaded even the sceptical Kirby. On 26 September, the day after Brundage's return from Europe, the 18 members of the American Olympic Association voted unanimously to send a team to the 1936 Olympic Games. Any hopes that this decision might terminate the controversy vanished as the *New York Times* reported, on the 27th, that the Anti-Defamation League, citing instances of Nazi persecution of Jewish athletes, was calling for a boycott of the Games. US Representative Emmanuel Celler of New York, a prominent Jew, began congressional hearings and charged that Brundage 'prejudged the situation before he sailed from America. The Reich Sports Commissars have snared and deluded him' [34] A number of American sports administrators agreed with Celler. In December, the annual convention of the Amateur Athletic Union (AAU) voted to postpone acceptance of the German invitation. For Brundage, who was accustomed to a more acquiescent AAU, the vote was tantamount to a declaration of no confidence. Passions flamed, lines hardened.

By mid-1935, an intensive boycott campaign was in full swing in the United States as well as in Canada, Great Britain and France. Everyone realized that the American campaign was the most important and that the embattled Brundage was the key figure. His position had always been that sport and politics should be strictly separated: 'The AOC must not be involved in political, racial, religious or sociological [sic] controversies.' [35] All that could reasonably be asked of the Nazi regime, from this perspective, was that it accept Olympic rules, which the highest officials had agreed to do.

What was good enough for Brundage was also good enough for Pierre de Coubertin, whom the German Organizing Committee had assiduously courted. Although de Coubertin in retirement was scrupulous about attending neither the IOC sessions nor the Olympic Games, he did agree, after a visit to Laussanne by Diem and Lewald, to spend some time in Berlin, where, on 4 August 1935, he recorded a radio message in which he declared his confidence in the arrangements for the Games. [36, 37] He was delighted when, at a reception in his honour at Berlin's Pergamon Museum, the musicians played the same 'Hymn to Apollo' that he had ordered performed for the delegates to the 1894 Sorbonne conference. And he was presumably pleased when the Nazi regime nominated him for the Nobel Peace Prize a few months later. (The anti-Nazi martyr Carl von Ossietzky was the eventual recipient.)

While Diem and Lewald were persuading de Coubertin that these Olympic Games would be an authentic embodiment of his dream, Brundage was busy explaining why a boycott would be a travesty of 'Olympism'. He set forth his view in a 16-page pamphlet entitled 'Fair Play for American Athletes'. He asked if the American athlete was to be made 'a martyr to a cause not his own' and he repeated his arguments about the separation of sport from politics and religion. American athletes should not become needlessly involved in what he misleadingly referred to as 'the present Jew–Nazi altercation'. In his eyes the entire problem was that opponents of the Nazi regime were not satisfied with Olympic rules; they really wanted a boycott in order to undermine Nazism; they meant to use the Games as a political weapon. Since Jews and Communists were calling for a boycott, Brundage reasoned illogically that all the boycotters were Jews or Communists.

Brundage was not wholly inaccurate. It was inevitable that the boycott movement attracted anti-Nazis of all sorts, including those totally uninterested in sports. The Communist Party was active in a number of anti-Nazi campaigns (until the Molotov–von Ribbentrop Pact of 1939) and American Jews were naturally eager to express their opposition to Hitler by whatever means were available. But in Brundage's mind, all the volunteers in the pro-boycott camp had enlisted for base political reasons and 'all of the real sport leaders in the United States are unanimously in favor of participation in the Olympic Games which are above all considerations of politics, race, color or creed'. [38] Criticism of his position he dismissed as 'obviously written by a Jew or someone who has succumbed to the Jewish propaganda'. [39] Writing to IOC president Baillet-Latour, Brundage referred to the 'Jewish proposal to boycott the Games', [40] as if only Jews had reason to oppose Nazism.

Brundage's relations with Charles Ornstein, a Jewish member of the American Olympic Committee, deteriorated into petty hostility and his friendship with Judge Jeremiah T. Mahoney, his successor as President of the Amateur Athletic Union, turned to outright enmity. Mahoney was a considerable figure. Once a law partner of New York's Senator Robert Wagner, the judge had served for more than a decade on the New York Supreme Court. Guido von Mengden, press secretary for the Nazis' *Reichsbund für Leibesübungen*, denounced Mahoney as a 'powerful Jewish financier'. [41] Brundage, somewhat better informed about ethnicity in the United States, characterized Mahoney's opposition as politically motivated, explaining that Mahoney, a Roman Catholic, had mayoral ambitions in New York and was seeking to woo Jewish voters. Brundage refused to see that Roman Catholics had excellent reasons to fear Hitler, who had made no secret of his neopaganism or his hatred for the Church into which he had been born. In fact, Mahoney was but one of many Catholics calling for a boycott of the Games. The Catholic War Veterans and the Catholic journal *Commonweal* were for a boycott (as were the Protestant publication *Christian Century* and a number of respected Protestant spokesmen such as Harry Emerson Fosdick and Reinhold Niebuhr). The boycott movement included a number of politically prominent Catholics, such as Governor James Curley of Massachusetts and Governor Al Smith of New York. Three nationally known journalists, Arthur Brisbane, Westbrook Pegler and Heywood Broun, also climbed aboard what began to look like an unstoppable bandwagon. [42] To the gamut of American voices those of a number of German exiles were added. Leon Feuchtwanger, Heinrich Mann and Ernst Toller all spoke out against participation in the Games. [43] A Gallup poll taken in March 1935 showed 43% of the entire American population in favour of a boycott.

Because black athletes were such a strong component of the American track-and-field team, Afro-American reaction to the boycott campaign was especially important. The *Amsterdam News* supported a boycott, but the *Pittsburgh Courier-Journal* and most of the other black newspapers were outspoken about their desire not to deny athletes the chance of a lifetime. The athletes were clearly anxious to go. Sprinter Ralph Metcalfe told the *Chicago Defender* that he and other black athletes had been treated well during a 1933 tour of Germany; he was ready to return. Regrettably, there was another side to the controversy. Historian David K. Wiggins, the closest student of Afro-American responses to the boycott, has indicated that some blacks were actually anti-Semitic. 'They frequently stereotyped Jews and blamed them for everything from economic exploitation to murder.' While anti-Semitism did not make Afro-Americans especially sympathetic to the

Nazis' racist ideology, it did leave them less indignant than they might have been about the discriminatory treatment suffered by Germany's Jewish athletes. [44]

Brundage refused to take notice of the obvious. He continued obstinately to see the opposition as nothing but a conspiracy of Jews and Communists. Having been assured by his German friends that their government accepted the Olympic rules, believing as he did that the Games were the most important international institution of the century, a force for peace and reconciliation among peoples, he simply failed to understand that there were men and women of good will who did not agree with him. He was unable to imagine honest opposition and attributed it to ethnic prejudice or political ideology. Once he had made up his mind, he suspected his opponents were guilty of the most despicable motives and an almost satanic insincerity. Refusing to look at the evidence, he simply repeated his nonsensical demands that Jews and Communists 'keep their hands off' American sport'. Brundage's hysteria reached the point where the exasperated Kirby wrote him one of the harshest letters he ever received: 'I take it that the fundamental difference between you and me is that you are a Jew hater and Jew baiter and I am neither.' [45, 46]

Throughout the controversy, Brundage had the strong support of Dietrich Wortmann, President of New York's German-American Athletic Club. Appealing for funds to support the American team, the German-born wrestler, who had won a bronze medal in the 1904 Games, referred to the athletes as 'apostles of truth and justice for the promotion of friendship between our two countries'. Although some have interpreted Wortmann's impulsive rhetoric as a defence of the Nazi regime, those who have looked most closely at his behaviour have concluded that his 'efforts toward Olympic participation were for the sake of American athletes, the Games, and the Olympic spirit'. [47]

In response to Brundage's unfounded assertions of Nazi innocence, Judge Mahoney published a pamphlet entitled *Germany Has Violated the Olympic Code* (1935). Writing in the form of an open letter to Lewald, Mahoney cited specific cases, such as the expulsion of Jews from sports clubs and from public facilities, the ban on competition between Jews and other Germans, the exclusion of world-class high jumper Gretel Bergmann from the Olympic team. Every one of Mahoney's allegations has been verified by subsequent scholarship. In fact, unknown to most of the participants in the debate, the US State Department knew at the time that the promises made to the IOC were worthless. George Messersmith, the American consul in Berlin, reported as early as 1933 that Jewish athletes were the victims of severe discrimination. In November 1935, six months before the Games were to begin, a dispatch from Messersmith informed Washington that Lewald had confessed to him, in tears, that he – Lewald – had lied when he assured Brundage and the American Olympic Committee that there was no discrimination against Jewish athletes. [48, 49]

Mahoney had the facts, Brundage had the votes. Strongly seconded by Ornstein, Mahoney offered a boycott resolution at the annual meeting of the Metropolitan Association of the Amateur Athletic Union, which took place on 8 October 1935.

The motion was tabled by a vote of 77–32. [50] When the national AAU met in New York on 6 December, Mahoney continued the fight. Brundage fretted about the venue. To William May Garland he complained: 'You can't imagine what the situation is in New York City where, because of the fact that 30% or 40% of the population is Jewish, the newspapers are half given up to the German situation.' [51] Carl Diem confided his worries to his diary: 'today, the American Olympic Committee [Diem confused the Amateur Athletic Union with the American Olympic Committee, which had already endorsed American participation] is meeting in New York to decide the question of its participation in the Olympic Games'. [52] Brundage and Diem had reason to worry, for the vote was close, but Mahoney's motion to investigate further before accepting the invitation failed by $58^{1}/_{4}$ to $53^{3}/_{4}$. The members then agreed to support sending a team to the Winter Games at Garmisch-Partenkirchen and to the Summer Games in Berlin. After the AAU's decision, the National Collegiate Athletic Association gave its approval, which had never really been in doubt.

Brundage's baseless allegations about a boycott movement led by Jews and Communists might have been true for the Canadian opposition to the Games. In Canada, 'the campaign leadership never really broadened beyond the ranks of the Communist Party'. While P.J. Mulqueen and other officials of the Canadian Olympic Committee indicated their satisfaction with the assurances they had received from the IOC, Eva Dawes, one of the stars of the track-and-field team, clashed with officialdom. Already barred from AAU athletics meetings because she had competed in the Soviet Union, Dawes and five other Canadian athletes went to Barcelona in the summer of 1936 to participate in a Communist-sponsored *Olimpiada*. [53] In fact, the *Olimpiada* never took place because of the outbreak of the Spanish Civil War (1936–9). [54]

European opponents of Nazi sports policy also mounted a boycott campaign. Louis Rimet, head of the French sports federation as well as of the *Fédération Internationale de Football Association* (FIFA), was among the influential spokesmen pleading for strong action. He was joined by the French presidents of the international federations for swimming (FINA) and ice-hockey (LIHG) and by Bernard Lévy, head of the prestigious *Racing-Club de France*. Late in 1935, a socialist deputy asked the *Chambre des Députés* to terminate the government's programme for training Olympic athletes. The motion was lost by 410–151. Early in 1936, however, Léon Blum led the socialists and their allies to victory in national elections, and his Popular Front government tried to satisfy both camps by appropriating 1.1 million francs for the Olympic Games and 600 000 francs for the *Olimpiada* in Barcelona. The compromise failed to calm the storm. The Communist newspaper *L'Humanité* was unhappy that government funds were sending 189 male and 11 female athletes to Berlin; at the other end of the political spectrum, the conservative newspaper *Le Figaro* expressed its disgust at the government's support for the 1300 athletes, officials and conference delegates preparing for the *Olimpiada*. The Barcelona-bound French contingent was, in fact, far larger than all the others put together. (The second largest group, the Swiss, numbered only 150.) [55, 56]

Although only 12 American athletes sailed to Spain for the *Olimpiada*, many others participated that summer in a World Labour Athletic Carnival that was staged on New York's Randall's Island with AAU sponsorship arranged by Mahoney and Ornstein. [57] Wortmann complained about the use of the AAU's name for this obviously political event, but AAU Secretary Daniel J. Ferris defended the dissenters' right to claim sponsorship. [58]

While Brundage was victorious in the United States, his American opponents had carried the battle elsewhere. The third American member of the IOC (in addition to Sherrill and Garland) was Ernest Lee Jahncke, a staunch Republican who had served as President Herbert Hoover's Assistant Secretary of the Navy. On 27 November, the *New York Times* printed his appeal to Baillet-Latour. Jahncke asserted that

> The Nazis have consistently and persistently violated their pledges. Of this they have been convicted out of their own mouths and by the testimony of impartial and experienced American and English newspaper correspondents . . . It is plainly your duty to hold the Nazi sports authorities accountable for the violation of their pledges . . . Let me beseech you to seize your opportunity to take your rightful place in the history of the Olympics alongside de Coubertin instead of Hitler. [59]

Baillet-Latour, who had previously promised Brundage that he was ready to come to the United States to combat the 'Jewish' boycott campaign, [60, 61] was furious. He had recently visited Hitler and was assured by the Führer that the charges against Germany were false. Baillet-Latour told Jahncke that the president's duty was to execute the will of the IOC, which was steadfastly committed to the Games. The Count saw Jahncke as a traitor who for inexplicably spiteful reasons accepted neither the word of Adolf Hitler nor the personal assurances of honourable men like Diem, von Halt and Brundage. Taking umbrage, Baillet-Latour asked Jahncke to resign from the IOC, which Jahncke refused to do. [62] Brundage later told Baillet-Latour that the reply to Jahncke was 'straight from the shoulder'. [63]

Sherrill, meanwhile, began to back away from his previous position. While still claiming to be a friend of the Jews, Sherrill warned them that continued agitation might increase popular anti-Semitism. He had what must have been a very difficult interview with Hitler on 24 August. When he mentioned to the Führer that members of his government had pledged, two years earlier, that *all* Germans would have the right to try out for the team, Hitler informed him, vehemently, that the German team would not include Jews. Either Hitler had not been informed of this pledge when it was given or he conveniently 'forgot' it when it was mentioned by Sherrill. After reporting to Baillet-Latour, Sherrill had another conversation with Hitler, this one over dinner. He was now assured that the pledge would be honoured. As a result of these two meetings, Sherrill was mesmerized by the force of Hitler's personality. Muting his criticism of Hitler's Germany and expressing a good deal of enthusiasm for Mussolini's Italy, Sherrill wrote to Baillet-Latour to ask sarcastically why Mahoney did not worry about the plight of the Negro athletes who suffered from discrimination not only in the South but even at the hands of the New York Athletic Club, of which both Sherrill and Mahoney were members. [64, 65]

The Winter Games, which began on 6 February, are usually forgotten by historians of the 'Nazi Olympics' (but see Richard Mandell, who discusses them in his book of that title [66]). Wet snow dampened spirits at the opening ceremony and there were nasty moments when boorish Bavarians and over zealous troops made foreign visitors feel less than welcome. Fair play and good sportsmanship also suffered a setback when the British ice-hockey team, strengthened by Canadian professionals, swept to victory. (Ironically, it was Canada they defeated in the final match.) On the other hand, there were fantastic performances, like that of Norway's Ivar Ballangrud, who won three gold and one silver medal in the four speed skating events. Sonja Henie, about to begin her career as a film star, edged Britain's Cecilia Colledge to win the figure skating title for the third time in a row.

Shortly after the Winter Games, on 7 March, Hitler sent his army into the Rhineland, an area demilitarized under the terms of the Treaty of Versailles. Hitler assumed that this defiant violation of the treaty would not jeopardize the Summer Games, and he was right.

Difficulties dogged the American team on its way to Berlin, but they were non-political. Eleanor Holm Jarrett was a veteran swimmer who had already competed in two Olympics. As a 15-year-old she had tied for fifth place in the 100-metres backstroke at the Amsterdam Games. Four years later in Los Angeles she won that event with a world record. Now a married woman of 22, she asked for and was denied permission to join the passengers in first-class accommodation (at her own expense). She made the best of a bad situation by drinking, dancing and staying up all night. After having been placed on probation, she was found drunk by the chaperone of the women's team. That Jarrett smoked, gambled and missed meals added to the officials' horror. The American Olympic Committee decided to expel her from the team and Brundage refused to alter the decision even after he was handed a petition signed by 220 coaches and athletes. Since Jarrett was considered a beautiful woman as well as a great athlete, the press reacted gleefully and newspapers published erotic photographs of the persecuted 'water nymph'. Brundage was pilloried as a mean old man, while Jarrett quickly obtained press credentials and attended the Games as a journalist. [67, 68, 69, 70, 71]

Brundage had more important worries than what to do about Mrs Jarrett. Counting on the repeated guarantees of his German friends and carried along by his belief in 'Olympism', he had risked his authority on behalf of the Games. If the Nazis failed to keep their promises, what then? In countless letters and speeches he later claimed that the Nazis *had* kept their word, that they had followed Olympic rules, that German Jews had been free to try out for the team, and that these had been the grandest and most successful of Olympics. he was wrong about at least the first three claims. It is true that the Nazis invited two athletes of mixed ancestry to join the team – Rudi Ball as an ice-hockey player and Hélène Mayer as a fencer. Mayer, who lived in the United States, won an Olympic gold medal in 1928 and was the American champion from 1933 to 1935. The statuesque blonde was an ironic choice because she did not consider herself a Jew.

Dark-haired Gretel Bergmann, however, was denied a place in the team despite the fact that she was Germany's best high jumper. On 16 July, less than a month before the Games were to begin, *Reichssportführer* von Tschammer und Osten informed her that her performance had been inadequate. Her jump of 1.6 metres was in fact 4 centimetres higher than that of her closest 'Aryan' rival. To von Tschammer und Osten's fallacious statement was added the absurd argument that Bergmann was not a member of an official sports club. How could she have been when Jews were banned from membership? Other Jews who might have won places in the team were intimidated or lacked facilities to train and failed to achieve their potential. Margaret Lambert, for instance, was called back to Germany from London, and was then told that her performance was inadequate. In all, 21 German Jews from the *Makkabi* and *Schild* organizations were 'nominated' as candidates for the team and invited to a training camp; none was selected.

One must give Baillet-Latour some credit for doing his best to hold the Nazis to their promises. Although he had written to Brundage that he was not personally fond of Jews, he did attempt to force the Nazis to admit qualified Jewish athletes to the German team and he did occasionally force Hitler to modify his policies. When Baillet-Latour heard, shortly before the beginning of the Winter Games, that the streets and roads of Garmisch-Partenkirchen were placarded with anti-Semitic placards, he demanded that they be removed – and they were. [72] Hitler and Goebbels went to great lengths to convince the world that their regime was benign and peaceable. Nazis were told not to wear their uniforms when they went to Olympic venues; the government radio was ordered not to play martial music; the *Sturm-Abteilung* was instructed to avoid provocative songs; and innkeepers were told to treat all their guests – even Jews – courteously. The Ministry of Propaganda announced: 'We desire in these weeks to prove to the world that it is simply a lie, a constantly repeated lie, that Germans have systematically persecuted the Jews.' [73]

If the Summer Games were not the triumph of 'Olympism' that Brundage and Baillet-Latour insisted they were, were they, on the contrary, a propaganda coup for the Nazis? The question is not easily answered. Hitler had told Diem and Lewald that he wanted to impress the world with the magnificence of the Games, and the world was impressed. The facilities were monumental. The magnificent *Deutsches Stadion* that was originally constructed for the 1916 Games was expanded to accommodate 110 000 spectators. At the open-air Olympic pool, 18 000 spectators were able to follow the swimming and diving events. The pageantry, which can still be vicariously experienced in Leni Riefenstahl's documentary film *Olympia*, was truly extraordinary. Among Diem's inspired innovations was an enormous iron bell inscribed with the worlds, '*Ich rufe die Jugend der Welt*' ('I summon the youth of the world'). It was also Diem's idea that a torch be lit at Olympia and carried by a relay of thousands of runners from there to the stadium in Berlin, where it was used to ignite the Olympic flame. Spiridon Louis, the Greek peasant who had won the first marathon in 1896, was invited to Berlin, where he presented Adolf Hitler with an olive branch. [74] In retrospect, the symbolism becomes a tragic irony. Other victors from 1896, like gymnast Alfred Flatow and his cousin Gustav, were murdered in the course of Hitler's monstrous 'final solution of the Jewish problem'. [75]

The most impressive of Diem's many artistic contributions was *Olympische Jugend* (Olympic Youth), a series of dances choreographed by Mary Wigman to music composed by Carl Orff and Werner Egk. The performers of *Olympische Jugend* included a chorus of a thousand, sixty male dancers, and eighty female dancers. The fourth part of this paean of youthful idealism was prophetically entitled '*Heldenkampf und Todesklage*' ('Heroes' Struggle and Lament for the Dead'). For these Games, the IOC wanted to use the music performed in Los Angeles, but Lewald had Richard Strauss set to music a poem by Robert Lubahn. The text was altered to make it more rather than less nationalistic. Similarly, the sculptors whose work adorned the main stadium and the other structures – Georg Kolbe and Arno Breker – were ordered to produce statues with suitably 'Aryan' physiques. They dutifully avoided the 'modernist' styles that the Nazis had condemned as 'degenerate art'. Whatever art historians think of the result (most are sarcastic), the spectators seem to have been impressed by all the marble muscles. [76]

Visiting dignitaries were invited to the Berlin opera and to a concert held in the Pergamon Museum, which exhibited, then as now, a stunning collection of Hellenistic art and architecture from the ancient city of Pergamon (near the present Turkish town of Bergama). Goebbels entertained two thousand guests at a magnificent country estate recently confiscated from a Jewish family. [77, 78] Small wonder that thousands of visitors left Berlin with a sense of aesthetic fulfilment and a vague impression that National Socialism was not as dreadful as they had thought. The swastika was much in evidence, but Hitler's role was minimized. Baillet-Latour told him that his duty as host was to utter a single sentence, which Baillet-Latour had typed for him. 'I declare the Games of the Eleventh Olympiad of the modern era to be open.' Intentionally or not, Hitler's response to Baillet-Latour's instructions was comic. The dictator, who was accustomed to delivering four-hour harangues, replied to Baillet-Latour, 'Count, I'll take the trouble to learn it by heart.' [79]

The athletes were impressed not only by the magnificent sports facilities but also by the Olympic village, where every effort was made to secure their comfort. (The second half of Riefenstahl's film begins with a pastoral sequence set in the village.) There were over one hundred buildings to house the athletes; their national cuisines were served in 38 separate dining halls; and runners were able to train on a 400-metre track, while swimmers and oarsmen used a specially constructed artificial lake. [80]

The strongest evidence for Brundage's claim that they were not a propaganda triumph is the fact that the Afro-American athlete Jesse Owens was undoubtedly the star of the Games. Setting a world record of 10.3 seconds for 100 metres and an Olympic record of 20.7 seconds for 200 metres, he went on to long jump an astonishing 8.06 metres and to help set another world record in the 400-metre relay. In photographs published in the German press during and after the Games, Owens appears in a favourable light. On 7 August, *The Spectator* in London commented: 'The German spectators, like all others, have fallen under the spell of the American Negro Jesse Owens, who is already the hero of these Games.' He was described in the text of one popular German publication as the *Wunderathlet* of the Games. [81] That is certainly the way Owens figures in Riefenstahl's [82, 83] documentary film, where he appears as if he really were an Olympian, a god of sports. The film was released in 1938 after two years of editing. A French journalist reviewed the film in an article aptly entitled, 'Les Dieux du stade' ('the Gods of the Stadium'). Owens was described as 'beau comme une statue de bronze animée'. [84] In the film, the camera follows Owens as it did no other athlete. When Goebbels, whose propaganda office secretly financed the film, protested that there were too many positive shots of Owens, Riefenstahl appealed to Hitler, who intervened to prevent the cuts ordered by Goebbels. [85] Ironically, no photograph of Owens (or of any of the other black athletes) appeared in the Atlanta *Constitution*, the most liberal of Southern newspapers.

Owens does figure in a famous story from the Games which the fog of time has turned into folklore. Hitler, we are told, refused to shake hands with Owens. In fact, when the Games began, Hitler personally congratulated a number of athletes, including the first German victors Hans Woelcke (shot-put), Gerhard Stock (javelin), and Tilly Fleischer (javelin), all of whom he invited to his private box. Two Afro-Americans, Cornelius Johnson and David Albritten, were first and second in the high jump, but Hitler left the stadium before the event was concluded. The following day, Baillet-Latour, accompanied by the German IOC member von Halt, cautioned Hitler and told him to invite *all* the victors to his box or none of them. Hitler decided to save his felicitations for a postgame celebration limited to the German athletes. If anyone was insulted, it was Johnson, not Owens. The latter told the *New York Times* 25 August: 'There was absolutely no discrimination at all,' but the story of the snub was (and is) too good to sacrifice at the altar of historical truth. [86]

This unexpected display of apparently unbiased treatment was actually part of a concentrated effort at shaping a favourable image of the new regime. The Ministry of Propaganda ordered, on 3 August, that 'the racial point of view should not in any form be part of the discussion of athletic results. Special care should be exercised not to offend Negro athletes.' When the editors of the rabidly racist *Der Angriff* were unable to restrain themselves from a much-publicized sneer at American's 'black auxiliaries', they were reprimanded by the ministry. There was, in the words of Hans Joachim Teichler, a 'temporary suspension of a core part of National Socialist ideology'.

Notions of 'Aryan' superiority began to seem quite ludicrous when Kitei Son of Korea won the marathon and the Japanese swimmers did almost as well as they had in 1932. (The Japanese swimming and diving team, which included athletes from conquered Korea, collected four gold, two silver, and five bronze medals.) The most annoying outcome for the Nazi host was probably the women's high jump. Having kept Bergmann from the German team, they watched Ibolya Czak, a Hungarian Jew, win that event with a leap of 1.6 metres – exactly the height that Bergmann had cleared shortly before the Games. Was it annoyance or a pleasure for Hitler and Goebbels when Hélène Mayer, the 'half-Jew' fencer, won a silver medal and raised her arm in the Nazi salute?

Ironically, in the light of expressed American concern for the fate of Jewish athletes, the most serious allegations of anti-Semitism to emerge from the actual competitions (as opposed to the pre-Olympic selection process) concerned the American team. Marty Glickman and Sam Stoller, the only Jews in the American track-and-field squad, were axed from the relay team although Glickman's times were faster than those of Foy Draper, who ran (with Owens, Metcalfe, and Frank Wykoff). The reason for this was probably not anti-Semitism. The American coaches, Lawson Robertson and Dean Cromwell, chose Draper because he was a student at the University of Southern California, where Cromwell coached. [87]

All in all, the United States did well enough in track and field and in diving for American journalists gleefully to claim that the United States had 'won' the 1936 Olympics. There was certainly reason to be proud not only of the black athletes but also of Glenn Morris, who won the decathlon, and Helen Stephens, whose time of 11.5 seconds in the 100-metres was faster than Thomas Burke's had been at the first modern Olympics in 1896. It was easy for the Americans to overlook the aquatic achievements of the Japanese men and Holland's champion swimmer, Hendrika Mastenbroek (three gold medals and one silver). How many readers, sitting over breakfast and scanning the local paper, realized that the Egyptians were superb in weightlifting, the Swedes and Hungarians in wrestling, the Italians in fencing, the French in cycling, and the Germans in just about everything? In fact, the Germans won 33 events, came second in 26 and finished third in another 30. *The Spectator* for 21 August contained that journal's quadrennial vintage of sour grapes: 'When to win the Olympic Games becomes an object of British, as it has German, policy, we shall really have reached the stage of senility, the true decadence.'

If most of the world's sports fans were but dimly unaware of German athletic superiority, it was not the fault of the government-controlled media. In addition to pre-Olympic newsletters and other publications, there was television transmission to 25 TV halls, and shortwave radio broadcasts that reached some 40 countries. Commentators from 22 countries sent the message. Finally, in 1938, Riefenstahl's *Olympia* was released with English and French as well as German narration.

The Nazi propaganda apparatus made much of the mostly favourable press coverage of the Games and exploited to the utmost the aged, infirm de Coubertin's remarks that these 'grandoise' Games, organized with 'Hitlerian strength and discipline', had 'magnificently served the Olympic ideal'. (This was de Coubertin's last public pronouncement. [88])

Propaganda coup or not, the Games were undoubtedly an important step on Brundage's path to Olympic leadership. On the first day of its thirty-fifth session, the IOC officially expelled its lone dissenter, Jahncke, by a vote of 49–0. Garland abstained from the vote. (Jahncke was also ousted, along with Ornstein, from the American Olympic Association.) In Jahncke's place the IOC elected the man who had fought successfully to block a boycott of the Games. The IOC minutes state explicitly that Brundage was elected not to take the place of the recently deceased Sherrill but rather 'en remplacement de M. Lee Jahncke'. [89] This petty vindictiveness continued when the American Olympic Committee published its official report on the Games. There were photographs of the American IOC members, including Sherrill but excluding Jahncke. Reporting to the AOC, President Brundage dismissed the boycott movement as 'radical propaganda'. A.C. Gilbert, *chef de mission*, also condemned the 'active boycott by Jews and Communists' that 'aroused the resentment of the athletic leaders, the sportsmen and [the] patriotic citizens of America'. In Brundage's eyes, the Games had been a great success. 'Fulfilling the visions of its founder, Baron Pierre de Coubertin, once again this great quadrennial celebration has demonstrated that it is the most effective influence toward international peace and harmony yet devised.' [90] But not, it seems, effective enough. Two years later, on 1 September 1939, the host of the 1936 Olympic Games ordered the invasion of Poland, and with that fateful action, began the most destructive war the world has ever known.

## References

1. Mayer, Otto (1966) *Á Travers les anneaux olympiques*, (Geneva: Cailler), p. 131.
2. Bernett, Hajo (ed.) (1966) *Nationalsozialistische Leibeserziehung* (Schorndorf: Karl Hofmann), for a representative sample of Nazi views.
3. Bernett, Hajo (1988) *Der Weg des Sports in die nationalsozialistische Diktatur* (Schorndorf: Karl Hoffmann).
4. Bernett, Hajo (ed.) (1982) *Der Sport im Kreuzfeuer der Kritik* (Schorndorf: Karl Hofmann), p. 218.
5. John, Hans-Georg (1976) *Politik und Turnen* (Ahrensburg: Czwalina).
6. Peiffer, Lorenz, (1976) *Die Deutsche Turnerschaft* (Ahrensburg: Czwalina).
7. Überhorst, Horst (1970) *Edmund Neuendorff* (Berlin: Bartels & Wernitz).
8. Krüger, Arnd (1975) *Theodor Lewald* (Berlin: Bartels & Wernitz).
9. Diem, Carl (1976) *Ein Leben für den Sport* (Ratingen: A. Henn).
10. Diem, Carl (1980) *Der deutsche Sport in der Zeit des Nationalsozialismus*, ed. Lorenz Peiffer (Cologne: Carl Diem Institute).
11. Lewald to Brundage, 29 April 1933 (Avery Brundage Collection, University of Illinois, Box 33).
12. Krüger, Arnd (1972) *Die Olympischen Spiele 1936 und die Weltmeinung* (Berlin: Bartels & Wernitz), pp. 12, 63.
13. Ibid., p. 49.
14. International Olympic Committee, *Bulletin du C.I.O.*, 8:24 (September 1933): 9.
15. Teichler, Hans-Joachim (1991) *Internationale Sportpolitik im Dritten Reich* (Schorndorf: Karl Hofmann), pp. 84–85.

16. Sherrill to Rubein, 11 June 933 (Brundage Collection, Box 35).
17. *New York Times*, 9 October 1933.
18. Brundage to Kirby, 31 May 1933 (Brundage Collection, Box 28).
19. Kirby, G. (1954) *I Wonder Why?* (New York: Coward-McCann), for Kirby's career.
20. Kirby to A.C. Gilbert, 14 December 1933 (Brundage Collection, Box 26).
21. Brundage Collection, Box 28.
22. Kirby to Brundage, 2 November 1933 (Brundage Collection, Box 29).
23. Steinhöfer, Dieter (1973) *Hans von Tschammer und Osten* (Berlin: Bartels & Wernitz).
24. Henri Baillet-Latour to Brundage, 28 December 1933, transmitting an English translation of an order dated 21 November 1933 (Brundage Collection, Box 42).
25. Brundage to Baillet-Latour, 28 December 1933 (Brundage Collection, Box 42).
26. International Olympic Committee, *Bulletin du C.I.O.*, 9:26 (October 1934): 8.
27. Teichler, Hans-Joachim (1982) Coubertin und das Dritte Reich. *Sportwissenschaft*, **12**(1), 25n.
28. Wenn, Stephen R., (1989) A Tale of Two Diplomats: George B. Messersmith and Charles H. Sherrill on Proposed American Participation in the 1936 Olympics. *Journal of Sport History*, **16**(1), Spring, 27–42.
29. Edstrøm to Brundage, 4 December 1933 (Brundage Collection, Box 240).
30. Bohlen, Friedrich (1979) *Die XI Olympischen Spiele in Berlin 1936* (Cologne: Pahl-Rugenstein), p. 52.
31. Diem, Carl, Reise nach Schweden 1934 (Carl Diem Institute, Cologne).
32. Brundage to Karl Ritter von Halt, 22 October 1934 (Brundage Collection, Box 57).
33. *New York Post*, 26 September 1934.
34. *New York Times*, 27 September 1934.
35. Brundage to Kirby, 3 March 1934 (Brundage Collection, Box 28).
36. Teichler, *op. cit.* pp. 23–4.
37. Callebat, Louis, (1988) *Pierre de Coubertin* (Paris: Fayard), pp. 206–7.
38. Brundage to Elias Brailas, 14 January 1936 (Brundage Collection, Box 153).
39. Brundage to B. Halback, 17 March 1936 (Brundage Collection, Box 153).
40. Brundage to Baillet-Latour, 24 September 1935 (Brundage Collection, Box 42).
41. Bernett, Hajo (1976) *Guido von Mengden* (Berlin: Bartels & Wernitz), p. 47.
42. Gottlieb, Moshe (1972) The American Controversy over the Olympic Games. *American Jewish Historical Quarterly* (61), March, 181–213.
43. Beier, W. (1974) The Struggle of the Antifascists against the Misuse of the 1936 Olympic Games. *History of Physical Education and Sport Research and Studies* (2), 129.
44. Wiggins, David K. (1983) The 1936 Olympic Games in Berlin: The Response of America's Black Press. *Research Quarterly*, **54**(3), September, 278–92.
45. Kirby to Brundage, 27 May 1936 (Brundage Collection, Box 29).
46. Krüger, Arnd (1978) Fair Play for American Athletes: A Study in Anti-Semitism. *Canadian Journal of History of Sport and Physical Education*, **9**(1) May, 48.
47. Gray, Wendy and Barney, Robert Knight (1990) Devotion to Whom? German-American Loyalty on the Issue of Participation in the 1936 Olympic Games. *Journal of Sport History*, **17**(2), Summer, 214–31.
48. Krüger, *Die Olympischen Spiele*, pp. 154–55.
49. Wenn, Stephen R. (1991) A suitable Policy of Neutrality? FDR and the Question of American Participation in the 1936 Olympics. *International Journal of the History of Sport*, **8**(3), December, 319–35.
50. *New York American*, 9 October 1935.

51. Brundage to Garland, 28 October 1935 (Brundage Collection, Box 56).
52. Diem, Carl, Tagebücher, 7 December 1935 (Carl Diem Institute).
53. Steinberg, David A. (1980) Workers' Sport and United Front, 1934–36. *Arena Review*, **4**(1), February, 1–6.
54. Kidd, Bruce (1980) The Popular Front and the 1936 Olympics. *Canadian Journal of History of Sport and Physical Education*, **11**(1), May, 1–18.
55. Holmes, Judith (1971) *Olympiad 1936* (New York: Ballantine Books).
56. Murray, William J. (1992) The French Workers' Sports Movement and the Victory of the Popular Front in 1936. *International Journal of History of Sport*, **19**(1), April, 29–49.
57. Ibid., pp. 44–9.
58. Ferris to Brundage, 5 June 1936 (Brundage Collection, Box 23).
59. *New York Times*, 27 November 1935.
60. Baillet-Latour to Brundage, 10 October 1935. (Brundage Collection, Box 42).
61. Ibid., 10 December 1935.
62. Baillet-Latour to Jahncke, 13 December 1935 (Brundage Collection, Box 42).
63. Brundage to Baillet-Latour, 6 January 1936 (Brundage Collection, Box 42).
64. Wenn, Tale of Two Diplomats, pp. 27–43.
65. Eisen, George (1984) The Voices of Sanity: American Diplomatic Reports from the 1936 Berlin Olympiad. *Journal of Sport History*, **11**(3), Winter, 56–78.
66. Mandell, Richard (1971) *The Nazi Olympics* (New York: Macmillan).
67. Statements by May Lou Petty and Ada Taylor Sackett (Brundage Collection, Box 235).
68. *Chicago Sunday Times*, 26 July 1936.
69. *Chicago Daily News*, 25 July 1936.
70. *Chicago American*, 25 July 1936.
71. *Chicago Tribune*, 28 July 1936.
72. Poplimont, André (1956) Berlin 1936. *Bulletin du C.I.O.*, No. 56 (15 October) 46–7.
73. Teicher, *Internationale Sportpolitik*, pp. 164–6.
74. Alkemeyer, Thomas (ed.) (1986) *Olympia-Berlin: Gewalt und Mythos in den Olympischen Spielen von Berlin 1936*. Proceedings of a conference held 16–18 October 1986.
75. Bernett, Hajo (1987) Alfred Flatow – vom Olympiasieger zum 'Reichsfeind', *Sozial- und Zeitgeschichte des Sports*, **1**(2), 94–102.
76. Adam, Peter (1992) *Art of the Third Reich* (New York: Harry N. Abrams), for a discussion of Nazi art and architecture, including that of the Olympic Games.
77. Dodd, Jr., William E. and Dodd, Martha (eds.) (1941) *Ambassador Dodd's Diary, 1933–1938* (New York: Harcourt, Brace), pp, 339–44.
78. Brundage to Heinz Schöbel, 7 January 1963 (Brundage Collection, Box 62).
79. Memoranda (Brundage Collection, Box 245).
80. Mandell, *Nazi Olympics*. For these and further details of life in the village.
81. *Die Olympischen Spiele 1936*, 2 vols. (Altona-Bahrenfeld: Reemtsma, 1936), **2**(17), 23, 26–7, 46–7.
82. Riefenstahl, L. (1993) *A Memoir* (New York: St. Martin's Press).
83. Graham, Cooper G. (1986) *Leni Riefenstahl and Olympia* (Metuchen: Scarecrow Press), for a more critical view of Riefenstahl.
84. de Houville, Gerard (1936) Les Dieux du stade. *Revue de Deux Mondes*, 8th series, 46, 15 August, 935.
85. Bernett, Hajo (1973) *Untersuchungen zur Zeitgeschichte des Sports* (Schorndorf: Karl Hofmann).
86. Baker, William (1986) *Jesse Owens* (New York: Free Press), for the definitive biography of Owens.

87. Oscar Johnson, William (1972) *All That Glitters Is Not Gold* (New York: Putnams), pp. 177–84.
88. Teichler, Coubertin und das Dritte Reich, pp. 35–6.
89. Procès-Verbale de la 35ième Session du Comité International Olympique, Berlin, 30–31 July and 15 August 1936, p. 2 (Archives of the International Olympic Committee, Lausanne).
90. *Report: 1936. Games of the XIth Olympiad*, ed. Frederick W. Rubien (New York: American Olympic Committee, 1937), pp. 27, 31, 73.

# Chapter 4

# The Foreign Office and the Football Association

## British sport and appeasement, 1935–1938

*Richard Holt*

From the outset modern sport has acted as a vehicle for national aspirations. The Olympic Games, for all its pretensions to global harmony, quickly became a focus for international rivalry and resentment. The British, for example, were disappointed in their meagre haul of medals in the London Games of 1908, taken as a sign of national decay, whilst after the 1912 Stockholm Olympics, the French vowed to reassert their national prowess in front of the Germans in Berlin in 1916. [1] Then the First World War intervened, chauvinism was further strengthened and the Allies promptly refused to invite their former enemies or the new Soviet Union to participate in the Antwerp Games of 1920 and again in Paris in 1924. [2] Clearly the idea that sport was apolitical before the advent of fascism and communism is misleading. In France, the gymnastics movement was violently anti-German and sport was split between the Catholic Church and an anti-clerical State before 1914. In Britain, sport was suffused with Darwinism and imperialism, especially amongst the products of the elite public school system.

Yet British sport *was* 'apolitical' in the more restricted sense of the role of the Government. It was a central tenet of the dominant amateur system of thought and values in British sport that the State had no role to play. British sport was Victorian; it reflected the wider liberal belief in minimal state intervention and small government. [3] This is not to say that there was no connection between organized sport and the State. On the contrary, there was extensive informal and social contact. Politicians, civil servants and even government ministers were often members of sporting bodies, such as the Marylebone Cricket Club (MCC), which controlled English cricket. But these organizations, including the British Olympic Association, received no money from the State. They more or less did as they pleased.

Of course, there were exceptions. No social phenomenon as vast as modern sport with its international dimensions could escape some contact with government. This, however, tended to be ad hoc, occasional and indirect. The lead in banning the Germans and their allies from Antwerp and from the Paris Games in 1924 seems to have come from British sports bodies spontaneously refusing to play those whom they had so recently faced in the trenches. The Foreign Office, it is true, had discouraged sporting contacts with the new Soviet Union and Cabinet members had moved quickly to heal the wounds inflicted by the 'Bodyline' cricket tour of Australia in 1932. [4] But these were isolated incidents. It was not until the mid- to late 1930s that there was more serious and continuing government involvement in organized sport. Why, in particular, did the handful of public school and Oxbridge politicians and diplomats, who shaped British foreign policy, suddenly take a new interest in football and other sports?

The reason was simple, although the policy was not. The fascist manipulation of sport changed the terms of the debate and made it effectively impossible to retain the strict separation of sport from the State. The first challenge came from Mussolini, who offended British public opinion by laying claim to world supremacy in Britain's national winter ball game. England's football team had never been beaten at home and resented the Italian claim to be world champions by winning the World Cup in Rome in 1934 – an event in which the insular British had refused to participate at that time. But the mandarins at the Foreign Office were initially slow to catch the public mood. Steeped as they were in amateur traditions, the thought of using a football match for domestic or foreign policy purposes was alien, even repugnant. The British Council in Turin had noted as early as 1928 that the Italians 'are a first class side and out to win and they expect us to give them a good game'. Yet Whitehall paid little attention when England drew with Italy in Rome in 1933 and a return match, to take place in London, was arranged for November 1934. [5] The Italian team were the objects of fascist fascination and control but the British Government did nothing more than make a perfunctory reply to Italian complaints about the distribution of tickets. The connection between British prestige abroad and British football had yet to be made in the official mind.

This was all the more remarkable in the light of the prevailing diplomatic situation in Europe. The rise of Hitler to power had not gone unnoticed in Whitehall. A Cabinet Defence Requirements Committee had been set up to plan rearmament and a policy of finding potential allies against German expansion was under way. Alongside France, Italy was the prime object of British interest. If Mussolini could be brought into a pact to support the Locarno agreements of 1925, which guaranteed the western terms and borders set after the First World War by the Treaty of Versailles, then the German threat would be much reduced. [6, 7, 8, 9, 10] It was not at all in British interests for a football match to foster a mood of popular acrimony, yet that is exactly what happened. Mussolini saw off the team with a rousing speech, crowds gathered in the streets of Rome to hear the radio broadcast of the match, aptly named 'The Battle of Highbury', in which England scored from a penalty in the first minute, an Italian went off with a broken toe and an Englishman got a broken nose; the 'robust' Arsenal centre forward, Ted Drake, outraged the Italians by charging the goalkeeper in what the *Daily Herald* called 'the most brutal and dangerous . . . international match played in this country for several decades'. [11] If the English had deliberately set out to use sport to antagonize Italy, they could hardly have done a better job. The Battle of Highbury of November was hardly the best preparation for 'the Stresa Front' against Hitler, which was set up at a meeting the following April, only to collapse in confusion with the Italian invasion of Abyssinia.

The point here is not that an acrimonious football match wrecked the chances of an alliance against Hitler; such a proposition is self-evidently absurd. It was Mussolini's attack on Abyssinia, a member of the League of Nations, which ended the Stresa Front. The issue is rather more subtle. Privately the British Government, like the French, wanted to do a deal with Mussolini to keep him away from Hitler. But when the Hoare–Laval Pact to arrange this was leaked to the press in December 1935, a public outcry against a deal with Italy forced the resignation of the Foreign Secretary and finished the Stresa Front. [12] Clearly, it was public support for the League of Nations, massively affirmed in the 'Peace Ballot' of June 1935, that was largely responsible. However, public dislike of Italy with its fascist swagger and pretensions to supremacy in England's national sport may have been an aggravating factor. The English public were not inclined to view Italian antics whether on the football field or in Africa with much sympathy; the unprecedented popular reaction, when the news of a secret agreement with Italy leaked out, was hardly surprising.

Britain was now a mass democracy and even the Foreign Office had to begin to take cognisance of popular culture. The British Government had let sport sour its relations with Italy in 1934 but it did not intend to allow the same thing to happen with Germany in 1935. This emerged in the controversy that broke out over the invitation of a German football team to play England in December 1935. [13] Whilst there is certainly no evidence of any positive initiative to promote good Anglo-German relations via football, there was a new determination to ensure that sporting contacts caused no unnecessary damage. Britain was embarking upon a policy of the 'appeasement' of Germany, that is, the active seeking of German goodwill and compliance whilst gradually strengthening home defences; [14] Britain was prepared, for example, to risk international disapproval by signing a bilateral naval pact with Germany in June 1935. Initially there was no suggestion that British prestige in sport should be used as a weapon in the critically important diplomatic manoeuvres that were in progress. Hitler, however, took a different view. At this time he favoured making overtures to the British, for whom he had some residual racial respect, in order to detach them from the French. Hence when the Football Association (FA) offered a return match, its German counterpart, which like all other sporting bodies had been 'integrated' under Nazi control, accepted enthusiastically. [15, 16]

When the news got out that England was to play what amounted to a Nazi team, a campaign of protest began which merged into a wider debate over participation in the Berlin Olympic Games of 1936. As the fixture approached a left-wing press campaign against it gathered momentum, focusing on the case of a Polish Jew who allegedly had been killed by Nazis at a football match. The German ambassador protested and the Foreign Office was drawn into discussions, offering to brief the press on the inaccuracies of the story. [17] The Foreign Office found itself drawn into the affair against its will. As Wigram, the desk officer dealing with Germany noted, a football match 'is a private affair, arranged by private individuals and it is not for the government to interfere in an affair of that kind any more than in any other contact between private individuals and Germans so long as it does not lead to a breach of the peace'. [18] Senior civil servants at first stuck to their liberal view of the State and their amateur view of sport as a autonomous and voluntary activity. But the threat of protests in the streets or at the match and, even worse, of violence and injury to visiting German players and supporters set alarm bells ringing, especially when it became clear that the German 'supporters' consisted of nearly 10 000 members of the 'Strength Through Joy' Nazi sports movement.

The Home Secretary was privately concerned. 'Why should we approve of this Nazi invasion? Is it not likely to lead to a violent demonstration in which the London police will have to defend a lot of Germans against a protesting British crowd?', noted the Permanent Secretary in a memo to Robert Vansittard, Permanent Secretary of the Foreign Office, and extreme Germano-phobe. [19] But the Home Office wanted the Foreign Office not only to comply with this but to help justify it. The Foreign Office was extremely reluctant to do so. 'Let us know or say as little as possible', the Foreign Secretary scrawled in the margin of the official minute, which concluded 'it is difficult, isn't it, to conceive a public statement in which we would say the match had not been put off because we were afraid of the effect in Germany'. [20] The ball was tossed between these two ministries with neither wishing to take the initiative. Banning the game ran deeply against the grain both in terms of the traditions of British sport and public life and the immediate needs of Anglo-German relations. It was one thing to seek to win German friendship through the explicit manipulation of sport – such a thing was not British – but it was quite another to risk a diplomatic incident by snubbing the Germans once the game had been agreed. To cancel the fixture would have been to admit that the British Government could not ensure the safety of foreign visitors; worse still, it would have been perceived as a propaganda victory for the Left over a Conservative government that had won the general election of November 1935 with a majority of 432 to 174.

The press were indignant at the prospect and left the Government with little room for manoeuvre. As the campaign against the match gathered momentum immediately preceding the game, a Trades Union Congress (TUC) delegation went to see the Home Secretary. The *News Chronicle* complained that 'the intrusion of politics into sport is so detestable a poisoning of the springs of human fellowship' that it must be resisted. [21] The *Evening Standard* noted that 'today, for the first time in history, football affairs have obtruded upon the Foreign Office and the Home Office'. [22] 'Since when has anybody except the TUC considered it necessary for foreigners to submit to a test of political rectitude before being permitted to watch their countrymen playing football in these islands,' thundered the Conservative *Morning Post*. [23] The *Daily Telegraph* thought opposition to the match 'strange and unhealthy'. [24] The *Daily Mail* branded it 'rancorous' [25] and *The Times* concluded that 'to think this way is abhorrent to the English spirit'. [26] Only the Labour paper, the *Daily Herald*, took a critical view of the fixture.

In this political context there was never any realistic possibility of getting the game banned unless the protesters were willing to raise the stakes much higher by the serious threat of violence. In such circumstances the police may have advised the Home Secretary that it was impossible to ensure public order and there would have been little choice but to accept the lesser of two evils and stop the fixture. Opposition to the match was well-organized but limited to a small number of Jewish and trade union activists and officials, along with some members of the small British Communist Party. There was no plan to do anything other than make a peaceful protest. Moral indignation was easier to deal with than sticks, stones and street demonstrations. Hence the Government belatedly acceded to the TUC's request to meet the Home Secretary in the hope of avoiding more serious trouble. At least the protesters could claim their case had been heard and might exercise a restraining influence on those who wanted to take direct action. This presumably is why the Government agreed to a meeting on an issue that normally would not have been considered official business. The lengthy transcription of the meeting shows how anxious they were that the motives of the Government should not be misunderstood and offers a rare and important insight into both left- and right-wing attitudes towards sport and international politics. [27]

The TUC delegation's objections to the match, which emerged in the course of the discussion, were threefold. They thought, first, that Germany was a barbaric state in which human rights had been flagrantly abused since the Nazis came to power. It was their contention that Britain should not be seeking to have friendly sporting contact with a regime using a systematic policy of racial and political persecution and that Britain's place in the civilized world would be damaged. Secondly, they felt that sport itself had been overtly and massively politicized in Germany in direct opposition to the dominant sporting values prevailing in Britain. Thirdly, they argued that the Germans had a more sinister purpose in bringing large numbers of Nazi supporters to London to march through streets so close to the Jewish immigrant areas of East London, where the British Union of Fascists were already causing trouble.

The Home Secretary, Sir John Simon, who until a few months before had been Foreign Secretary, was able to deal with the first issue quickly and effectively. The playing of a game against a foreign power implied no official support for that country's policies. Moreover, the game, he stressed from the outset, was *not* suggested by the British Government. 'It is important to note that the fixture was negotiated and settled upon quite privately . . . That is a fact. It would not have been at all a fair thing for me to say if it had been begun diplomatically, but it was not so . . . We did not know at all. No Government Department was communicated with until it had been done. I do not think we even heard of it until some time later.' [28] The Government had not sought this match and there was no secret policy of courting dictators through sport.

The second and third issues, however, proved rather more difficult. The Government was perfectly well aware of the extent of Nazi infiltration into German sport. By late 1935, the policy of absorbing private cultural bodies into the State was already well advanced; the preparations for the Olympic Games were in their final stages and the Winter Games at Garmisch only a couple of months away. The TUC delegation had an apparently strong hand to play. The meeting had begun with one of the delegates, Mr Bromley, introducing himself as 'an old footballer and former sprint runner', going on to underline that 'we are not at all against sport' but 'simply very much in favour of keeping it unpolluted'. [29] This set the TUC delegation clearly apart from the Communist-backed British Workers Sport Federation, which had not only advocated a political struggle against fascist sport but also denounced amateurism as 'bourgeois'. [30, 31] Walter Citrine, the head of the delegation, was particularly indignant at press accusations that the TUC was bringing politics into sport. 'I want immediately to repudiate that; it had never been our purpose; it is not our present purpose and it is not likely to be our future purpose . . . the very absence of protest to you on former occasions when teams have played in this country with whose governments we did not entirely agree is evident that we ourselves do not import politics into sport.' [32] The proposed match against Germany was 'unique and distinct' because 'the German Government have imported sport into politics so grossly that today it is practically impossible for any sort of organisation, which is not under the direct auspices of the Nazi government, to take part in sport'. [33]

The TUC had a strong card to play here but they did not press home their advantage. The reason was soon apparent. Although what they said about the 'nazification' of sport was undeniable, they were open to the counter argument put by the *News Chronicle* that 'the true answer to that attitude is to refuse to follow what we hold to be a bad and foolish principle'. [34] This clearly struck home with some of the delegation who, as the discussion proceeded, seemed to be in genuine difficulty and confusion over the whole question. One member, Mr Dukes, in an extraordinary outburst, went as far as to say 'Frankly, I welcome the fact that the team is coming over; I want to see as much international sport as can be arranged.' [35] The values of fair play, amateurism and the maintaining of sport as a private activity which permeated the ruling elite also strongly influenced the Labour movement; like the Right, the democratic Left also tended to see sport in rather idealized terms as a means or moral improvement. They were almost as thoroughly impregnated with a belief in apolitical sport as the Conservative Party and press. All an experienced politician like Simon had to do was keep quiet and let the protest break up under the weight of its own contradictions.

Hence, it was fear of German supporters that proved most contentious and which occupied the bulk of the meeting. Here the opponents of the match had a powerful argument with which Simon himself had privately expressed some sympathy. [36, 37] The thought of up to 10 000 members of the Nazi Youth and similar bodies posing as supporters of the German football team was no more acceptable to the Government than to the opponents of the match. It is doubtful if such a political demonstration was ever intended, given Hitler's desire to stay on good terms with the British. However, it was widely believed on the Left that such a demonstration would take place and that British fascists would use the occasion for a display of strength. 'If a British team were visiting Germany . . . nobody would think of going there waving Union Jacks or Red Flags, but the Germans when they go to a tea party have flags and swastikas . . . That is what we really fear,' as one delegate remarked. [38] Clashes between fascists and anti-fascists in the East End were among the most violent of the 1930s and the game ironically was sched-uled to be played at White Hart Lane, a ground which attracted a significant number of Jewish supporters to watch Tottenham Hotspur.

The Police Commissioner was on hand to indicate that no such march of Nazi supporters would be allowed. Without giving away operational details, which were carefully worked out and kept secret until just before the game, he made it clear that German spectators would be bussed to the ground and no 'procession' would be permitted. In this limited sense, perhaps, the protest movement had made their point; they had concentrated the official mind on the possible political abuse of the fixture and ensured that a fascist demonstration would not take place. Simon gave repeated assurances that he had personally checked the arrange-ments, which did not involve a 'procession'. The meeting drew to a close with a semantic argument over the definition of a 'procession', to the evident irritation of the Home Secretary and his officials. Despite this anticlimax, the meeting was important and historic. The links between sport and politics had been brought into the open for the first time and the Government had been required to state that it would at least try to enforce its declared principle of the separation of sport and politics by taking steps to stop the German supporters turning a sporting event into a Nazi rally.

As it happened the match went off smoothly. The fears of the Left that there would be a major Nazi demonstration proved groundless and the arrival of the Germans did not result in a large demonstration of support from the British Union of Fascists. There were, in fact, no major incidents. Even the *Jewish Chronicle* noted that a number of Jewish fans went along to the game and others made money as tour guides or interpreters. [39] There was a capacity 60 000 crowd, most of whom would have been manual workers. Clearly the Labour movement was far ahead of its rank and file, an awareness of which may well have weakened their determination to press home the campaign against the game. As it turned out, the Germans had the good grace to lose the match 3–0, having announced in advance that they expected to do so. Stanley Matthews was playing only his second match for England and George Camsell scored twice, with Cliff Bastin of Arsenal adding a third. The crowd rather took to the blond-haired German captain whom they nicknamed 'Greta' and the match passed off in a friendly and satisfactory fashion for both sides.

Unlike the Italians the previous year, the Germans were on a goodwill mission to 'honour' the founders of the game. The German sports minister, von Tschammer und Osten, who had accompanied the team, toasted the British at the dinner held in the evening after the match and the Football Association con-demned the efforts that had been made to stop the fixture. More importantly, however, many of those present were invited to another dinner the following night hosted by the newly formed right-wing Anglo-German Fellowship, recently set up by Lord Mount Temple, who 'referred to the match as a turning point in relations between the two countries'. [40]

What were the implications of this unprecedented public airing of the relationship between sport and politics? From the Government's point of view their strategy had been a success. The challenge had been successfully resisted without it appearing that any special concessions had been given to Germany. The Foreign Office had been alerted to the potential political sensitivity of sport. Henceforth its main strategy would be to intervene to ensure non-intervention, that is, to arrange things so that Britain did not offend other powers through sport and to keep the British Government well away from direct involvement. Where possible, international sport should promote goodwill and British prestige – bad publicity abroad arising from sport was to be avoided at all costs – but this should be done behind the scenes by dropping a word in the ear of the main sporting bodies via the 'old boy' network.

An immediate casualty of the match was the move to oppose British participation in the 1936 Olympics. If a Nazi team could not be stopped from visiting Britain, how much less was it likely that a British athletics team would be banned from going to Germany? The campaign to boycott the Berlin Olympics had in any case been noticeably weaker in Britain than in the United States or in France. [41, 42] This was partly because Britain had a much smaller and less politically well-organized Jewish community than America; it also had no black athletes, whose participation in Berlin was openly criticized in the racist Nazi press. Amateurism was most deeply entrenched amongst British athletes themselves and a move to boycott the Games at a meeting of the Amateur Athletic Association (AAA) was overwhelmingly defeated. [43] Harold Abrahams, the Jewish sprinter who had won a gold medal in the Paris Games of 1924, was against a boycott. Ex-Cambridge, a member of the AAA general committee and athletics correspondent of the *Sunday Times*, Abrahams was an influential figure. If, as a Jew, he had taken a leading role in opposing the sending of a team to Berlin, the question at least would have been put properly on the agenda. By taking the opposite line and accepting the assurances of the Germans to the International Olympic Committee that there would be no discrimination in the picking of the German team, Abrahams and the British athletics establishment made opposition to the Games in Britain even more marginal and ineffective. Predictably the Nazis promised there would no barriers to German-Jewish athletes and predictably none were selected despite several individuals with an outstanding claim to a place. [44]

The British Government, alerted to the dangers of becoming openly involved in the politics of sport by the England–Germany match, took the trouble to see that the Olympics did not damage Anglo-German relations whilst trying as far as possible to stay out of the picture. Dispatches from the British ambassador in Berlin, Sir Eric Phipps, left the Foreign Office in no doubt of the 'enormous importance' attached to the Games by the German regime. Writing in February 1936, Phipps stressed the 'considerable anxiety' in Germany over an American ban and the 'relief expressed when it was heard that the American team had actually arrived'. [45] The Foreign Office carried on a double game during the months leading up to Berlin in August. To an inquiry from the Spanish Government in April as to 'whether the British . . . are going to take part in the Olympic Games at Berlin and whether . . . they will receive assistance of any kind from the Government', the Foreign Office frostily referred the Spanish ambassador to the British Olympic Association, a private organisation with whom His Majesty's Government have no connection, and there is no question of any official patronage or assistance (financial or other wise) being given to British teams participation'. [46] This 'hands off attitude', however, did not extend as far as refusing to intervene when Phipps sent a coded telegram (marked 'very confidential') on 16 May pointing out that the French ambassador was extremely worried that 'Left parties in France are putting pressure on the French Government to refuse to send French candidates to the Olympic Games' and that this 'would mean the end of any hope of agreement between France and Germany.' [47] Vansittart himself 'put in a word against the idea that France ought to boycott the Olympic Games' with the French ambassador pointing out that it 'could do no possible good'. [48]

The British were clearly concerned that the Games should go ahead but they were also unwilling to say so in public and nervous about any kind of official endorsement of the event. This attempt to combine the traditional policy of keeping sport and politics apart with the wider policy of appeasement made it difficult to decide on doing anything. When, for example, Prime Minister Stanley Baldwin received a perfectly innocuous request from Lord Burghley to attend an Olympic dinner in May, the Foreign Office was asked for a view. At first they agreed, noting that 'the Prime Minister would not be going against the tradition of non-intervention by attending' but seeking clarification over exactly who was issuing the invitation and who else would be attending. [49] This was 3 March 1936. Ten days later when the matter was reviewed, it was clear that Baldwin would be a guest of the British Olympic Association and there was no obstacle to his going. However, in the intervening period, the Germans had marched into the Rhineland. Officials were unwilling to commit the Prime Minister to the dinner until 'the present crisis resolves itself' but it was striking that no one suggested he publicly refuse to attend, still less that a boycott might now be considered. [50]

At about the same time, in early March, the German Navy had issued an invitation to the Admiralty to send a warship to Kiel during the Olympics and to enter a team for a sailing event in the week after the Games. Again a decision was deferred because of the re-occupation of the Rhineland; however, when the Foreign Office learned that the Swedes, Danes and even the United States were sending ships, it agreed to the idea, providing the Admiralty could spare one. The whole trivial episode dragged on and on with Navy worries about pulling forces out of the Mediterranean, where Britain was supposed to be imposing sanctions against Italy. Eventually it was decided to send a ship for part of the time and a crew by train for the naval races – a confused and half-hearted compromise, which encapsulated the ambivalence of official thinking. [51]

The dinner and the naval invitations reveal the conflicting interests that beset the government when it was called upon to take a position over international sport, especially in connection with Germany. It was important that Britain should not be seen trying to win favour with the Germans through sport; but it was even more important they should not give any unnecessary offence. When the Foreign Secretary, Anthony Eden, was asked in the House of Commons in July 1936 if he would 'ask for an assurance that they [the Germans] do not propose to use the Olympic Games for the purposes of political propaganda, and as implying recognition and support for the Nazi regime', he replied, 'No, sir'. Similarly, he refused to be drawn by the other side when asked if he viewed 'with disfavour these impertinent pinpricks against a friendly nation'. [52]

So British attendance at the Summer Games in Berlin went ahead despite detailed knowledge of what the Germans were doing. It was perfectly obvious that Goebbels was drawing maximum propaganda value from the event to show the achievements of National Socialism and that the 'Olympic pause' in racist persecution was superficial and purely temporary. But with the collapse of the Stresa Front and the re-militarization of the Rhineland, Britain was in a weak position. If Germany could not be opposed, then she would have to be appeased and Neville Chamberlain, the strongest advocate of a policy of negotiation and concession, was becoming ever more powerful in the government, taking over as prime minister the following year. [53]

The Berlin Games, of course, did not produce the results either Hitler or the fanatically nationalist crowds had hoped. Far from being a demonstration of Aryan superiority, Jesse Owens dominated the prestige sprint events whilst the Finns won the longer distances and a New Zealander, Jack Lovelock, who had studied in London, won the 1500 metres. Britain took a splendid gold in the 4 × 400 relay with a young army officer, Godfrey Rampling, running an outstanding third leg and the team came back moderately satisfied with British honour intact. The Nazis had temporarily suspended their Jew-baiting and arrest of political opponents. The Germans were pleased with the Games despite their relative lack of success in the big events and it looked as if the regime would be more easy to deal with as a result of this massive exercise in public relations. Goebbels seems to have come away with the impression that Robert Vansittart, who attended the Games, 'was deeply impressed by Germany'. [54, 55] Nazi appreciation of upper class English manners and irony was limited, to say the least; Vansittart was certainly struck by the scale of the undertaking but his hostile view of Nazism was unchanged – indeed this led to his removal as Permanent Secretary of the Foreign Office the following year on Chamberlain's orders.

The impact of the Berlin Games and the wider awareness of fascist sport in Britain were twofold: first, they focused attention powerfully on the question of national fitness; secondly, they encouraged British diplomats to take a closer interest than before in the role which sport might play in foreign policy. In terms of British domestic policy towards physical education, there is no doubt that the example of mass fascist youth movements exploiting the possibilities of sport for physical fitness, paramilitary training and national motivation had a sharp impact on both the major West European liberal democracies. The Popular Front in France appointed a junior minister for sport and combined a national fitness policy with a socialist stress on shorter hours, better holidays and public facilities. The British, whilst denying that the Strength Through Joy of Dopolavoro systems had spurred them into action and stressing the popular demand for improving the existing system, began a remarkable period of activity. This ran from 1936 to the outbreak of war and saw the issuing of a new and much expanded physical education syllabus for schools and a national plan for improved facilities; the involvement of the British Medical Association in assessing dietary and exercise needs; and most importantly, the passing of the Physical Education and Training Act of 1937 establishing a National Fitness Council with a budget of two million pounds over three years. [56, 57, 58] Some of this, of course, came from the slow growth of physical education as a subject in schools combined with the 'outdoor movement' of the 1930s which saw greatly increased numbers of people going walking in the countryside or taking other kinds of exercise. But it is doubtful if these desirable developments alone would have produced such sudden official enthusiasm for expensive legislation from a Conservative government committed to tight controls on public spending. Hitler concentrated the mind wonderfully.

In terms of British diplomacy, the challenge of fascist football and the political mobilization of sport at the Berlin Games clearly had an impact. As a status quo power with vast global commitments to its Empire and trade routes, the British did not want problems close to home. Apart from Hitler, they had the Italians strad-dling the Mediterranean and the Japanese threatening investments in China and, possibly, the defence of India and Australia. Having dropped their alliance with the Japanese in 1922 to please the Americans, the British were very anxious to avoid a conflict in the Far East. As early as January 1936 the Japanese had contacted the British to see if they would support a bid to host the 1940 Olympics in Tokyo. The British ambassador noted that 'although it may seem unimportant I believe it may contribute to peace in the Far East' and an excited Eden wrote 'then for heaven's sake let us encourage it. I could even run in the mile myself!!' [59] When the advantage was great enough, the sacred principle of non-political sport went out the window at the precise moment it was being used against those who opposed contact with Germany. A problem, however, emerged over the Japanese bid. The British Olympic Association (BOA) itself was planning to put in a bid for the 1940 Games. The Government did not learn of the London bid until June and found itself once again in a difficult spot, caught between its principles and political expediency. After some intense behind the scenes discussion, the BOA were urged to withdraw in favour of Japan who were duly awarded the 1940 Games. The Japanese were delighted. The volte-face 'for reasons of high policy and contrary to normal rule [sic] of non-intervention', as a telegram to the British Embassy in Tokyo described it, seemed justified. [60]

The British began to realize that in their sporting heritage they had a valuable resource in the eyes of the rest of the world, even amongst otherwise dangerous or unfriendly powers. After the Japanese bid and the Berlin Games, British ministers did not intervene directly in the Olympics, although they pointedly refused to endorse the BOA's bid for the 1944 Games on the grounds that it might offend the Italians who were trying to get the Games for Rome. Rather the Foreign Office sought to use sport to enhance Britain's prestige generally. Success in sport gave the impression of a physically vigorous nation and countered fascist notions of a racially degenerate democracy whilst stressing the special role accorded to moral qualities in sport. Upholding ideals of sportsmanship came to be seen as increasingly important. Vansittart became chairman of a committee to oversee British foreign propaganda and, as his Private Secretary wrote, 'in that capacity takes a special interest in the question of Association football matches between British and foreign teams'. [61]

This had two aspects. The first was to avoid the British reputation for sportsmanship being harmed by the bad behaviour of British sides abroad. There had been minor incidents in France, Germany and Austria but the most indignant complaint came from the Secretary General of the British Council, Lt.-Col. Charles Bridge, to the Foreign Office 'about the unfortunate effect produced in Poland by the bad behaviour of visiting British football teams'. In this case a player spat at a referee who had sent him off in front of 50,000 spectators, including several leading members of the Polish government. Whilst recognizing 'that the Football Association is a private undertaking over which the Government cannot exercise control . . . something can and must be done to try and protect the British reputation for sportsmanship . . . Otherwise why waste the taxpayers' money on trying to disseminate among foreigners an appreciation of the glories of British culture!' [62] Vansittart saw Stanley Rous, secretary of the FA, and asked him if more care could be taken in the preparation of teams and he agreed to help. The real difficulty was the limited control of the FA over teams making foreign tours.

In the international sphere, where the FA had more control, the results were more favourable. In particular, a good deal of interest was taken in a return football match played in Berlin in 1938. The British were anxious that the national team should perform well and create a good impression. The diplomatic service was pressed into a little scouting, with Vansittart writing to Rous 'to let you know that the German team to play against the British (*sic*) football team in Berlin about a fortnight from now has already been practising for some time'. [63] Rous was left in no doubt that England expected him to do his duty. 'It is really important for our prestige that the British team should put up a really first class performance.' [64] As it happened, the England team surpassed his highest expectations with a brilliant 6–3 victory and further impressed the Germans by reluctantly following the advice of the British ambassador, Sir Neville Henderson, and giving the Nazi salute.

At the time even an opponent of Chamberlain's form of appeasement such as Vansittart thought the whole event a great success. The Consular Report of Current Events in Berlin during May 1938 noted that 'the splendid game played by the English team was thoroughly enjoyed by the huge crowd and it is now recognised that the excellence of English football is still something to be admired and coveted. The game undoubtedly revived in Germany British sporting prestige.'[65,66] Vansittart passed on the good news to Rous 'appreciating the co-operation which the FA has offered' and looking forward to discussing 'further measures to ensure a good impression is made abroad by British participation in such matches'. [67] However, there were clear limits to their interest. The government showed little initiative in these matters. The sports authorities set the programme; the State merely saw it did not conflict with the wider national interest. The government was not proactive. It did not, for example, apply pressure on the FA to enter the World Cup, the finals of which were played in Paris in 1938 and won again by Italy.

All the same, in terms of its attitude to sport, the Foreign Office had come quite a long way in a short time. From almost entirely ignoring the Italian fixture in 1934 and finding themselves caught off guard by the arrangement of a match with Germany in 1935, they had moved towards keeping much more closely in touch with the FA. They had retained the broad principle of sport as a private activity. However, they had also become much more aware of the potential threat to the delicate balance of foreign policy if fixtures were allowed to be cancelled as a result of pressures from radical minorities. The England–Germany game went ahead without a problem and, much more important, the Berlin Games themselves were a success. This, of course, is not to say that the official policy was morally right or effective; an Olympic boycott might well have embarrassed Hitler and have shown a collective resolve that was lacking elsewhere. But this is not the point. Despite the inevitable differences between departments and individuals – the State was not monolithic – the British government came to have a clearer perception of how to use sport to further its interests as the manipulation of the Japanese Olympic bid made clear. But for most of the time the aim was more general. It was to begin, albeit tentatively, to promote British interests more actively by using a hitherto untapped cultural resource: the unique position and prestige of Britain in the world as the founders of modern sport.

## Acknowledgements

I would like to acknowledge my gratitude to Pierre Arnaud, who first suggested the topic to me and who, with Alfred Wahl, organized both the research project on Sport and International Relations through the CNRS and a colloquium in Metz. I am also very grateful to Tony Mason, with whom I wrote an earlier version of this paper, for his help and his permission to quote from his work on Italy. Brian Stoddart's Sport, Cultural Politics and International Relations: England versus Germany, 1935 in N. Muller and J.K. Ruhl, *Sport History*: Olympic Scientific Congress, Oregon 1984 (Niederhausen 1985) proved an exceptionally helpful and perceptive piece of research that deserves to be more widely known. Re-reading Stephen Jones, *Sport, Politics and the Working Class* (Manchester University Press 1988) I was again struck by the loss to the scholarly community of so energetic a scholar, killed tragically at the age of 30 in 1987, who pioneered British work in this area. Finally, I thank Jan Tolleneer of the KU Leuven for hosting a valuable preparatory research seminar in Kortrijk and the editors of this volume for their efforts in the difficult task of multi-national publishing.

## References

1. Holt, R. (1995) Contrasting nationalisms: sport militarism and the unitary state in Berlin and France, 1870–1914. *International Journal of the History of Sport*, Sept.
2. Arnaud, P. (1994) Des jeux de la victoire aux jeux de la paix, in P. Arnaud and A. Wahl (eds), *Sports et Relations Internationales* (Centre de Recherches Histoire et Civilisation de l'Université de Metz).
3. Holt, R. (1992) *Sport and the British: a modern history* (Oxford University Press), esp. pp. 344–5.
4. Sissons, R. and Stoddart, B. (1984) *Cricket and Empire: the 1932 Bodyline tour of Australia* (London).
5. Holt, R. and Mason, T. (1994) Le football, le fascisme et la politique étrangère britannique: L'Angleterre, l'Italie et l'Allemagne, 1934–5, in Arnaud and Wahl, *op. cit.*, pp. 78–80.
6. Adams, R.J.Q. (1993) *British Politics and Foreign Policy in the Age of Appeasement 1935–9* (Stanford) gives a summary of what is a vast literature.
7. Taylor, A.J.P. (1961) *Origins of the Second World War* (London).
8. Gilbert, M. (1966) *The Roots of Appeasement* (London).
9. Middlemas, K, (1972) *The Diplomacy of Illusion: the British Government and Germany, 1937–39* (London).
10. Parker, R.A.C. (1993) *Chamberlain and Appeasement: British Policy and the coming of the Second World War* (Macmillan).
11. Holt and Mason, *op. cit.*, p. 80.
12. Adams, *op. cit.*, pp. 20–3.
13. Stoddart, B. (1985) Sport, Cultural Politics and International Relations, in N. Muller and J.K. Ruhl, *Sport History* (Niederhausen).
14. Rock, W. (1977) *British Appeasement in the Thirties* (London) gives a good historiographical survey and discussion of the team.
15. Carr, G.A. (1979) Sport and Party Ideology in the Third Reich. *Canadian Journal of the History of Sport*, Dec.
16. *Journal of Sport History*, **17**(2), 1990, special German issue.
17. Stoddart, *op. cit.*, pp. 389–90.
18. FO 371 18884/C7757 Minute by Wigram summarizing FO position.
19. HO 45 16425 memo Permanent Secretary of Home Office on 11 Nov. 1935 to Vansittart.
20. FO 371 18884/C7757 Vansittart remarked that it would be 'difficult to cancel without causing an incident for certain, although there may be worse incidents still if there is an unchecked Nazi influx'.
21. *News Chronicle* 28 Nov. 1935.
22. *Evening Standard* 29 Nov. 1935.
23. *Morning Post* 29 Nov. 1935.
24. *Daily Telegraph* 30 Nov. 1935.

25. *Daily Mail* 30 Nov. 1930.
26. *The Times* 3 Dec. 1935.
27. HO 45/16425 Notes of the Deputation from the Trades Union Congress to the Home Secretary, 2 Dec. 1935.
28. Ibid.
29. Ibid.
30. Jones, Stephen (1988) *Sport, Politics and the Working Class* (Manchester University Press), on the relationship between Communist and Labour sport, esp. pp. 182–4.
31. Hill, Jeff (1994) Le sport socialiste en GB et ses relations avec l'Europe, in P. Arnaud and A. Wahl, *op. cit.*, pp. 173–86.
32. HO 45/16425 Notes of the Deputation.
33. Ibid.
34. *News Chronicle* 28 Nov. 1935.
35. HO 45/16425 Notes of the Deputation.
36. FO 3771 18884/C7757 Minute by Wigram summarizing FO position.
37. HO 45/16425 memo Permanent Secretary of Home Office on 11 Nov. 1935 to Vansittart.
38. Notes of the Deputation, *op. cit.*
39. *Jewish Chronicle*, 6 Dec. 1935.
40. Stoddart, *op. cit.*, p. 403.
41. Guttmann, A. (1992) *The Olympics: a history of the Modern Games* (Illinois University Press), pp. 53–72, for a concise survey.
42. Murray, Bill (1992) Berlin in 1936: old and new work on the Nazi Olympics. *International Journal of the History of Sport*, April, provides a good bibliographical review.
43. Davis, Duff Hart (1986) *The Berlin Games* (London) looks at the event perceptively from the British angle; unfortunately it has no notes.
44. FO 371/19940/C5645 note from British Embassy on exclusion of Grete Bergmann from the German team because she was Jewish.
45. FO 371/19940 Phipps to Eden 13 Feb. 1935.
46. FO 371/19940/C3697 reply to Spanish Ambassador 30 April 1936.
47. FO 371/19940/C3697 Phipps to Vansittart 16 May 1936.
48. Ibid., Vansittart's reply to Phipps 20 May 1936.
49. FO 371/19940/C1721 3 March 1936 Invitation to Prime Minister to attend British Olympic Dinner.
50. Ibid. Notes of a reply 12 March 1936.
51. FO 371/19940/C1639 memo 23 June 1936 summarizing position over invitation to send a warship to Kiel for Olympic Games.
52. Extracts from Hansard with the file on Olympic Participation in FO 371/19940.
53. Parker, *op. cit.*
54. Bernett, H. (1988) Nazi Physical Education as reflected in British Appeasement Policy. *International Journal of the History of Sport*, Sept., 170.
55. Mandell. R. (1987) *The Nazi Olympics* (Illinois University Press), for a general account.
56. Ibid.
57. Smith, W. David (1974) *Stretching Their Bodies: the History of Physical Education* (Newton Abbot), pp. 144–8.
58. FO 371/22933/C19398.
59. Polley, M. (1992) Olympic Diplomacy: The British Government and the projected 1940 Olympic Games. *International Journal of the History of Sport*, August, 176.

60. Ibid., 182.
61. FO 395/568/P3341 Vansittart to Rous 27 July 1938.
62. FO 395/568/P2241 Secretary General of British Council 12 July 1938.
63. FO 395/568/P1718 Vansittart to Rous 6 May 1938.
64. Ibid.
65. FO 395/568/P1718 Extract from Consular Report on Current Events in Berlin during May 1938.
66. Beck, P. (1982) England versus Germany, 1938. *History Today*, 32, for a discussion of the match and its context.
67. FO 395/568/P1718 Vansittart to Rous 25 June 1938.

# Chapter 5

# The sports policy of the Soviet Union, 1917–1941

*James Riordan*

The policy pursued by Soviet leaders in international sport in the period following the October 1917 Revolution in Russia up to 1941 was unique. Not only did the Communist leaders turn their backs on world sport, including the Olympic Games, they attempted to form a new pattern of sports relations based on 'worker (i.e. 'communist worker') sport' or 'physical culture'. For the first time a major state declared sport to be a political institution which played a significant part in the class war between workers and bourgeoisie, between the new socialist state and the capitalist world.

This was an analysis and policy that was to have worldwide repercussions not only on other Communist Parties, which tended to follow whatever line Moscow advocated for the 'Communist International', but on anti-communist governments and sports movements in reaction to the Soviet policy (including those in fascist Italy, Germany and Spain).

We may usefully delineate the interwar period into separate eras in which the policy pursued by the Soviet leadership (and, therefore, 'world communism' and reacting opposition forces) markedly differed: i) 1917–28; ii) 1928–39; and iii) 1939–41. In summary, the first period saw the promotion of 'proletarian internationalism' through sport and the undermining of bourgeois and social-democratic authority, in order to advance world revolution. Following the obvious failure of world revolution, however, the policy changed in 1928 to one of reinforcing the USSR as a nation-state. With the signing of the Molotov–von Ribbentrop pact in 1939, the policy then veered to one of collaboration with facist states in sport and postponement of Soviet involvement in world war.

## Promoting proletarian internationalism, 1917–28

The overriding assumption of this period was that world revolution was on the horizon and that, until then, the world would be split irreconcilably into two hostile camps. The Declaration on the Formation of the USSR, adopted on 30 December 1922, stated unequivocally the fundamental preconceptions of Soviet leaders in international affairs:

> Since the foundation of the Soviet republics, the countries of the world have been split into two camps: the camp of capitalism and the camp of social-ism . . . The USSR is to serve as a decisive new step on the way to uniting the workers of the world into a World Socialist Soviet Republic. [1]

The spreading of communism throughout the world was regarded not simply as an ideological precept, but as a practical necessity on which depended the very existence of the Soviet state.

Thus, in sport, the Soviet leaders at first ignored bourgeois sports organiza-tions, refused to affiliate to their international federations and boycotted their competitions, especially the Olympic Games which were characterized as designed 'to deflect workers from the class struggle while training them for new imperialist wars'. [2]

In any case, there was strong pressure from various quarters within the Soviet Union during the 1920s against the development of organized competitive sport in the new worker state. To one group, the 'hygienists', 'sport' implied competi-tion, games that were potentially injurious to mental and physical health. Such pursuits as boxing, weightlifting and gymnastics were, in their opinion, irrational and dangerous, and encouraged individualist rather than collectivist attitudes and values – and as such, were contrary to the desired socialist ethic. To another group, the *Proletkult* (Proletarian Culture), all organized sports that derived from bourgeois society were remnants of the decadent past and emanations of degen-erate bourgeois culture. A fresh start had to be made through the revolutionary innovation of proletarian physical culture. To these and others, just as during the Renaissance the bourgeoisie had developed a substantially new pattern of sport imbued with their values, it was thought perfectly natural after the Russian Revolution that a fundamentally new pattern of recreation would emerge, reflect-ing the requirements and values of the working class and the new socialist state. Exactly what this new pattern would be was unclear, but few thinkers felt that it should be governed by the types of sports, rules and regulations embedded in the Olympic Games, which reflected the social distinctions and privileges current in Western society.

Initially then, excursions beyond Soviet borders were largely confined to playing against foreign worker teams and to the sport the USSR was best at – soccer (having inherited well-equipped clubs from many of the foreign factories in Russia). Nonetheless, the need to coexist (especially with the USSR's neighbours), a desire to compete against the world's best teams and the consideration that the bour-geoisie in certain backward states were playing a progressive role brought some limited contacts. The contacts might well have been more extensive but for the refusal of certain governments to grant visas to Soviet athletes (e.g. Spain, Czechoslovakia and Lower Austria in 1926 and 1927).

Limited participation in other sports began to take place in the late 1920s, even in bourgeois tournaments, as long as Soviet representatives stood a reasonable chance of winning. As a Soviet periodical wrote at the time:

In certain circumstances, the participation of working-class chess players in bourgeois tourneys would be politically advantageous, inasmuch as it would unite working people around the idea of class solidarity and of opposition as a class to the bourgeoisie. The Chess Section therefore deems it possible for the proletarian chess organisations to take part in international matches so as, through victories over bourgeois masters, to enhance self-respect among the proletarian masses and faith in their strength and youthful talents. [3]

For the most part, however, as long as the USSR remained isolated and weak internationally, foreign sports relations were restricted to worker sports organizations and reflected the policy of the Communist International or Comintern. The Third or Communist International was set up in Moscow in March 1919, with the avowed objective of working to spread communism throughout the world. As Trotsky put it; 'If today the centre of the Third International lies in Moscow, tomorrow . . . it will shift westwards – to Berlin, Paris, London.' [4] From the first, as the historian Max Beloff has written, the Comintern 'was dominated by the Russian Bolshevik Party'. [5]

Soviet foreign sports policy, in fact, was largely identical with and conducted through the International Association of Red Sports and Gymnastics Organisations, better known as Red Sport International (RSI). The RSI was formed at the First International Congress of Representatives of Revolutionary Worker Sports Organisations as an affiliate of the Comintern in Moscow in July 1921, two years after the Comintern's inception. Founder members were worker sports organizations from eight countries: Czechoslovakia, Finland, France, Germany, Hungary, Italy, Soviet Russia and Sweden. By 1924, it had 2 214 000 members in nine sections distributed in Bulgaria, Czechoslovakia, Estonia, France, Italy, Norway, Uruguay, USA and USSR. Its first president was Nikolai Podvoisky, then concurrently head of the Soviet sports movement; its secretary was Fritz Reissner of Germany.

The RSI was formed partly to counterbalance the social-democratic (Lucerne-based) Worker Sport International (WSI – in 1929 renamed the Socialist Worker Sport International), which had been set up in 1920 on the initiative of Belgian, French and German social democrats and was composed of worker organizations from these three countries plus others in Britain, Czechoslovakia, Finland and Switzerland. The RSI made its concern for sport and the class struggle manifest in the second article of its statutes:

The Red Sport International embraces all worker and peasant sports associations which support the proletarian class struggle . . . Physical culture, gymnastics, games and sport are a means of proletarian class struggle, not an end in themselves. [6]

Relations between the two socialist sports internationals were hostile from the start, with the RSI accusing its 'reformist' rival of diverting workers from the class struggle by preaching that athletes should be neutral and that sport should be apolitical. The RSI further charged it with preventing its members from competing against Soviet and other revolutionary sports bodies (the WSI counterclaimed that the RSI was bent on the 'militarization' of sport). [7]

Following the WSI-sponsored First World Worker Olympics of 1925, which excluded Soviet athletes (the WSI actually invited RSI athletes to compete on condition that the two internationals amalgamated; the RSI declined), Moscow staged its first great international sporting event in 1928 – the First Worker Spartakiad dedicated to the tenth anniversary of the Soviet sports movement. The Spartakiad was intended to demonstrate proletarian internationalism in sport by being a *universal worker Olympics* and a counter balance to the bourgeois Olympics being held the same year in Amsterdam. Although the Spartakiad was dominated by Soviet athletes, a sizeable foreign contingent arrived – in spite of the WSI ban on its members attending and the difficulties put in the way of worker athletes by Western governments.

Some 600 foreign athletes (about 15% of all the participants) from a dozen or more countries are said to have taken part in the games (although Soviet sources put the figure at a dozen nations: Austria, Britain, Czechoslovakia, Estonia, Finland, France, Germany, Latvia, Norway, Sweden, Switzerland and Uruguay. [8] Another source adds Algeria and Argentina. [9]

The programme ranged over 21 sports, approximating to the programme of the bourgeois Olympics. It differed from the latter, however, in that, besides team and individual competitions, the Spartakiad contained two innovations thought to be appropriate to such a novel socialist sports festival: first, a variety of pageants and displays, including an elaborate ritual of opening and closing ceremonies, carnivals, mass games, motor-car and motor-cycle rallies; and second, demonstration of folk-games, folk-music and folk-dancing. In addition, there were displays of sports that were unfamiliar to many of the participants (e.g. Rugby, tennis, field hockey), poetry readings and mock 'battles' between the 'world proletariat' and the 'world bourgeoisie'. [10]

## Strengthening the USSR as a nation-state, 1928–39

Shortly after the 1928 Moscow worker Olympics, the USSR and the Comintern underwent a radical change in foreign policy. Concerned at the ebb of the world communist movement and convinced that it was only a matter of time before the capitalist powers renewed attempts to destroy the Soviet regime (following their failure in the attack on Soviet Russia from 1918 to 1921), the Soviet leaders felt it necessary to build up defence capacity and try to postpone the coming assault as long as possible so as to permit the consolidation and strengthening of Soviet defences through the country's rapid and extensive industrialization. The growing weight attached to the defensive aspects of Soviet foreign policy was greatly reinforced by the triumph of Stalin's doctrine of 'socialism in one country' first put forward in 1924–5. Trotsky and other leaders who saw the strengthening of the world revolutionary movement as the only real guarantee of maintaining the gains of the Russian Revolution had, by the end of 1927, been driven into the political wilderness; henceforward, there could be no doubt that it was the Russian Revolution rather than the international revolution which was dominant in the minds of Soviet leaders. The work of the Comintern thus became defensive in object – the aim being to prevent or frustrate an anti-Soviet coalition rather than to further and lead revolution.

Not only did Soviet foreign policy alter in relation to bourgeois states; it changed towards the social democrats too. Since 1920, Communist Parties abroad had been acting under the slogan of a 'United Front' which indicated a readiness, at least in theory, for some sort of cooperation with other parties of the Left. However, it was in the name of this policy that the Chinese communists had collaborated with the Kuomintang and met with disaster when Chiang Kai-shek had turned on his communist partners. In Europe, Communist Parties had encountered little success in their approaches to social-democratic parties. A new policy in relation to social democrats went into operation after the Sixth World Congress of the Comintern in the summer of 1928. As the British historian, E.H. Carr, describes it:

> The manifesto issued by the Congress, ranging the Social Democrats with the Fascists, denounced them as being 'on the side of the exploiters, on the side of the imperialists, on the side of the imperialist robber states and their agents', and called on workers everywhere to fight 'against reformism and Fascism for the proletarian revolution'. [11]

The new policy was, of course, applied in all areas, including sport. It was taken up immediately by the RSI which appealed for 'a relentless fight against the social-fascist leaders'. [12] Subsequent events – economic depression in Europe and the growth of fascist regimes in Italy and Germany – led to a great reduction in, if not decimation of, the ranks of both the WSI and the RSI. By the mid-1930s, their feud had become an anachronism, with the backbone of the WSI (the nearly two-million-strong sports association of Germany) broken by Hitler, and the RSI virtually confined to the USSR. [13, 14]

Although no sports ties linked Germany and the Soviet Union during the 1930s, Soviet athletes were now venturing into contests with bourgeois states. Thus, in the first Soviet chess venture abroad, Mikhail Botvinnik drew with the world champion, the Czechoslovak Flohr, in 1933; three years later, his tie for first place with the Cuban Capablanca at the world championship held in Nottingham merited a picture and full-length article on the front page of *Pravda*. Following the signing of a mutual assistance pact between Soviet Russia and Czechoslovakia in 1935, three soccer matches were played by Prague against Leningrad, Moscow and the Ukraine.

The turning-point for Soviet soccer came the next summer. At the height of the Spanish Civil War, an all-star team of Basque players drawn from leading clubs of Spain toured Europe to raise funds for the Republican cause. The Basques arrived in Moscow on 16 June 1937 to huge acclaim. They won all their initial matches, including a 2–1 defeat of Dinamo Moscow before over 90 000 fans in the Dinamo Stadium. Finally, Spartak Moscow won a much-disputed victory 6–2 against an extremely weary team that had played a dozen matches in almost as many days. This was the first defeat of a first-class professional team by any Soviet side. [15]

Following Hitler's announcement in March 1935 of what he called 'the restoration of German sovereignty' and unlimited rearmament, the fear of fascism became very real and Soviet foreign policy veered once more towards cooperation between social democrats and communists. In July 1935, the Seventh and last Congress of the Comintern was summoned for the purpose of generalizing the new line. The main resolution declared that: 'In the face of the towering menace of fascism, it is the principal and immediate task of the international worker movement at the present phase of history to establish a united fighting front of the working class.' [16] The defence of democracy against fascism was sold to be the supreme task. Sport, too, was to play its part in 'safeguarding democracy and constitutional government'. [17]

The Soviet side advocated the unification of the international worker sports movement and, although the two sports internationals could not agree on a popular front, they did reach some measure on consensus on certain points: they issued a joint appeal for all athletes to boycott the 1936 Berlin Olympics; and Soviet athletes were permitted to take part in the WSI-sponsored International Worker Olympics held in Antwerp in 1937. Nevertheless, strong disagreement, notably over competition with bourgeois athletes: while the WSI leaders were now opposed to such 'fraternization' with the class enemy, Soviet leaders pressed for contacts with 'all organisations opposed to the fascist danger'. [18]

Soviet leaders saw a difference between the earlier united front and the current popular front in that the latter extended to the anti-fascist bourgeoisie, and Soviet leaders played down the class struggle against them. But international events, particularly the gathering of war clouds over Europe, were to bring to an end the period in which the policy of 'popular fronts' was pursued.

## Promoting good-neighbourly relations

Alongside the 'class' use of sport in the interwar period, one relatively stable element in sport's role as a diplomatic and propagandist medium throughout the Soviet period was to promote relations with the USSR's neighbours. The immediate neighbours comprised six states in Europe (Czechoslovakia, Finland, Hungary, Norway, Poland and Romania), in addition to the three Baltic states (Estonia, Latvia and Lithuania), and six in Asia (Afghanistan, China, Iran, Korea, Mongolia and Turkey). Countries whose geopolitical situation brought them within the category of strategically important 'neighbours' were Denmark and

Sweden in the Baltic region, Albania, Bulgaria and Yugoslavia in the Balkans, Austria in Central Europe, Japan in the Far East, and several countries in the Middle East.

The Soviet leadership made no bones about the tasks of its sports organizations in

> uniting progressive forces in the international sports movement, consolidating the united front of sports organisations of socialist states, young independent countries and worker sports groups in capitalist states for the purpose of reaching progressive decisions on issues facing the international sports movement, and employing sport as a weapon in the campaign for peace and mutual understanding. [19]

In the period 1917–39, contacts with developing states were naturally limited by the hold that the imperial nations still had over Africa, Asia and Latin America. In any case, the USSR's ability to bargain with the 'great powers' was severely restricted by its weakness and isolation as the world's sole, beleaguered, communist country, as well as by the mistrust in which it was generally held. On the other hand, the USSR was less handicapped in dealings with its immediate neighbours, all of whom were relatively weak and vulnerable; some, like Turkey and Persia (Iran), saw it as vital for their own survival and independence to pursue good-neighbourly relations with the USSR as insurance against Soviet encroachment and as a warning to other 'big powers' not to trespass into Soviet border areas.

The overall Soviet objective from the outset in regard to the neighbours and those states within strategically important areas close to the USSR was, as Max Beloff has written, 'to link these (states) to Russia by treaties embodying the three major principles of "non-intervention", "non-aggression" and "neutrality"'.[20]

Furthermore, it has to be borne in mind that as the revolutionary fires faded in Europe (Germany, Hungary) in 1918, Soviet leaders began to turn their attention eastwards, seeing the East rather than the West as the centre of the revolutionary stage, and the national liberation movement in those states (headed mainly by the national bourgeoisie) as a bulwark against Western colonialism. As the first Soviet Minister of Foreign Affairs, Lev Trotsky, put it:

> The road to India may prove at the given moment to be more readily passable and shorter for us than the road to Soviet Hungary. The sort of army which, at the moment, can be of no great significance in the European scales can upset the unstable balance of Asian relationships, of colonial dependence, give a direct push to an uprising on the part of the oppressed masses, and assure the triumph of such a rising in Asia. [21]

Sports contacts reflected these diplomatic and strategic considerations. Indeed sport, in cutting across social, ethnic, religious and language barriers, was seen as one of the most suitable vehicles for Soviet cultural diplomacy.

Contacts with 'neighbouring' states after 1917 took two forms: between Soviet and foreign national teams – e.g. between the USSR and Finland, Turkey or Sweden – and between local Soviet and local and national foreign teams from just across the border – e.g. between Baku and Iran, Odessa and Turkey, Leningrad and Finnish town clubs.

Nonetheless, sports relations tended to be confined to the sport that the USSR was best at – soccer; the first international soccer match was against the Finnish labour federation team TUL in 1922, which the old Moscow Zamoskvoretsky Sports Club won 7–1. The following year, two Soviet teams played a total of five matches in Finland (Kotka, Turku, Kuopio, Helsinki and Tampere), winning all of them, two with the demoralizing scores of 19–0 and 13–1. Fixtures continued until 1929, with a total of 16 more matches played, mostly by Leningrad against Finnish city teams (Soviet teams winning 10, losing 3 and drawing 3). [22]

The interesting feature of these contacts is that they took place despite the official animosity prevailing between the two countries. Finland had been an autonomous Grand Duchy of the Russian Empire (though maintaining independent sports relations – it took part as a separate nation in the Olympic Games, for example), but had declared itself an independent state in 1917 and sustained itself under General Mannerheim, supported by the Germans, against the Red Army in the Russian Civil War, before establishing a republic in 1919. Soviet–Finnish sports relations existed notwithstanding official hostility and Finland's refusal to sign a non-aggression pact with the USSR.

During 1923, the Russian Federation soccer team undertook a tour of Sweden, playing ten matches, including a drawn game against Stockholm and a win against the Swedish national side. The same team played four matches in Norway in 1923, including two against Oslo and the Norwegian national team – winning all its matches. Parallel with these 'official' contests, Soviet teams were competing against foreign worker teams. During its 1923 foreign tour, for example, the Russian Federation soccer team also played worker teams in Szczecin (Poland) and in Berlin – games that became annual fixtures until relations with Poland and Germany were severed in 1933, on Hitler's assumption of power. In 1924, a Leningrad team played Finnish, Norwegian and German worker clubs (winning all three). The following year, it played two games against Estonia's capital Revel (now Tallinn) and eight games against Finnish teams.

In the south, following the overthrow of the Ottoman Empire by Kemel Ataturk in 1922 and the proclamation of the Turkish Republic in October 1923, good-neighbourly treaties were signed with the USSR, envisaging sports exchanges. In fact, no other country received so many Soviet sports delegations in the period 1924–5 and 1931–6. In soccer alone, 10 matches were played against Soviet teams in 1924–5, and as many as 31 between 1931 and 1936. Interestingly enough, despite the relative disparity in skill between the two countries, no Soviet team humiliated its Turkish rival, as occurred, for example, in regard to Finnish teams. Of the 41 matches played between Soviet and Turkish sides between 1924 and 1936, Turkish clubs won 6, 9 were drawn and 13 were won by Soviet sides by the odd goal. The inevitable conclusion is that Soviet teams played under instructions to lose, draw or to win by a margin that would not offend Turkish national pride. It is noteworthy that many matches were given the status of full 'internationals' – USSR v Turkey, or the Ukraine, Moscow or Leningrad v. Turkey. Occasionally, however, matches were played between geographically close towns on either side of the Black Sea – Batumi and Odessa on the Soviet side, Trabzon and other Turkish teams on the Turkish side.

Following the *coup d'état* of 1921 in Persia by Reza Khan, his assumption of the title Reza Shah Pahlavi in 1925 and his modernization programme, relations with the USSR were gradually normalized. Despite disputes over the territory of Azerbaijan, sports exchanges were inaugurated in 1926 as examples of good-neighbourliness. Thus, four matches were played in the Soviet Caspian city of Baku in 1926 by the Persian national team against Baku and Azerbaijan (three won by Soviet teams, one drawn). This was followed by visits in 1927 and 1928 to Meshed, just across the Soviet–Persian border, by a team from Ashkhabad, capital of the Soviet frontier republic of Turkmenia (both matches won 2–1 by Ashkhabad). And in 1929, Baku won its three matches against Tehran.

Prewar sports contacts with other neighbours or near-neighbours were inhibited by the backwardness of sport in adjacent countries – Afghanistan, China, Korea and Mongolia – and by problems of establishing sports relations. For example, relations with Czechoslovakia were hostile and intended sports tourneys were aborted in 1926 and 1927 owing to the refusal of the Czechoslovak Government to grant entry-visas to Soviet athletes. Following the mutual assistance pact signed between the USSR and Czechoslovakia in 1935, however, a Prague soccer team toured the USSR (in 1935), drawing two matches against Moscow and Leningrad, and beating the Ukraine.

Despite the so-called Litvinov Protocol on renunciation of war, signed in Moscow in 1929, by the USSR and its neighbours, including Poland and the free city of Danzig (now the Polish city of Gdansk), virtually no official sports exchanges took place between Poland and the USSR because of the hostile attitude of the Pilsudski regime to all cultural exchanges with the USSR. A similar situation pertained in respect of Romania, also a signatory to the 1929 Litvinov Protocol; implacable hostility to cultural exchanges prevented any sports contracts, especially after the establishment of a fascist dictatorship by King Carol II in 1930. Even after the Molotov – Ribbentrop Pact of 23 August 1939, the Romanian regime steadfastly refused all Soviet overtures for sporting and other exchanges (as did the strategically close states of Albania, Hungary and Yugoslavia).

There was yet another role assigned to Soviet sport from the 1920s – regional contacts with bordering states, especially in the Asiatic part of the country, were used for demonstrating the advances made by kindred peoples under socialism. It has to be remembered that in 1922, of the 140 million Soviet citizens, some 30 million, mainly Turkic people (Turkic by language, Islamic by culture, Muslim by religion), still pursued a semi-feudal, pastoral or tribal form of life, similar to that followed by kindred ethnic groups across the border in Turkey, Persia, Afghanistan,

Mongolia and China. At this time, cultural, economic and health levels were roughly analogous on both sides of the divide. From the outset, Soviet policy was for the relatively economically advanced parts of the USSR to help bring about a major social change in Soviet Central Asia (the republics of Turkmenia, Uzbekistan, Kirghizia, Tadjikistan and Kazakhstan). The epoch introduced by the five-year plans (from 1928 onwards) brought rapid economic and social development – official indexes of industrial production show a twelve fold increase in these regions between 1926 and 1940. [23] A revolution similarly occurred in literacy and vital health statistics. Contacts between kindred peoples on either side of the border increasingly demonstrated, therefore, the great strides forward being made by Soviet peoples under socialism. As an Uzbek sport minister put it: 'The attainments of Soviet Uzbekistan and its entry into world sport are of immense significance; they demonstrate graphically the triumph of Lenin's national policy. Today, Uzbekistan has become a beacon of mature socialism in the East, attracting the attention of young developing states.' [24]

## Relations with the Axis powers, 1939–41

The signing of the Munich agreement on 28 September 1938 (there had been no prior consultation with the Soviet Government), the apparent bankruptcy of the Soviet Union's Western policy and the need to come to terms with Hitler all dictated a radical change in Soviet foreign policy in 1939. As a result, the German–Soviet Non-Aggression Pact, negotiated by the respective foreign ministers, Molotov and von Ribbentrop, was signed on 23 August 1939; a secret Protocol was signed the same day outlining German and Soviet spheres of interest. [25, 26, 27, 28, 29, 30, 31] In return for 'non-intervention', Stalin secured what the British historian E.H. Carr called, 'a breathing space of immunity from German attack . . . and German agreement to the existing Soviet frontiers in Eastern Europe'. [32]

The events of the first few months after the signing of the pact – and the subsequent commercial and cultural (including sport) exchanges – provide ample evidence of the ease with which a state of the Soviet type could carry into effect a new policy, whatever the magnitude of the apparent change involved. Internal propaganda conformed to the new line and all anti-fascist expressions vanished (for example, even guards in labour camps were forbidden to call prisoners 'fascists'!). [33] Of course, communists throughout Europe were thrown into confusion – though most eventually toed the Moscow line.

This volte-face found its echo in sport. The first ever sports agreements signed between the USSR and a West European state were those concluded with Germany shortly after the signing of the pact. They envisaged a wide exchange of athletes: German fencers, swimmers, gymnasts, soccer teams, track and field athletes and tennis players came to the Soviet Union, while Soviet gymnasts, swimmers and weightlifters all competed in Germany. In fact, more sports contests took place between Soviet and German athletes during 1940 than between the athletes of the USSR and all 'bourgeois' states in all the preceding years since 1917 put together. Some 250 German athletes competed in the USSR and 175 Soviet athletes competed in Germany between September 1939 and the end of 1940.[34] All this was to reinforce the newly established, if somewhat remarkable, friendship.

Following the German invasion of Norway in April 1940, and the establishment there of the Quisling fascist regime, a Soviet–Norwegian sports agreement was signed; it brought an exchange of skiers to compete in bilateral skiing contests in December 1940. [35] Sports contests with the Baltic states followed the division of Soviet and German spheres of interest, the signing of mutual assistance pacts with the three Baltic states and the establishment of Soviet military bases there. In the period between the signing of these pacts in late 1939 and the incorporation of the three Baltic states into the USSR in August 1940, sports agreements resulted in Estonian boxers and wrestlers, Latvian skaters and Lithuanian basketball players competing in the Soviet Union. [36]

## Some conclusions

With its control over the sports system, the Soviet leadership was able to mobilize resources to use sport to perform what it believed to be salient political functions in foreign policy. As we have seen, this included initially promoting proletarian internationalism, and then switching to a policy of strengthening the Soviet Union as a nation-state. In regard to neighbouring states, the policy was consistently to promote good neighbourliness and to demonstrate the progress made by a kindred peoples under socialism. Perhaps the most amazing volte-face of all was the sudden turn to sporting competition with fascist regimes between 1939 and 1941.

It is, of course, impossible to measure the impact of sport on the behaviour of states – to discover whether sport can ever affect policies, let alone hearts and minds. All that can be said is that once the USSR entered the sporting arena, sport could no longer be, if it ever was, the neutral, apolitical medium that some people once attributed to it.

## References

1. *Syezdy sovetov. Sbornik dokumentov* (Moscow, 1960), vol. 3, p. 16.
2. Kozmina, V.P. (1969) Mezhdunarodnoye rabocheye sportivnoye dvizhenie posle Velikoi Oktyabrskoi sotsialisticheskoi revolyutsii (1917–1928), in F.I. Samoukov and V.V. Stolbov (eds), *Ocherki po istorii fizicheskoi kultury* (Moscow), p. 165.
3. Editorial in *Shakhmatny listok*, 7 October 1925, p. 3.
4. Trotsky, Leon (1964) *The Age of Permanent Revolution* (New York), p. 131.
5. Beloff, Max (1947) *The Foreign Policy of Soviet Russia, 1929–1941*, (Oxford), vol. 1, p. 3.
6. Kozmina, *op. cit.*, p. 171.
7. *Freihe Sportwoche*, 12 December 1923, no. 40 (Leipzig).
8. *Pravda*, 13 August 1928.
9. *Fizkultura i sport*, no. 33, 1928.
10. *Pravda*, 22 August 1928.

11. Carr, E.H. (1951) *German–Soviet Relations between the Two World Wars, 1919–1939* (Oxford), p. 99.
12. *Krasny sport*, 12 May 1929.
13. Arnaud, Pierre (ed.) (1994) *Les origines du sport ouvrier en Europe* (Paris), for a fuller history of worker sport in individual European states and Europe generally.
14. Krüger, Arnd and Riordan, James (eds) (1985) *Der internationale Arbeitersport. Der Schlussel zum Arbeitersport in 10 Landern* (Cologne), for a fuller history of worker sport in individual European states and Europe generally.
15. Edelman, Robert (1993) *Serious Fun. A History of Spectator Sports in the USSR* (New York).
16. *Seventh World Congress of the Communist International* (in Russian) (Moscow, 1935), p. 7.
17. *Fizkultura i sport*, no. 7, 1935, p. 3.
18. *Pravda*, 27 June 1938.
19. Romanov, A.O. (1973) *Mezhdunarodnoye sportivnoye dvizhenie* (Moscow), p. 185.
20. Beloff, *op. cit.*, vol. 2, p. 5.
21. Trotsky, L.D. (1964) in Jan Meijer (ed.), *The Trotsky Papers, 1917–1922*, vol. 1 (New York), p. 623.
22. Perel, A. (1958) *Football in the USSR* (Moscow).
23. Lane, David (1985) *State and Politics in the USSR* (Oxford), p. 90.
24. Ibragimov, Y.I. (1977) Sportivnye dostizheniya uzbekskoi SSR, *Teoriya i praktika fizicheskoi kultury*, (10), 10.
25. For details of the Pact and secret Protocol. Grenville, J.A.S. (1974) *The Major International Treaties, 1917–1973* (Methuen, London), pp. 194–202.
26. *Pravda*, 21 August 1939.
27. Ibid., 24 August 1939.
28. Ibid., 1 September 1939.
29. Ibid., 28 September 1939.
30. Ibid. 29 September 1939.
31. Ibid. 30 September 1939.
32. Carr, *op. cit.*, p. 136.
33. Communication from a British communist, Len Wincott, incarcerated in a Soviet labour camp from 1939 to 1956.
34. Romanov, *op. cit.*, p. 192.
35. Ibid., p. 193.
36. Ibid.

Chapter 6

# The role of sport in German international politics, 1918–1945

*Arnd Krüger*

## Introduction

Germany was to have staged the 1916 Olympics in Berlin. There were even negotiations to have the first ever Olympic Winter Games in Berlin and on the Feldberg in the Black Forest in the same year. The job of selecting and preparing the athletes and first full-time administrator for the German Olympic Committee and Sports Federation was given to Carl Diem (1882–1962). Raising the standard of track and field to the highest level was to be undertaken by a professional coach from the United States, Alvin Kraenzlein (1878–1928), formerly of Princeton University, and a four times Olympic Gold Medallist. The German parliament discussed the funding of international sports and decided that the federal government was responsible and that it should pay not only for staging the Olympic Games but also for the selection and preparation of athletes for international competitions leading up to the Games. [1] The Secretary of the Interior was made responsible for elite sport as international cultural representation and is still responsible on the basis of this decision today (1997). Germany was the only country in Europe where such clear-cut decisions were made by the central parliament, and where a government was willing to implement the funding of national representation through elite sports. Why? The sporting press was very obvious:

> The Olympic Games are a war, a real war. You can be sure that many partic-
> ipants are willing to offer – without hesitation – several years of their life for
> a victory of the fatherland . . . The Olympic idea of the modern era has given
> us a symbol of world war, which does not show its military character very
> openly, but – for those who can read sports statistics – it gives enough insight
> into world ranking. [2]

It was not much later that the Olympic idea was no longer a symbol, but reality. World War I saw all sports organizations cooperating willingly, even if they had different political interests, to further the military readiness of German youth. During this period of the imperial *Burgfrieden* (peace inside the besieged castle), there seemed to be more pressing things than international sports. Germany had the largest physical exercise organization in the world, the Deutsche Turnerschaft (DT), which had 1 400 000 fee paying members in 1914 – but they resented international competitions. They espoused the doctrine of F.L. Jahn (1778–1852), the 'Turner father', who had proclaimed his *Turnen* for the benefit of military readiness and the strengthening of the Germanic race. The internationally minded sports movement, on the other hand, had only been started in the 1880s, and although it had received some support from the imperial household (the German Emperor Wilhelm II was a grandson of Queen Victoria of England and his Anglomania included a love of athleticism [3]), was outnumbered by the *Turners* 7:1 before the outbreak of the War.

As of 1892, there was also a social-democratic Workers' *Turner* Movement (Arbeiter Turner Bund (ATB)) doing exercises and proclaiming international brotherhood against the nationalistic bourgeois movements. [4] Although they were supposed to be progressive, [5] their point of view in regard to competitions, specialization and the striving for records, was identical to the *Turners*:

> *Turnen* has to become the general possession of the people. *Turnen* has to be performed simply and systematically, emphasizing the hygienic conditions and stressing the general physical education . . . Competitive *Turnen* has to be used as a means of propaganda to further our *Turner* movement and to serve as educational means for the participating *Turners* . . . This agitation and instruction can only serve its end when the class is emphasized and not the individual. [6]

Competitive *Turnen* and all of sport are furthering egoism was the major argument. [7, 8] The workers' *Turner*, however, was able to keep sport in perspective, after all class consciousness was the driving force within its ranks. So, in order to placate many of its sports minded members, one unified organization for *Turnen* and sport, the ATSB, was created while the bourgeois *Turners* and sportsmen split into separate federations and stayed that way until they were unified by the Nazi Government in 1933.

The sports movement did receive a considerable impetus in the latter stages of the war when the military demanded that sports should replace *Turnen* in the school system. It seemed that British military preparations for war were superior to the German – the British embraced sports rather than *Turnen*. It is an open question whether the German military believed the British war propaganda – or whether the British really were better. [9] But this decision was the beginning of a process of 'sportification', which continued for the next twenty years. In 1933, when the last comparable data are available, the ratio was 5:1 in favour of membership in sports organizations.

## Isolation and international growth

Even before the First World War had ended, the dominant personalities of German sport were considering their postwar options. They realized that the

Olympic Games organizing committee, seemingly dominated by the French, the 'arch enemy', was unlikely to allow them to compete after the war. They were proved right when Germany was excluded from the Games of 1920 and 1924 after being held responsible for starting the war. Even Carl Diem, a great advocate of the Olympic Games and a strong sports movement in Germany, advised Germany not to take part in the international Games – even if permitted to do so – 'as long as Negroes in French uniforms are stationed at the German Rhine. In this time the *Kampfspiele* (national Olympic Games) are a valuable *Ersatz*'. [10] It should not be overlooked that the Olympic Games have always been very important for Germany, the country that excavated the Olympic sites. Being part of the Olympic movement was highly symbolic and meant being part of the civilized world. [11, 12] International sporting competitions have the chance to promote international understanding, but they can also be used to hide one's real intentions: both points of view are relevant in the case of Germany and international sports. [13]

At the end of the war, Germany experienced a socialist revolution, which eventually became a less extreme social-democratic majority in parliament. The constitution of the Weimar Republic maintained Germany as a federal state with its cultural rights vested into twenty-five separate states. Many of the older generation and especially the Civil Service considered themselves monarchists at heart but were forced by the conditions of the day to become democrats. Having to pay for much of the damage Germany had caused in the war, having lost most of its border regions to its neighbours, strictly reducing its military might, and losing the right of compulsory military service, the conditions of the Treaty of Versailles, which had ended the war, were considered by most a humiliating disaster. Germany was excluded politically from the international scene until 1925–6. Only the Locarno Treaty and entry into the League of Nations brought Germany back into the international political community. But militarily, Germany was still a nonentity.

In terms of sport, Germany had to reorganize internally – as many international sport federations isolated Germany at the time. This was most prominent in the case of the International Olympic Committee (IOC). It should not be overlooked, however, that while the Olympic movement played strictly the diplomatic card of Britain and France, other countries were ready to accept German competitors directly after the war.

The situation was even more difficult in international workers' sport. After the Socialist Revolution in Russia the international federation – founded in Belgium with German participation in 1912 – split into two federations – one led by the communists, the other by the social-democrats. Germany played a leading role in both. [14] While Germany was still excluded from the regular Olympic movement, it staged the First Workers' Olympics in Frankfurt/M in 1925. There were 150 000 spectators, and 60 000 people joined in a mass demonstration of international worker solidarity. [15, 16]

Whether Germany was in or out depended on the composition of the executive boards of the various federations. On the whole, Switzerland and the Scandinavian countries were sympathetic and accepted Germany as their natural partner in sports. Consequently, winter sports saw German participation early on. [17] What was more important from a German point of view was soccer, which was becoming the most popular sport in Europe. In 1920 England appealed to FIFA (Fédération Internationale de Football Association) to exclude Germany, Austria and Hungary because these countries had been responsible for the First World War, but FIFA turned down the request. As a result all the British Isles representatives resigned from FIFA in protest. Germany, however, could continue to play international football. [18]

The sports movement used this period to strengthen its domestic hold and to gain assurances that the social-democrat government would support sport as much as the monarchy had. The social-democrats – then a minority party – had voted against government funding in 1914, [19] but in government they followed the same reasoning as the monarchist government had done before the war: a winning national team is a good advertisement. The only difference was that social-democratic city governments also extended their support to workers sports clubs, thus improving the chances for mass participation.

Carl Diem continued as head administrator. He possessed the most active and most creative mind in the sports movement. [20] Theodor Lewald (1860–1947), who had been under-secretary of state in the Home Office until he was forced out because he was too conservative for the democratic government in 1921, became the president of the central sport organization (*Deutscher Reichsausschuss für Leibesübungen – DRA*) and the German Olympic Committee. [21, 22] Both aligned the sports movement with the interest of the state and organized the DRA as if it was a section of the central government.

Diem needed a solid base from which he could strengthen the German sports movement, so he founded the *Deutsche Reichshochschule für Leibesübungen* (Central Institute of Physical Education and Sport). An ardent fan of everything in American sport, he copied the American way of running their physical education and athletic departments. [23] He became the head administrator and lecturer for organizational theory. It was here that sport-related research was ahead of its time. The athletic heart, previously considered a physical risk, was thought to be an asset. The American spirit of the roaring twenties [24] was inspired by behaviourism and so the athletes were considered 'Mortal Engines'. [25]

In 1921 a Sport Badge was introduced for men, women, and young people. It created considerable interest and has been in existence ever since. Daily physical education lessons were demanded but a small increase was all that could be achieved. A Reich's school conference for physical education in 1920 helped to strengthen the role of sport versus *Turnen* in the school system and eventually in the rest of society. [26] A *Turnen* and sport duty year was demanded to replace compulsory military training banned after the war. Although it did not become mandatory, it increased the public awareness of sport. Annual school championships were successfully introduced for both sexes emphasizing mass participation and athletic quality in a wide range of track and field events. Tax deductions and reduced railway fares for sports clubs were introduced. A Sports Space Bill demanding 5 sq. m. of space for everyone was brought in – and failed. But it encouraged cities to increase considerably the amount of sports space available for everybody. The democratic Germany had laid the basis for all the country's future developments in sport. [27]

## Crises and chances

After 1925 it seemed as if Germany would become a stable country, mastering national and international crises. Along with political pacification came economic recovery. How then could German democracy collapse and bring the Nazis to power in 1933? Of course, sport is only a small part of this shift, but the same symptoms are present.

On the one hand, there was an enormous upsurge in the potential of Germany, on the other, a downfall in the years of an economic crisis caused by the highest inflation rate ever. The upsurge is best shown in sport by Germany's second place in the 1928 Amsterdam Olympics. After so many years of isolation this seemed to be quite a surprise to many, but it should not be overlooked that Germany sent the largest team, had large crowd support and had a well-organized sports system. In 1932, however, Germany was suffering economically, and it was being discussed publicly whether in a time of economic crisis a team should be sent to Los Angeles at all. A small team was eventually sent, but finished only seventh. It would prob-ably not have gone, if Germany had not been given the Olympics of 1936 in a close vote over Barcelona at the IOC meeting in 1931. As host of the next Olympic Games it was expected to send a team, although many of the athletes and officials paid their own way.

German sports science was quite progressive by European standards. Even before the turn of the century universities accepted doctoral dissertations in sports-related fields, particularly sport history. [28] Therefore the standards in some disciplines were quite high. This emphasis on sports-related subjects guaranteed that there were enough highly qualified staff to run the first university departments of physical education whey they were formed in 1922. Dr. Hermann Altrock (1887–1980) became the first university professor of sports science in Leipzig in 1925. German scientists were among the pioneers for coaching sports science. Their anthropometric work laid the basis for how talented individuals would be selected in the future.[29] They were very active in forming international organi-zations for physical education and sports medicine. [30]

Why then were German physical educators among the strongest supporters of Nazism in most schools, to such an extent that – after the Nazi era – the Nazi phys-ical educator was almost a caricature of a Nazi? Nazism not only promised them higher status, it offered many of the attributes they had found serving with other men in the First World War trenches. [31] Courage and strength to them were more important than the attributes of the traditional German intellectual. This compared favourably to the time of financial crisis: when physical education took a back seat in the education system; when young physical educators were no longer hired; when the ones in service had their pay drastically reduced; and when physical education was no longer considered useful and often abandoned.

The situation was even worse in sports medicine and other academic fields; where the high percentage of Jews practising in these professions was out of proportion to the rest of the population. The Nazis promised to kick out the Jews and provide jobs for the young people of 'Aryan' descent. On the whole Jews were not very prominent in sport. There were two Jewish sports federations, Maccabi and *Schild*. Maccabi had been founded as a national Jewish organization to further *Muscular Jewishness* and the emigration to Palestine in 1889. *Schild* was the organization of Jewish participants in the First World War and a nationalistic organization. In 1933, there were 25 Maccabi sports clubs with some 8000 members, 90 *Schildclubs* with some 7000 members and 18 independent *Vintus*-clubs with an unknown number of members. The majority of Jews practised their sport in the normal sports clubs. [32] The political and cultural fragmentation of the Weimar period is best characterized by the fact that there were also separate Catholic and Protestant sports organizations (totalling about 20 times as many members as the Jewish organizations), but in sports such as cycling there were as many as 20 federations all claiming that they were national.

The question of anti-Semitism led to a split in the *Turner* movement. While the majority accepted German-Jewish members, the great number of *Turners* in Austria and in some other parts of Germany did not. This led to a breakaway by the Austrian *Turners* because they were so anti-Semitic that they excluded their German–Jewish members, while the others accepted them. The breakaway *Deutsche Turnerbund* (founded 1889) also accepted the notion of a greater Germany with seven Austrian and five German voting provinces. [33, 34] If you look at history backwards, it is obvious that the Turners were the first in 1933 to exclude their Jewish members, months before they were asked to do so. But in 1889 they were willing to lose 15% of their membership over the anti-Semitic question.

During this time of relative stability a young generation of sport leaders became prominent. They had an athletic background, a relatively good education, but were mostly influenced by the experience of the war years. For the trench generation that had fought together in the First World War, comradeship and honour had strong personal meanings. Quite a number of them turned to national socialism, as it gave their lives meaning. The young Nazi movement used this male brotherhood of the trenches as a basis of their far-reaching network. Dr Carl Krümmel (1895–1942), physical educator, a German cross-country and 5000 metres champion, responsible for military training in the central army camp in Wünsdorf, a professed Member of the Nazi Party, was elected president of the German Organization of Physical Educators in 1925. [35] The Swimming Association elected Hans Geissow, a stout Nazi, as president in the same year. [36] The presidents of many of the other *Turner* or sports organizations were close to the Nazi ideas, but were not members of the Nazi party. Being a professed Nazi had stopped being a hindrance for election to office.

As the workers' sport organizations stayed outside mainstream sport, it is obvious that the bourgeois sport movement was more conservative than average. On the other hand, many people on the far right joined paramilitary groups that were only nominally active in sport, but used them as a front to receive state funding as a sports organization, while preparing to overthrow the democratic government – whether from the Left or the Right. [37]

Germany did not have many professional sportsmen or women. The amateur code was strengthened by the ideology of the *Turners* and resulted in a general resentment of professionals in many sports – including the most popular, football. But there were Germans who took part in professional sports events, cycling and boxing. Indeed Max Schmeling (1905– ) was the heavyweight champion of the world from 1930 to 1932 and from 1936 to 1938.

## A coordinated sports movement

When the Nazis came to power in early 1933, no one knew what they stood for in many areas – including sports. It soon became obvious that the same personnel as before would continue to work for the Nazis, and that only minimal changes would be made in the general bourgeois sports movement. The students of the famous Berlin Physical Education and Sports Academy had asked many prominent sports leaders, for the winter issue of their student paper 1932–3, what they anticipated for the coming year. There were conflicting views, but it was obvious that the *Turners* expected their organization to regain prominence while sports people hoped for a model more like that of the Italian fascists, who had improved their sports under the strong influence of the Mussolini government. The students themselves drew the conclusion that the 'terror of the measuring tape' would come to an end. When the Nazis came to power only weeks later, they dug up the Academy's fast cinder track and planted oak trees, the symbol of Jahn and Germanicness. [38]

The immediate questions for the Nazis were, on the one hand, who would run the Nazi sports movement and, on the other, whether the international cultural isolation would include the Olympic Games which they had 'inherited' from the democratic government. Already, in August 1932 at the Los Angeles Olympics, the IOC had expressed concern about a potential Nazi takeover. The *Völkischer Beobachter*, the Nazi party paper, carried little sports coverage, and often used the press service of the *Deutsche Turnerbund*, thus giving the impression that the exclusion of Jews, no competition against foreigners and exercises for military readiness were the main priorities of the Party. [39] Ritter von Halt, president of the German track and field federation, IOC member for Germany, and a banker close to the Nazis, volunteered to ask Hitler what his intentions were towards the Olympics. [40, 41] He was granted a personal interview and was able to report back to the IOC president Baillet-Latour that Hitler was in favour of the Olympics and would honour international obligations. [42]

The question of the way to run sport under Nazism raged for about four months. Finally, those sports leaders who did not want German isolation but preached the Italian model and demanded a leading position for Germany in the sports world won the argument. They readily copied the successful fascist model of a state sport where federations were no longer democratically elected, but hierarchically structured from above and 'coordinated' by the government, and later on (1938 onward) by the Nazi Party. [43] The sports leaders of most federations and clubs followed willingly as this brought them more influence. [44] The Italians had demonstrated as soccer world champions in 1930 and with a second place in the Olympic Games of 1932 that a state-supported sport would provide the basis for a culture of consent. [45] Krümmel became responsible for school physical education and fulfilled a promise to the physical education teachers that there would be daily physical education. Physical education became as important as intellectual subjects in school. The only shift in the curriculum was the introduction of boxing for boys and paramilitary exercise. [46]

When the IOC put the Nazi question on its agenda for the June 1933 annual meeting in Vienna, it wanted assurances from its German members that things were progressing as usual and that the Games could be staged. Vienna would have been the last chance to relocate the Olympic Games, as in many of the previous Games a four-year cycle was considered sufficient. The German IOC members were still the same – and they gave the assurances with the consent of the German government. Lewald, now president of the organizing committee, and Diem, his secretary general, tried to calm the international concern. Even when General Charles Sherrill (1867–1936), IOC Member for the United States, insisted that one should be very specific that 'on principle, German-Jews would be part of the German team'– and not just Jews would be welcome – the German members enlisted the help of the secretary of the office still responsible for sport, the newly installed Reichssport-Leader, Hans von Tschammer und Osten (1887–1943) [47, 48] to confirm that this was in line with German thinking on the matter.

As the IOC had some prominent fascists in its own ranks, [49] everybody was happy. Although the declaration was not published within Germany, it calmed international public opinion until the summer of 1935. In 1933 the German workers' sports organizations had been banned – but that did not worry the IOC. To avoid any discontent from the average sportsman, the Nazis permitted the individual worker sportsman and woman to join a bourgeois sports club, provided he or she brought two sworn statements that he or she was not a 'Marxist'. No bourgeois sports club was permitted more than 20% of these as new members, to make sure that the workers were dispersed and would not be able to form larger groups elsewhere. When the Catholic and Protestant organizations were forced to close down two years later in 1935, American public opinion became active again.

## Fooling the enemy

In October 1933 Hitler had guaranteed to stage the Games in a grandiose fashion, irrespective of the cost involved. Together with Goebbels, his Minister for Propaganda, they wanted to conquer world public opinion with the help of the Olympic Games – and stage the biggest sport show that the world had known thus far. While the Los Angeles Olympics were the first Games to surpass one million spectators, Berlin eventually had more than three million. [50]

Between 1933 and 1936 many foreign teams visited Germany and the number of international sports meetings Germany participated in increased. Sport was used explicitly to break the cultural isolation that Germany had experienced from many groups because of its racial atrocities. Between 1920 and 1930 Germany had participated in fewer than 20 international sports meetings per year, under the Nazis this increased to over 30, and in preparation for the 1936 Olympics there were 78 in 1935 alone. In March 1933 the Swastika became an additional official symbol of the State and these meetings were also used to show off this. At first, the German authorities attempted to fly both Germany's flags (the Black-White-Red of the monarchy and the Swastika) at all the meetings Germany attended, but this created problems where foreign organizers permitted only one flag per country. Thus from February 1935 the Black-White-Red of the monarchy was discarded in favour of the Swastika, which was accompanied by the *Deutschland-Deutschland über alles* (Germany, Germany above all) as the national anthem.

In this respect the soccer match between England and Germany in December 1935 in London is significant. It was part of a cultural offensive and determined to give the British public a favourable impression of Germans. Labour, Jewish, and German emigrants combined to assure an anti-German propaganda. Five thousand German fans attended, England won 3–0, and the British press was full of praise for the decent behaviour of the German fans – not common in England when your team had lost – and the high standard of play. Although the German anthem was booed, the rest of the match continued without incident. [51]

After the Berlin Olympic Games, France met Germany in more international sports meetings than any other country, including the fascist countries. They met 24 times in 1937 and 17 times in 1938. Franco's Spain – favourable politically to the Nazis – also forged close sporting links with Germany.

With more German sports officials taking active roles on the international stage than ever before, it is not surprising that most of the international sports federations were in favour of going to Berlin in 1936: the only strong reservations coming from the United States and the Netherlands. [52] Eventually the AAU of the US voted in December 1935 about participation in the Games and the result was $58^{1}/_{4}$ to $53^{3}/_{4}$ in favour of all eligible sports going. [53] Avery Brundage, then president of the AAU [54], played a major part in this decision and was rewarded when the IOC made him the new member for the US, replacing Lee Jahncke whom the IOC had excluded for speaking out against American participation. [55]

On the other hand, the Dutch decided that the decision whether or not to go should be taken by the individual federations – and all but two decided to go. [56]

Thus, Germany could claim that it had the overall consent of the Olympic movement to stage the Olympic Games. It staged the Winter Olympics in Garmisch-Partenkirchen and the summer Olympics in Berlin and both were enormously successful with more participating nations, athletes and journalists than ever before. Goebbels' Ministry and the Olympic Committee formed a working group to provide and coordinate German propaganda and regular pre-Olympic press releases in many different languages were sent to newspapers around the globe. A torch relay was invented by Goebbels' staff to transport an Olympic flame from Mount Olympia to Berlin so that attention could be focused on Berlin in the last days before the Games, and also show that the Nazi regime respected ancient Olympic tradition. 'Note you, of Sparta, and not of Athens'. [57] Many of these propaganda ideas became a permanent feature at future Olympic Games. Tourists were also encouraged to travel to the Games in order to attract much needed foreign currency.

## Optimal preparation

Surprisingly, Germany, for the first time, finished top of the medal table ahead of the US and Italy. Although the German authorities had publicly laid more emphasis on demonstrating Germany's organizational strength, the *Reichssportführer* had created the conditions for optimal preparation: whoever was pre-selected for the German Olympic team, in some cases as early as 1934, received favourable working conditions in the various services of the public sector, thus providing the basis for as much free time for training as necessary. Many worked for the military or paramilitary organizations, but some, like the famous Rudolf Harbig, later to become the world record holder for 800 metres, worked for the city gas company in his home town of Dresden. He is also an example of the improving cooperation between sports science and coaching, as he was the first truly interval-trained athlete, improving on the previous world record by almost three seconds in 1939. He was also fully government supported. [58] Full-time national coaches were hired whose knowledge of sports science was based on a broader spectrum of research. This was a great boost, particularly to those sports that were internationally rather amateur. However, in sports like soccer, which at international level had only semi-professional training methods, the Germans did not improve all that much. But, competing in many international sports meetings did help to strengthen team spirit. The fact that the *Turners* participated officially in the Olympic Games for the first time since 1904 also helped. Some of the best former workers' athletes also improved the quality of the German team. Considering that Germany had already been second in 1928, a second place could reasonably be expected – but being first was above expectation and helped German internal and external propaganda enormously.

The Games presented to the world a picture of peace, and fulfilment of all the

Olympic ideals, an image furthered by the fact that only official German photographers were permitted at the Games sites, thus giving only one view. Leni Riefenstahl's famous film about the Berlin Olympics, which has won many international prizes, even today propagates the myth, but was a perfect piece of Nazi propaganda. [59] Race was a much discussed subject, particularly as Jesse Owens, the black American sprinter, became the superstar of the Games, thus questioning Nazi theories of the racial superiority of the 'Aryan' race. [60] But the German 'full' Jews had no chance to participate in the Games, while the 'half-Jews' could still represent Germany. This was in accordance with the Nuremberg racial laws and calmed international public opinion which did not realize the subtle difference between the two. The German authorities also made use of Pierre de Coubertin (1863–1937), the founder of the Olympic movement. He not only made some radio broadcasts for propaganda purposes, but gave a press interview after the Games, stating that in his view it did not make any difference whether the Olympic Games served the purpose of propaganda for the tourist industry as it did for Los Angeles in 1932 or for a political regime as it did in 1936. Most important for him was that the Games were progressing. De Coubertin, who was broke at the time, was financially supported by the Nazis. [61]

## Approaching war

As was feared before by many abroad, the SA-slogan 'Wenn die Olympiade vorbei, schlagen wir die Juden zu Brei!' ('when the Olympic Games are over we beat the Jews to hash')[62] soon became a reality. Jews had had to leave the general sports organizations in 1933, but many had joined Jewish organizations which soon had more members than ever before. But from 1935 onwards membership of many of these organizations, and in particular of the Maccabi, began to stall, so that by the time all Jewish sports organizations were dissolved in 1938, they had ceased to be of any consequence. [63]

Theodor Lewald, himself a 'half-Jew', was asked by the German government to step down as a member of the IOC, and allow von Tschammer to take his place. However, Diem and Lewald succeeded in getting their old friend General Walter von Reichenau (1884–1942) into the post. Ignoring this setback, von Tschammer made a lot of goodwill tours all over Europe, using Diem who had become the head of foreign affairs for the sports federation, [64] as his main contact with foreign sports organizations. Diem was also chosen by the IOC to edit their new trilingual journal *Olympische Rundschau*, sponsored by the Nazis, who, by sponsoring the journal, were able to increase their hold on the Swiss-based organization.

Inside Germany, the sports movement was getting closer to the Nazi Party and in 1938, its status changed from a somewhat independent organization to one which was 'supported' by the Party. It also changed its name to *nationalsozialistisch*. In practice this meant that at a time when everybody had to perform a public service of some sort, being a club official or coach came into this category. It also meant, that instead of negotiating with a government official to obtain sports grounds and subsidies, all negotiating had to be done through Party channels. Because of this rule, after the war all sports officials were considered to be members of Nazi organizations, and the sports movement was banned.

Appeasement was the international watchword of the day after the 1936 Olympics. Thus, what was so prominent in the political arena leading to the infamous 1938 Munich Agreement, can also be seen in sport. Germany tried to act according to the notion that sport and politics were separate, that Germany was only claiming its birthright, and this was readily accepted by the IOC. [65] When Norway and Switzerland could not organize the Winter Olympic Games of 1940, Garmisch-Partenkirchen stepped in and offered the best Games ever. The IOC voted to accept with only two members abstaining, even though Germany had already marched into Czechoslovakia, breaking the Munich accord that was supposed to have ended all Hitler's territorial claims. [66]

Germany tried to compete in as many international sports meetings as possible during this period so as to maintain an air of normality: in July 1939 France competed against Germany in track and field in Munich, and on 12/13 August, two weeks before the start of the Second World War, the French sent swimming and water polo teams to compete again in Munich. Germany also participated with one thousand gymnasts in the *Lingiade* in Stockholm in July 1939. The largest gymnastic festival in the world gave a friendly welcome to the German team. Although the Reich authorities had made sure that Czech Sokol clubs would not participate, this was only commented on by social-democratic sections of the Swedish press, leaving the conservative organizers and the German team very happy. [67] Sweden was a strong supporter of the Nazis in sport in spite of the fact that it remained neutral throughout the war. [68]

## International sport during the Second World War

When Hitler started the war in 1939 it was considered by physical educators as much as by sports leaders to be the *true test* of their system of physical education: 'This struggle is at the same time the test of the national-socialist education. It will be a proof of character of the first order. Who could know in advance that our political physical education could show its quality so soon?' [69]

The *Reichssportführer* von Tschammer decreed immediately that everybody should continue with sport, 'being an indispensable condition for the education of youth for military readiness'. [70] Of course, this was welcomed by the coordinated sporting press. After two months of war Cavalier told the track and field clubs that the enemy was surprised about the number and quality of the German sports meetings, that the clubs were an important link with their members at the front and all correspondence should encourage them to keep fighting, and finally, that the clubs would be having more social meetings than ever before to boost morale at home. [71]

The outbreak of war meant that it was no longer feasible for Germany to hold the Winter Olympic Games in Garmisch-Partenkirchen. However, Germany did wish to carry on sporting competition and the Minister for Foreign Affairs von Ribbentrop informed the Minister of the Interior that if possible Germany would compete against the neutral powers. He confirmed in a letter to the *Reichssportführer* in October 1939 that German teams should compete abroad and that foreign teams should compete in Germany as often as possible. [72] The sports movement obliged. In 1939 Germany held the most sports meetings it had ever held in a year (106) against 19 different countries. This dropped to 50 against 11 countries in 1940 and 50 against 9 in 1941. There was a slight increase up to 51 against 9 in 1942. Nevertheless, these were twice the number held in 1932 and 1933. Thus for the German population the message seemed to be business as usual. [73] What applied to sports meetings also applied to other sporting competitions. In 1942 Germany even staged the European Boxing Championships, and international professional cycle races were held in Germany as late as 1944. [74]

Up to 1942, while it looked as if Germany might win the war, German sports officials tried to reorganize international sports so that they could be run by Germans or those sympathetic to the German cause. European federations were founded which were under German influence. These included not only those in the fascist countries, but also those in the neutral countries, which tended to lean towards Germany.

The IOC was in a unique situation. Its president Henri de Baillet-Latour (1876–1942) was more or less a hostage in occupied Belgium – under a commanding general who was an IOC member. Carl Diem went to see Baillet-Latour in July 1940. He was tasked by the Führer himself to transfer the IOC into German hands. [75] Baillet-Latour was quite willing to help the Germans – if they won the war. As they had not, and they were still fighting, he decided that the IOC should be a non-active organization for the time being. This was against the interests of the majority of the executive committee (Brundage, Bonacossa, Edström, von Halt), who had favoured an executive committee meeting in Berlin, but in the interest of Lord Aberdare; and a doubtful Marquis de Polignac. [76] The IOC did not become officially active again until the death of the president in 1942. He was replaced by the Swedish vice-president Sigfried Edström (1870–1964), but by that time the chances of a German victory were becoming remote. In spite of Edström's pro-fascist stand, he was too smart to run the risk of a Nazi take-over of the IOC or the IAAF (International Amateur Athletics Federation) of which he was also in charge. Against the wishes of the Germans and Italians he also declined to hold the 1942 European Track and Field Championships. [77]

The war was now taking its toll on sport. As of 1 January 1942 all skiing competitions ceased, and all skiers were sent to help the German army fight on the Eastern Front. The First European Sports Conference which was to take place in Garmisch-Partenkirchen at the occasion of the Ski-World Championships in February 1942 was cancelled together with the championships. This demonstrated to Edström, who had been invited, that the chances of a German victory were growing slimmer. With Germany now fighting total warfare on all fronts, most international sporting competitions ended.

Karl von Halt became Hitler's last *Reichssportführer* in 1943. German championships took place in almost all sports until 1944. In 1944 DSC Dresden won the German soccer championships in the Berlin Olympic Stadium in front of 75 000 spectators, beating the Airforce SV Hamburg 4–0. It was, however, not only elite sport which flourished. Traditional meetings attracted many athletes. The *Maschseelauf*, a cross-country relay, attracted 142 teams totalling over 2000 runners in May 1943. [78]

Also by 1943 Germany had tens of thousands of non-Germans in the country, i.e. foreign workers, prisoners of war and forced labourers. The prisoners of war and forced labourers spent most of their time in camps, but they were differentiated in that the prisoners of war did not have to work, whereas the forced labourers provided free labour for the war effort. Conditions in the prisoner-of-war camps did not differ from those in the concentration camps, [79] but as far as sport was concerned, there was a difference between POWs and forced labourers. For Poles and other Eastern workers, sport was prohibited. For others, sports grounds could be provided, but no equipment. In the city of Hanover, for example, 600 came every week to the Hindenburg Stadium to take showers. Fraternizing with POWs or foreign workers was prohibited for German sportsmen. Sport between Germans and foreigners was not planned. Sports meetings between POWs of different nationalities took place for propaganda purposes under the auspices of the sports federations (NSRL). [80] Therefore, some sort of *international* sports did take place in Germany until the end of the war.

At the very end of the war, when Berlin was being attacked by the approaching Soviet forces, we find many of our leading actors again. Carl Diem was giving pep talks to 15- and 16-year-olds, persuading them to fight against the Russians as a personal sacrifice in the spirit of the ancient Spartans. [81] Karl von Halt led a group of elderly gentlemen (including Diem) near the Olympic Stadium against Soviet tanks, was captured and spent five years in a Soviet POW Camp, the former Nazi concentration camp of Buchenwald. [82]

## Conclusion

Germany was one of the countries that made use of international sport earlier than most others on a high governmental level. With a considerable degree of continuity in personnel from Imperial Germany, through the Republic into the Nazi period and afterwards into the German Federal Republic, the knowledge and skill of international competitions and the propaganda that went with it was thoroughly maintained. With sporting organizations cooperating closely with the various levels of government, the Nazis did have some streamlining and coordinating to do to increase efficiency, but mainstream sports and *Turnen* willingly followed the Nazis along their path of using sport as a means to an end.

The Nazis put even more emphasis on the role of sport in international relations, referring to the athletes as 'soldiers in track suits, fighting for the fatherland'. Sport to them was one of the few ways, and the most efficient, to break the cultural isolation of the Third Reich. In the early years of the war, Germany tried also to become the leader of the European sports movement, but failed in 1942, because their efficient war machine was grinding to a halt – not because many international sports leaders were actively opposed to the Nazis. When we look back at that period, it is clear that sport was considered an efficient means for national representation; governments went a long way to support it and the sports movement was proud to serve that function – no matter what the government stood for.

# References

1. Krüger, A. (1994) 'The Olympic Spirit of the Modern World has given us a Symbol of World War.' Sport and National Representation at the Eve of World War I, in P. Arnaud and A. Wahl (eds), *Sport et rélations internationales*, vol. 19, Centre de Recherche Histoire et Civilisation de l'Université de Metz, Metz, pp. 47–64.
2. Berner, M. (1913) Der olympische Gedanke in der Welt. *Fußball und Leichtathletik* (14), 495–6.
3. Mangan, J.A. (1981) *Athleticism in the Victorian and Edwardian Public School*, Cambridge University Press, Cambridge.
4. Krüger, A. and Riordan, J. (eds) (1985) *Der internationale Arbeitersport*, Pahl-Rugenstein, Köln.
5. Krüger, A. (1989) Is there any sense in competition, specialization and the striving for records? The struggle between Turnen, sports and Swedish gymnastics in Germany, in G. Bonhomme (ed.), *La place de jeu dans l'éducation. Histoire et pédagogie*, FFEPGV, Paris, pp. 123–40; French version: Quelle signification peut-on accorder á la spécialisation á la compétition et à la recherche de la performance: Les lutte d'influence entre turnen, le sport et la gymnastique suédoise en Allemagne, in G. Bonhomme (ed.), *Supplément en français de l'édition bilingue*, FFEPGV, Paris, pp. 3–14.
6. von Wisoczky, A. (1897) Zur Frage des Preisturnens. *Arbeiter Turn-Zeitung*, (7), 4/15 Jan., 79–80.
7. Krüger, A. (1975) *Sport und Politik. Vom Turnvater Jahn zum Staatsamateur*, Fackelträger, Hannover, pp,. 25ff.
8. Krüger, A. (1987) *Sieg Heil* to the most glorious era of German sport: Continuity and change in the Modern German sports movement. *Int. J. His. of Sport* **4** (1), 5–20.
9. Veitch, C.R. (1986) Play up! Play up! And Win the War! The Propaganda of Athleticism in Britain, 1914–1918, in G. Redmond (ed.), *Sport and Politics*, Human Kinetics, Champaign, pp. 93–8.
10. Diem, C. (1923) *Sport ist Kampf*, Hackebeil, Berlin, p. 34.
11. MacAloon, J.J. (1981) *This Great Symbol. Pierre de Coubertin and the Origins of the Modern Olympic Games*, University of Chicago, Chicago.
12. Krüger, A. (1990) The ritual in modern sport. A sociobiological approach, in J. M. Carter and A. Krüger (eds) *Ritual and Record*, Conn., Greenwood, Westport, pp. 135–52.
13. Galtung, J. (1984) Sport and International Understanding: Sport as a Carrier of Deep Culture and Structure, in M. Ilmarinen (ed.), *Sport and International Understanding*, Springer, Berlin, pp. 12–19.
14. Dierker, H. (1990) *Arbeitersport im Spannungsfeld der Zwanziger Jahre. Alltagserfahrungen auf internationaler, deutscher und Berliner Ebene*, Klartext, Essen.
15. Arnaud, P. (ed.) (1994) *Les origines du sport ouvrier en Europe*, Harmattan, Paris.

16. Krüger, A. and Riordan, J. (eds), (in press) *The Story of the International Workers' Sport*, Human Kinetics, Champaign.

17. Holmäng, P.O. (1992) International Sports Organizations 1919–1925: Sweden and the German Question. *Int. J. Hist. Sport* **9**, issue no. 455–66.

18. Huba, K. -H. (ed.) (1973) *Fußball-Weltgeschichte*, Copress, München.

19. Krüger, The Olympic Spirit, in Arnaud and Whal, *op. cit.*

20. Carl Diem Institut (ed.) (1968) *Bibliographie Carl Diem*, Hofmann, Schorndorf. His bibliography contained more than two thousand titles, including 59 monographs, 14 books as editor and 5 journals as editor.

21. Krüger, A. (1975) *Dr. Theodor Lewald. Sportführer ins Dritte Reich*, Bartels & Wernitz, Berlin.

22. Pfeiffer, R. and Krüger, A. (1995) Theodor Lewald: Eine Karriere im Dienste des Vaterlands oder die vergebliche Suche nach der jüdischen Identität eines 'Halbjuden', in *Menora Jahrbuch für deutsch-jüdische Geschichte*, Piper, München, pp. 233–65.

23. Krüger, A. (1991) We are sure to have found the true reasons for the American superiority in sports. The Reciprocal Relationship between the United States and Germany in Physical Culture and Sport, in R. Naul (ed.), *Turnen and Sport. The Cross-Cultural Exchange*, Waxman, New York/Münster, pp. 51–82.

24. Becker, F. (1993) *Amerikanismus in Weimar. Sportsymbole und politische Kulur, 1918–1933*, Dt. Universitäts Verl, Wiesbaden.

25. Hoberman, J. (1992) *Mortal Engines. The Science of Performance and the Dehumanization of Sport*, Free Press, New York.

26. Krüger, A. (1997) Turnen und Turnunterricht zur Zeit der Weimarer Republik Grundlage der heutigen Schulsport-Misere?, in A. Krüger and D. Niedlich (eds), *Ursachen der Schulsport-Misere in Deutschland*, Arena, London, pp. 13–31.

27. Ueberhorst, H. (1986) Sport, Physical Culture and Political Action in Germany During the Weimar Republic 1925–1933, in G. Redmond, pp. 109–16.

28. Krüger, A. (1990) Puzzle Solving. German Sport Historiography of the Eighties. *Journal of Sport History* **17**(2), 261–77.

29. Krümmel, C. (ed.) (1930) *Athletik. Ein Handbuch der lebenswichtigen Leibesübungen*, Lehmann, München.

30. Bernett, H. (1979) Anfänge sportwissenschaftlicher Vereinigungen, in *Geschichte der Sportwissenschaft. Internationales Seminar*, vol. 2, DHfK, Berlin, pp. 246–57.

31. Czech, M. (1993) *Frauen und Sport im nationalsozialistischen Deutschland. Eine Untersuchung zur weiblichen Sportrealität in einem patriarchalen Herrschaftssystem*, Tischler, Berlin.

32. Drüger, A. (1994) Wenn die Olympiade vorbei, schlagen wir die Juden zu Brei. Das Verhältnis der Juden zu den Olympischen Spielen von 1936, in *Menora 5th Jahrbuch für deutschjüdische Geschichte 1994*, Piper, München, pp. 331–48.

33. Mehl, E. (1930) *Grundriß des deutschen Turnens*. Deutscher Turnerbund, Vienna.

34. Becker, H. (1990) *Anti-Semitismus in der Deutschen Turnerschaft*, Richarz, St Augustin.

35. Ueberhorst, H. (1976) *Carl Krümmel. und die nationalsozialistische Leibeserziehung*, Bartels & Wernitz, Berlin.

36. John, H. -G. (1986) Die Affaire Geissow und der Deutsche Schwimmverband – auf dem Wege ins Dritte Reich? in G. Spitzer and D. Schmidt (eds), *Sport zwischen Eigenständigkeit und Fremdbestimmung*, Hofmann, Schorndorf, pp. 154–70.

37. Nitsch, F. (1985) Der 'proletarische Wehrsport' in der deutschen und internationalen Arbeitersportbewegung, in H. Becker (ed.), *Sport im Spannungsfeld von Krieg und Frieden*, DVS, Clausthal, pp. 97–121.

38. Krüger, A. (1985) 'Heute gehört uns Deutschland und morgen . . . ?' Das Ringen um

den Sinn der Gleichschaltung im Sport in der Ersten Jahreshälfte 1933, in W. Buss and A. Kruger (eds), *Sportgeschichte: Traditionspflege und Wertewandel*, Duderstadt, pp. 175–96.

39. e.g. *Völkischer Beobachter* 19 Aug. 1932.

40. He was later tried as a war criminal, see OMGUS (ed.) (1985) *Ermittlungen gegen die Deutsche Bank 1946/1947*, Nördlingen, pp. 57–9.

41. Joch, W. (1991) Kontinuität und Wandel, Elend und Würde. Karl Ritter von Halt (1891–1964), in A. Luh and E. Beckers (eds), *Umbruch und Kontinuität im Sport – Reflexionen im Umfeld der Sportgeschichte*, Bochum, Brockmeyer, pp. 442–57, for his importance for track and field.

42. Krüger, A. (1972) *Die Olympischen Spiele 1936 und die Weltmeinung*, Bartels & Wernitz, Berlin.

43. Krüger, A. (1984) Der Einfluß des faschistischen Sportmodells Italiens auf den nationalsozialistischen Sport in A.M. Olsen (ed.), *Sport und Politik 1918–1939/40*, University of Oslo, Oslo, pp. 226–33.

44. Krüger, A. (1991) Fasci e croci uncinate. *Lancillotto e Nausica. Critica e storia dello sport* **8**(1/2), 88–101.

45. de Grazia V. (1981) *The Culture of Consent. Mass Organization of Leisure in Fascist Italy*, Cambridge University Press, Cambridge.

46. Peiffer, L. (1989) *Turnunterricht im Dritten Reich. Erziehung für den Krieg?* PahlRugenstein, Köln.

47. Steinhöfer, D. (1973) *Hans von Tschammer und Osten – Reichssportführer im Dritten Reich*, Bartels & Wernitz, Berlin.

48. Teichler, H. -J. (1991) *Internationale Sportpolitik im Dritten Reich*, Hofmann, Schorndorf, pp. 59ff.

49. Scherer, K.A. (1974) *Der Männerorden. Die Geschichte des Internationalen Olympischen Komitees*, Limpert, Frankfurt/M.

50. Krüger, A. and Murray, B., (eds) (1996) *The 1936 Olympics in World Perspective*, University of Illinois Press, Champaign.

51. Stoddard, B. (1985) Cultural Politics and International Relations. England vs. Germany, 1935, in N. Müller and J.K. Rühl (eds), *Olympic Scientific Congress. Sport History* Schors, Niedernhausen, pp. 385–411.

52. Krüger, A. (1978) Fair Play for American Athletes. A study in anti-semitism. *Canadian Journal of the History of Sport and Physical Education*, **9**(1), 42–57.

53. Wenn, S.R. (1988) *The Commodore Hotel Re-Visited: An Analysis of the 1935 AAU Convention.* Proceedings of 6th Canadian Symposium on the History of Sport and Physical Education, London, Ontario, pp. 188–201.

54. Guttmann, A. (1984) *The Games must go on. Avery Brundage and the Olympic Movement*, Columbia, New York.

55. Lucas, J.A. (1991) Ernest Lee Jahncke: The Expelling of an IOC Member. *Stadion*, **17** (1), 53–78.

56. Swijtink, A. (1992) *In de Pas Sport en lichamelijke opvoeding in Nederland tijdens de Tweede Wereldoorlog*, DE Vriesborch, Haarlem.

57. Krüger, A. and Ramba, D. (1991) Sparta or Athens? The Reception of Green Antiquity in Nazi Germany, in R. Renson, M. Lammer, J. Riordan and D. Chassiotis (eds), *The Olympic Games Through the Ages: Greek Antiquity and its Impact on Modern Sport*, Hellenic Sports Research Institute, Athens, pp. 345–56.

58. Harbig, G. (1949) *Unvergessener Rudolf Harbig*, Verlag der Nation, Berlin.

59. Graham, C.C. (1986) *Leni Riefenstahl and Olympia*, Scarecrow, London.

60.  Baker, W. J. (1986) *Jesse Owens. An American Life*, Free Press, New York.
61.  Murray, W.J. (1992) France, Coubertin and the Nazi Olympics: The Response. *Olympika*, (1), 46–69.
62.  *Neues Tagebuch*, Paris, 2 May 1936, p. 431.
63.  Atlasz, R. (1977) *Barkochba. Makkabi – Deutschland 1898–1938*, Makkabi, Tel Aviv.
64.  Teichler, H. -J. (1987) Der Weg Carl Diems vom DRA-Generalsekretär zum kommissarischen Führer des Gaues Ausland im NSRL. Ein Beitrag zur Erforschung der Rolle der bürgerlichen Funktionselite in der nationalsozialistischen Diktatur. *Sozial- und Zeitgeschichte des Sports*, **1**, 42–91.
65.  Krüger, A. (1982) Deutschland und die Olympische Bewegung (1918–1945), in H. Ueberhorst (ed.), *Geschichte der Leibesübungen*, vol. 3/2, Bartels & Wernitz, Berlin, pp. 1026–47.
66.  Bernett, H. (1980) Das Scheitern der Olympischen Spiele von 1940. *Stadion*, (6), 251–90.
67.  Bernett, H. and Teichler, H. -J. (1979) *Die deutsche Mannschaft bei der Lingiade in Stockholm. Eine sportpolitische Expedition.* Proceedings of Hispa 8th International Congress, HISPA, Uppsala, pp. 83–108.
68.  Holmäng, P.O. (1988) *Idrott och utrikespolitik: Den svenska idrottsrörelsens internationella förbindelser. 1919–1945*, University of Göteborg, Göteborg.
69.  Dannheuser, J. (1966) Die politische Leibeserziehung im Krieg, *Leibesübungen und körperliche Erziehung (1939)*, *488*, quoted in H. Bernett *Nationalsozialistische Leibeserziehung*, Hofmann, Schorndorf, 217. There are many more quotes of the same kind in this collection by Bernett.
70.  von Tschammer, H. (1939) Sport der inneren Front. *NS-Sport* (1) 17 Sept., 15.
71.  Cavalier, H. (1939) Aktivität der Herzen Eine Betrachtung über den Einsatz des deutschen Sports im Krieg. *Leichtathletik* (16), 6 Nov., 2–3.
72.  Teichler (1991) *op. cit.*, p. 271.
73.  Krüger, A. (1993) Germany and Sport in World War II. *Can. Journal of the History of Sport*, **24**(1), 52–62.
74.  Krüger, A. (1991) 'Leibesübungen jetzt erst recht!' Sport im Zweiten Weltkrieg, in A. Krüger and H. Langenfeld (eds), *Sport in Hannover. Von der Stadtgründung bis heute*, Die Werkstatt, Göttingen, pp. 185–8.
75.  Carl Diem's Diaries, 17 July 1940, Carl-Diem-Institute, Cologne.
76.  Letter Edström to Brundage, Stockholm 29 July 1940, Brundage Collection on Microfilm (IfS Göttingen), Reel 24.
77.  Krüger (1978) Fair Play, *op. cit.*
78.  Turn-Klubb zu Hannover, *Rundschreiben*, vol. 32 (June 1943), 6, p. 1.
79.  Herlemann, B. and Sommer, K.L. (1988) Widerstand. Alltagsopposition und Verfolgung unter dem Nationalsozialismus in Niedersachen. *Nieders. Jahrbuch Landesgeschichte* (60), 291ff.
80.  Rundschreiben des Kreissportführers vom 26.8.1943 and die Vereinsführer des Sportkreises Hannover. *Archives VfL Hannover*, Akten (1940–45). (unerledgt).
81.  Dokumentation. Aus einem Referat von Reinhard Apel vom 28. April 1984 in der Führungs- und Verwaltungsakademie in Berlin. *Soz Zeitges. d. Sports* **1**(1) (1987), 105.
82.  Diem, L. (1982) *Fliehen oder bleiben? Dramatisches Kriegsende in Berlin*, Herder, Freiburg.

## Chapter 7

# Spanish sports policy in Republican and Fascist Spain

*Teresa Gonzalez Aja*

The historical period which extends from the First Republic (1873) up to the consolidation of the Franco dictatorship is extremely complex. The political and social changes which took place were often so dramatic that they influenced every sphere of life, regardless of the group to which people belonged. This is reflected in sport, thereby making it necessary to study sport in the context of the different events, and of social groups that practised it or had the power to control it.

The main cycles are clear. Between 1877 and 1886 there was a period of optimistic growth during an era of depression in Europe. When Europe recovered, Spain suffered the crises of the 1890s. Its recovery, in spite of a series of bad harvests and minor industrial crises, continued almost without interruption between 1900 and 1914, while the 1914–18 war converted neutral Spain into a favoured country. Primo de Rivera had the good fortune to govern during a period of prosperity which suddenly came to an end in 1929. Isolated to some extent from the consequences of the world crisis, the economy remained stagnant or declined during the 1931 Republic. The Civil War was a terrible blow from which Spain would not easily recover after 1939. For these reasons, 1929 can be seen as the climax of the growth which had begun in the 19th century; agricultural production was not to regain the levels of the last year of Primo de Rivera's dictatorship until the 1950s. [1]

## From the First to the Second Republic

The Spain of the last years of the 19th century gives us an image full of contrasts, which delighted romantic travellers. [2] Sports activities were the privilege of a few individuals who belonged to the highest social classes. Horse riding, shooting and fencing constituted the most frequently practised activities by this sector of the population, while the lower classes took part, above all, in their local festivals. In fact, bullfighting, the national festival par excellence, became a commercial proposition, once the railways made possible the regular transport of spectators and fighting bulls, and large bullrings were built in the provincial capitals, beginning with Murcia in 1886.

This contrast between social classes would not only be maintained, but would be intensified at the beginning of the 20th century, because of the unequal economic growth of the country. The Spain of small towns and local festivals would prevail over the Spain of the big cities and modern mass sports spectacles.

The economic behaviour of the aristocracy was often, although to a lesser extent, that of the village *cacique*, except that it enjoyed social, and, to a certain extent, political influence. Its number had grown continuously throughout the 19th century through the incorporation into its ranks of eminent military figures, important bourgeois and politicians. It decidedly supported traditional Roman Catholic values, trying to impose these values on the upper layers of society, in the same way that it imposed its own lifestyle. Its amusements were more and more modern following those of the most solid English sporting nobility. 'English-style' hunting became a passion with Alphonse XIII, as did polo. The lists of the guests at royal hunting parties are an index of the social forces which influenced the private thinking of the King: the parties were made up mainly by court aristocrats with the odd professional politician patrician like Romanones, a terrible shot but a frequent guest. Proust noted the social importance that Alphonse XIII gave to hunting. He used three shotguns with which he would shoot two birds in front of him, two above him and two behind him. He was as excellent a shot as George V. [3]

Alphonse XIII was a born sportsman and enthusiast. As well as hunting and polo, he practised pigeon shooting, motor racing, skating, etc.

This link between the aristocracy and sporting activities was clearly reflected in the interest shown in the Olympic Games. In 1902, thanks to the contacts of some aristocrats with Pierre de Coubertin, the Marquis of Villamejor was nominated a member of the International Olympic Committee, and was succeeded in 1922 by Baron de Güell. Alphonse XIII himself showed his interest in the Games by presiding over the Honorary Committee for the Candidacy of Barcelona to host the Games in 1924. However, the Barcelona bid was unsuccessful; it was given the 1936 Games instead. But even this was not to be, with the rise to power of Hitler, the IOC changed its mind, and Berlin became the seat of that Olympiad.

In Spain, the government of the Second Republic was not in favour of its athletes participating in Games which it considered tainted with a political ideology to which it was clearly opposed, and thus refused the subsidies which the Spanish Olympic Committee requested in order to participate. Consequently, there was no alternative but to follow the official line of non-participation and reject the Berlin Olympics. A group of military horsemen did decide to take part, but the war which overwhelmed the country after the military revolt in Morocco, prevented them from attending.

At the same time there began a movement, promoted by various communists, socialists and Jewish groups, to celebrate some alternative Games. This project was welcomed by the Left, both inside and outside Spain. The so-called Popular Olympics attracted a total of 4500 entries from many nationalities including the British, Swiss, Dutch, Norwegian and French. The opening ceremony was planned for 19 July 1936; the military uprising in Morocco broke out on 18 July of the same year. The Popular Olympics were, therefore, never held. Most of the foreign athletes who were already in the country were evacuated.

The Republic tried, for political reasons, to democratize and proletarianize the Olympic Movement which was closely linked to the ruling and aristocratic classes. However, the aristocratic influence was already clearly disappearing. The court and the old aristocracy did not realize that their situation was seriously threatened because of the unpopularity of a king whose position they could hardly defend, and yet whose existence was their *raison d'être*. In the Republic of 1931 the aristocracy was a solitary, idle and isolated caste. This estrangement had already become obvious in 1920 and had intensified during Primo de Rivera's dictatorship.

If the Civil War prevented the holding of parallel Games to the Olympics, it also put an end to the attempts of the Second Republic to implement educational programmes that would permit qualitative and quantitative changes in public education. Up until that time, the country's political, economic and social situation had not permitted any attempt to establish a strongly structured state school system. Physical education had only been introduced in small élitist circles. Alphonse XIII in 1883, created the Central School for teachers of theoretical and practical gymnastics. In 1887 the school, which belonged to the University of Madrid and which admitted both male and female students (an unusual characteristic for the era), was inaugurated. This school was closed down for economic reasons in 1892.

In 1919 the Army Gymnastics School was founded in Toledo. Up until then, the only way the non-aristocratic classes could live a life which included some physical training was during military service. Faced with this situation, it was necessary for the army to have a school for teaching and practising military physical education in civil life. The enormous interest that the army had in instilling the idea of physical exercise in the minds of the troops was evident. And it was this institution that was the first to introduce physical education as such, with the aim of maintaining and improving the fitness of soldiers and, at the same time, of ensuring the development of future generations. 'The army, an ideal school of Physical Education, serves to prolong the life of the citizens who make up a country, and is a powerful instrument for progress and civilization,' stated Eduardo de los Reyes in 1921. [4]

Several efforts were made to achieve this objective, the majority of which had few repercussions, like the gymnastics school created by the Engineering Corps of Guadalajara, which lasted barely two years. In 1911 Captain Gómez de Salazar and Captain González Deleito were sent to Stockholm to study the Swedish gymnastics system which had been structured by Hjalmar Ling. In the same year, provisional gymnastics regulations came into force for the infantry.

In spite of the wide horizons and good intentions which accompanied this project, it failed to achieve any practical physical activity. The fundamental reason was the lack of qualified staff; to be able to teach physical education, it was necessary not only to know the current regulations, but also the subjects which had served as a basis for their drafting, otherwise it was impossible to interpret them correctly.

All this serves to emphasize the enormous importance that the creation of the Army Gymnastics School had for physical education.

The initial idea for such a school came from the then Minister of War, José

Villalba Riquelme, who suggested to the King the need to have a gymnastics and sports school to keep military personnel fit and to extend this knowledge to civilians to promote physical education in Spain. On 29 December 1919, the Army Gymnastics School was created by Royal Decree; it would be referred to by the son of its founder, General Ricardo Villalba Rubio in his *History of Sport in Spain*, as the Spanish 'Joinville'.

Its purpose was to train a small staff of officer teachers of gymnastics so that the infantry could be taught physical education with a group of instructors to help them. It was intended not only physically to train the soldiers, but also to create individuals who were qualified to educate all youth. Thus the need was established to give special drilling to state school teachers who came to do their military service.

The admiration which was felt for the Swedish system was evident in the course developed by the school's creators. This is witnessed by the fact that to gain entry onto the course, the completion of which would enable a candidate to obtain an administrative position in the future institute, the desirability of knowing foreign languages, like French or English, was specified, but it was recommended that priority be given to those who spoke German or Swedish.

The influence of the Swedish system was not only evident in this school. In 1933, when the Navy Minister published his Physical Education Regulations, he based his fundamental method on Swedish gymnastics, applied gymnastics and games and sports. The same year, the Army Gymnastics School taught its courses not just to officers and non-commissioned officers of the Army, but also to officers and non-commissioned officers of the Navy.

From 1936 until 1939, life at the school came to a standstill because of the Civil War. On 23 October 1939 it reopened under a new name, the Central School of Physical Education.

However, until its bourgeois and optimistic reformism was overcome by socialism, the most serious attempt to introduce a new educational concept was promoted by the Free Teaching Institution.

The intellectual concept which gave birth to the institution was the philosophy of Krause in the 1860s and the radical-liberal beliefs of the 1868 Revolution. It was founded in Madrid by University professors who had lost their chairs in 1875, and by their supporters in liberal bourgeois circles. It was to be a free university, dedicated to the ideal of a non-official, non-dogmatic education which would mould the élite necessary to modernize Spain. After its failure as a university, the institution devoted its energies to primary and secondary education.

From its beginnings, the institute's president was Francisco Giner. The fact that Giner never abandoned his Krause dogmatism did not prevent him from creating an educational system directed against the teaching of traditional subjects on the basis of rote learning by teachers who were indifferent to the morals and intellectual personality of the students. His school tried to establish personal contacts between teachers and students, to adopt all the advances made in European educational methods, and to broaden the curriculum with courses in art, folklore and technical subjects; the students were encouraged to practise sports and to make trips into the countryside.

There was some development as regards physical education, starting from a closer study of the ideas current in other countries, but they basically meant further advances in ideas that were already prevalent in the institution. Its interest was due not to foreign influence but rather in its own pedagogy, in its anthropology and in its idealistic metaphysics, and especially in Giner and in Cossio, that is to say, in its 'humanistic ideal of an integral education'.

For the Free Teaching Institution muscular education was understood to be connected to the education of the will and to the senses. In order to achieve this, it used both indirect methods – the physical building of the school with all its facilities, its furniture, its school materials and its general teaching routine – and direct methods – exercises, gymnastics, games, walks, excursions and holiday camps. It was a first attempt (in general, a failure because the French influence was closer and traditionally better known in Spain) to divert Pro-European intellectuals from French models and to lead them towards Anglo-Saxon methods.

In 1882 football made an appearance. The teachers and students of the Free Teaching Institution and those of the Irish Schools in Valladolid and Salamanca were the first to practise this sport in Castile. That is to say, it began to be practised in élite schools, where games were encouraged, in contrast to the majority of schools, institutes and colleges, where physical education was practically unknown.

Football was, in fact, the only Western sport which eventually became a national passion. In spite of the attempts of reformers to introduce cycling and excursions as part of Western living, their supporters were confined to quite a small group; Lerroux, for example, was a cycling enthusiast, but the average Spanish worker could not hope to buy a bicycle.

In Spain, as in other countries, there has been no end of controversy about where football was first played. Huelva, Tarragona, Barcelona, Vigo and Bilbao, all claim seniority. However, everything seems to indicate that it was thanks to the leasing by the First Republic government of the copper pyrite mines of Rio Tinto to British capital, and the consequent arrival in the Andalusian region of British engineers and technicians, which introduced the game.

The Rio Tinto company promoted football, tennis and cricket, giving up land for pitches and complementary facilities, and paying for their construction. Another 'sportsman' who supported the newly introduced sport was Guillermo Sundheim, a mining engineer, who gave up some land in 1890 which was used to build a cycle track and a football pitch, where the first society, the Huelva Recreation Club, played. That same year another new society appeared, the Rio Tinto Football Club, a team about which little is known except that it was completely made up of British company employees.

A little more to the south east, in Gibraltar, the Gibraltar Civilian Football Club organized from 1895 onwards a championship which bore its name, was held annually and in which only English teams, like the Jubilee, the Gibraltar Albions

FC and the Exiles or the Prince of Wales, took part. The Spanish teams of that time were not good enough to compete for this trophy.

Owing to Anglo-Saxon influences, the first teams adopted English names, like The Sport Club or The Modern Club, and those that chose a Spanish name always added the word football, which had still not acquired its Castilian form, like the Iberia Football Club, and the Victoria Football Club.

Thus, football was introduced into Spain, as it was into Europe and South America, on the one hand, for pedagogical reasons – with the return of students and teachers from the United Kingdom who came back with an interest in football and sport in general – and, on the other, for economic reasons – the creation of new companies. The big clubs of today were created thanks to the joint efforts of Spaniards and foreigners.

In Barcelona, it was the Swiss Hans Gamper, an outstanding sportsman in his own country, who, on arriving in Barcelona as an accountant for the tram company of Sarriá, put an advertisement in the weekly *Los Deportes* in October 1899, inviting all football enthusiasts – football was already being played on open ground in Sarriá – to get in contact with the editorial office of the weekly. Twelve young men answered the advertisement, and a month later, in the Solé Gymnasium, they formed FC Barcelona.

Regenerationism, which was very much alive in Madrid, favoured a modernizing concept which promoted the development of football. The Spanish people, then open to all things foreign, began to take an interest in athletic exercise. The press began to encourage everything to do with sporting activities and physical exercise, because it was thought that it was thanks to these that the more advanced nations had managed to create strong and vigorous generations. 'For a nation to flourish, it is necessary to have men, but it is necessary to make those men, and they will be best found in sports centres where each one physically educates himself, strengthens his muscles and develops his understanding, in the sport which he prefers,' stated the *Heraldo del Sport*. [5] In general, the press considered that the level of physical education in Spain was deplorable and some of its members suggested that football might be the answer. Among those in the press who supported football were Francos Rodríguez, the Director of the *Heraldo de Madrid*, Luis Zozaya, editor of the same newspaper, Barner of *El Imparcial* and Vicente Castro Lés, director of the illustrated sports magazine *Gran Vida*. They supported football because they considered it to be a healthy sport, as it was played in the open air, as well as educational and manly. However, there were others in the press who favoured different 'sports' such as pelota, hunting, shooting, cycling, horse racing, and the Hispanic spectacle par excellence, bullfighting. It was precisely the Madrid bullfighting supporters who disapproved of those men with rolled up trousers running after a ball on an improvised pitch located in the middle of the avenue which led to the bullring.

However, the joint forces of the press and many of the aristocracy, together with Alphonse XIII himself, who patronized the Spanish Championship and created the King's Cup, and who, in succeeding years would be named honorary president of several teams, helped football to become more and more important.

Thus, at the beginning of the 20th century, in the regenerationist context of putting new heart into a shattered and neglected people, football grew in stature with the implantation of clubs being founded in Madrid and in all the important cities. The Barcelona club was formed in 1899, a year after Athlétic de Bilbao. Real Madrid was founded in 1902 and Atlético de Madrid in 1903.

The first international match was organized in 1905, on the occasion of a visit by the French President M. Loubet to Madrid, between the French champions Gallia FC and the Spanish champions Madrid FC.

The biggest hindrance to this sport was finding a suitable ground. In principle, any open piece of ground could be used for informal matches, but when the regulations had to be applied, the pitches needed to have the appropriate dimensions. This was solved by using the central areas of several horse-racing tracks, like the ones in Seville, Madrid and Bilbao.

Remarkable differences can be observed in the development of the game from one place to another in the Peninsula. While in Castile a style of football was practised which was similar to the Scottish one, technical and with short passes, Vizcaya was a clear example of English football, direct and aggressive play, with a profusion of high centres towards the head of the centre forward, and with which the best results were achieved on the field. More than half the cups played before 1936 were won by the Basques.

Moreover, if on the periphery of Spain, industrial demands and contacts of Spaniards with foreigners made the establishment of football possible, in Madrid it was educational centralism because that meant that a large number of people who played the game, especially from Biscay and Guipúzcoa, moved to the capital to study in the special schools of engineering and architecture. In fact, the universities were certainly the best breeding ground for footballers before the advent of professionalism, the first traces of which appeared at RCD Español, and the economic consequences of which city clubs began to notice around 1927. Indeed, officials of Barcelona Football Club admitted in 1926 that they were running a professional club. With the growing number of supporters, players and clubs there was a need for a federation to lead them; thus the Spanish Football Federation was founded in 1902. It was granted the title of 'Royal' in 1913.

The 1920s saw the beginning of the construction of large stadia. Barcelona had 20 000 members who lent money to built their new stadium in 1922, [6] in 1924 the Chamartin Stadium was built in Madrid, and the same year Granada built Los Cármenes, and Murcia built its stadium, followed by Gijón in 1928 and Alicante in 1932.

One sports event was to be fundamental for the definitive popularization of football: the Antwerp Olympic Games in 1920. Spain had been playing for about twenty years and had never played abroad. Compared with the Norwegian, Swedish, Danish and Belgian teams which were participating, it did not appear to have a chance, but it won its first match against Denmark, and played in the semi-finals against Holland. It won, and the press began to talk about the great success of the Spanish footballers and their 'fury', a term which served to define the characteristics of the Hispanic game for many years, even after the Civil War. But apart from Antwerp, the national team had little success on the international scene. After succumbing to Italy in the quarter-finals of the World Cup in 1934, it was hoped that it would do well in the 1938 tournament in France. For political reasons the team never made the journey.

Successful centre forwards took the place of bullfighters in popular mythology, especially in regions in which, like the Basque country and Galicia, bullfighting had never managed to achieve a popular mystique. Aguirre, the Basque politician and president of the autonomous Basque government in 1936, became famous as a centre half. Before the Civil War there was a close relationship between regionalism and football, truly the only form of politicization of the game before Franco. From its very early days, Athlétic de Bilbao presented the image of a club which represented its region, and this was reinforced by the decision taken by its board of directors in 1919 to create a team made up exclusively of Basques, excluding, therefore, Spaniards from other areas and foreigners. This club clearly supported the campaign for Basque autonomy.

However, before the Civil War, the place where football reflected regionalism in a much more intense form than in the Basque country, was Catalonia. In spite of having been founded by a Swiss, Barcelona always gave the image of a much more Catalan club than the other local team, RCD Español. The majority of Barcelona supporters considered Español a club of Castilians who had deliberately chosen a name which was a provocation to Catalans. The political rivalry of both teams thus began practically with their creation and made a considerable contribution to the violence of the matches. However, Español was not the principal object of contempt for Barcelona fans, who had an even greater aversion towards the royal manifestations of Castilian centralism. This was especially true during the dictatorship of Primo de Rivera. In June 1925, the military governor of Barcelona closed Les Corts Stadium for six months after supporters had whistled at and booed the Spanish royal march, when it was played before the match by a band of the British Royal Navy, something which contributed to increasing their hostility.

When the Civil War broke out, both the Barcelona players and those of Bilbao did not hesitate to enlist in the ranks of those who fought against the military uprising, although their incorporation did not last long, as in both cases the players embarked on the formation of football teams whose aim was to hold matches abroad to collect funds and spread propaganda. When the war finished very few of these players opted to return to Franco's Spain. From a sporting point of view the Civil War represented the end of an epoch. For many years afterwards Spain did not appear on the international scene.

## Sport in Franco's Spain

Up until his death in November 1975, General Franco continued to be, as was proclaimed on his coins, 'Caudillo of Spain by the Grace of God' and answerable, according to his apologists, only to God and history. Although in the last years he distanced himself from direct intervention in daily politics, it is certainly true that no important decisions could be taken without his consent. Right to the end, thanks to what was called the 'Francoist Constitution' he kept the power to appoint and dismiss ministers, a power which he used whenever he saw fit.

The period which began with the end of the Civil War was marked by the personality of this man who considered that the liberalism of the 19th century had been the cause of the final eclipse of Spain's greatness and that the party egoism of liberal politicians had been responsible for the disaster of 1898 and the anarchy into which Spain had fallen in 1936, which had placed the country on the brink of being taken over by the communists.

He considered that 'when you command the troops properly, they obey; and if they don't, they should be punished for mutiny. If you govern your subjects well, they will obey; and if they don't they should suffer the consequences of their sedition.' [7] He therefore carried out a systematic purge of men and ideas. The régime of freedoms characteristic of the previous system was replaced by a régime in which one had to obtain authorization to undertake any type of activity. Furthermore, the media and the teaching system were used to inculcate ideas and values which would ensure acceptance of the new régime. The only values which were taken into account were religious and patriotic ones. In order to inculcate them suitably in the new generation the Church and the Falange were incorporated into the teaching system.

With these premises it would appear logical to use sport to serve the political ideal.

An attempt was made to follow the German Nazi model. But several aspects should be borne in mind: Franco was never willing to build a totalitarian state with only one party after the Italian or German model. After the powers of the Axis were defeated, Franco understood the need to abandon the Fascist image of his régime. And with regard to the specific sports question, Franco was never willing to spend money on it, like Hitler or Mussolini.

On 22 February 1941, Franco signed a decree which created the National Sports Delegation of the Traditionalist Falange and of the JONS (National Syndical Offensive Juntas). The decree entrusted 'the direction and promotion of Spanish sport' to the Falange.

The Falange had been founded in 1933 by José Antonio Primo de Rivera, son of the military dictator of the 1920s. The party's ideology adopted many concepts from Fascist Italy: the defence of Christian values against the peril of Marxism, a totalitarian state which would create a classless society promoting the interests of the workers, and an imperialistic destiny at the expense of the weaker races.

The Falange was a small body until the outbreak of the Civil War; but during the conflict its membership increased – in a similar way to that of the Spanish Communist Party – to nearly two million, many of whom fought against 'the reds' in the different Falangist militia. But the rise of the Falange was thwarted by two fundamental blows which would give rise to eternal political frustration: the execution of José Antonio Primo de Rivera in the Alicante prison in November 1936, and Franco's incorporation of the Party into the 'ambiguous' Movement, together with the monarchists and the Carlists, in April 1937. This is the Party which was entrusted with sport by Franco, through the creation of the National Sports Delegation (NSD). The NSD was presided over by the National Delegate of Physical Education and Sports, who was also President of the Spanish Olympic Committee (clearly contravening the rules of the IOC which declare that national committees should be strictly non-political), and responsible for the sports medicine, legal, transport, press and propaganda sections, which made up the department of military sport and sports in the Movement; he was also head of the department of national federations, and his control over the different federations was total. The NSD not only appointed the presidents and vice-presidents of the various Spanish federations, but also the members of their boards of directors and, in addition, the presidents and vice-presidents of all the regional branches of these federations. And as if this was not enough, Article 4 of the Decree conferred on the NSD the right to veto the decision of any federation with which it did not agree. With all this it completely controlled the whole of Spanish sport. As Cazorla Prieto states: 'all the social organizations of sport were subject if not to an absolute state or parastate control, then to a rigid discipline imposed by the public authorities, which practically stifled any trace of social protagonism.' [8]

The new organization was going to be a delegation or agency of the General Secretary of the National Movement, the only political party permitted, an uncomfortable alliance of Falangists, monarchists and Carlists. Its mission was to use the international sports ambit to exhibit Spanish virility and 'fury', the same as the Italian and German régimes had done between 1930 and 1940. Therefore, any possibility that sport could have a certain degree of independence from the new political power was discarded from the outset.

The National Sports Delegation was a Falangist institution, whose staff was made up mainly of Falangists. However, the first National Sports Delegate was an Army General, General Moscardó, the hero of the siege of the Alcazar fortress in Toledo in 1936, and whose links with sport was limited to his enthusiasm for horse riding and clay pigeon shooting. He introduced a series of Falangist customs and symbols into the world of sport; for example, he changed the customary red shirts of the national football team to blue, and instituted the Fascist salute by athletes at the beginning of competitions.

His term of office lasted until his death in 1955, and he was succeeded by José Antonio Elola Olaso, a voluntary Falangist officer during the Civil War, who had served since 1940 as head of the Youth Front of the Falange. In 1966 he was dismissed from his post by the Ministerial Secretary José Solís, officially for health reasons, although it was thought that it was due to the continual failures of Spain in international competition. He was succeeded by Juan Antonio Samaranch who became a popular figure in Spanish sport and stood out in the NSD as a good Falangist. He was dismissed in 1970, causing a general feeling of surprise and sadness. This dismissal came a month after Solís was also dismissed from his post as Ministerial Secretary. His successor, Torcuato Fernandez Miranda, a long-standing

Falangist, appointed his good friend Juan Gich as head of the NSD. However, José Solís was later restored to his post, and he promptly dismissed Gich, replacing him with Tomás Pelayo Ros, who stayed in the post until 1976.

As can be seen, the post of national delegate was occupied by war heroes, Falangists and politicians on their way up, and it is thus not surprising that the NSD failed in almost everything that it tried to do. It certainly failed in its attempt to make Spain a nation of athletes, in spite of its slogan 'Practice sports and improve the race', as part of the 'Sports for All' campaign which began in the 1960s. It failed in its attempt to achieve glory for Falangist Spain in international competitions; the very few Spanish sports successes, especially those of Real Madrid, were the product of a massive import of foreign stars, who were mainly recognized as such abroad. It also failed in its attempt to win the respect of both athletes and the public in general, as was witnessed by the general rejection which became evident when censorship was lifted in 1976.

The blame for this depressing situation falls to a large extent on the Franco régime. One of the reasons why the NSD failed stands out clearly from what has already been said: the unfortunate system of appointing people whose capacity for sports administration left much to be desired (with the exception of Samaranch), but who were totally reliable to the régime. This selection system not only affected the administrators, it also influenced the civil servants who worked in the NSD.

The other reason for failure is the scant investment which Franco considered suitable for sport, which meant that the NSD had to exist on money collected from the football pools.

The sports press did what it could to hide the painful truth; that the brilliance of Real Madrid and the excellent image of a handful of outstanding individuals, like the gymnast Blume, the cyclists Timoner or Bahamontes, or the tennis player Manuel Santana, partially hid the poor level of sport in general. With a few exceptions it was content loyally to reproduce the short-sighted speeches of the ministers and civil servants of the National Sports Delegation and (in the best tradition of Spanish exaggeration of triumphs) expressed an over-the-top enthusiasm when it gave information about the scanty victories which were achieved, even though they were internationally insignificant, in sports like clay pigeon shooting and hockey on roller skates.

But the facts speak for themselves. In the six Olympic Games in which Spain participated during the Franco years, it won only one gold medal, two silver and two bronze. It is a pathetic record, worse than that of small countries like Finland, New Zealand or Ireland, and it is far from emulating the sporting feats of Fascist Italy or Germany. Franco wanted to emulate these feats, but he was not willing, in contrast to Hitler or Mussolini, to make any sort of economic investment in sport.

Within the educational programme, sport was affected by the same problems as education in general. The régime's attitude to education was marked by the total rejection of laicism, and of any innovatory or pro-European tendency, and a complete affirmation of what was most traditional and Roman Catholic in Spain. An extensive set of characteristics that persons responsible for teaching should possess was drawn up, and provincial commissions were charged with purging all teaching staff of primary, secondary, university and special centres of education who did not meet the criteria; these commissions had been formed on the basis of a decree published on 8 May 1936. The schools, as in sport, were left in the hands of persons loyal to the régime, and who in many cases lacked qualifications. Thus, not only were their services rewarded, but also, given their proven loyalty on the battlefield, it was guaranteed that they would inculcate in the new generations the values for which they had fought.

When coeducation disappeared, the physical training of both sexes became totally different. The boys would do rigid, virile exercises of a marked military nature. The girls would practise Swedish and rhythmic gymnastics and the popular dances characteristic of the different Spanish regions. The lack of teachers made it necessary for the students at the Toledo Physical Education School (an institution for the military mentioned in connection with the previous period) to enter civil education; and for many years this centre would supply almost all Spanish physical education teachers. From 1941 on, the specialism of physical education was taught at the José Antonio Academy for high-ranking officers, exclusively for men. In 1945, the 'Julio Ruiz de Alda' Higher School of Physical Education was established for women only. Opened originally on a temporary basis, it became permanent only in 1957. Both these schools were placed under the control of the General Secretariat of the Movement, a situation which lasted until the creation in Madrid of the first National Institute of Physical Education in 1965.

The old summer holiday camps were replaced by camps or hostels organized by the Youth Front, the Feminine Section or the Syndical Works for Education and Rest. The ideology of these camps was far from the hygienic postulates which gave birth to the holiday camps. The accommodation in tents, the wearing of the Falangist uniform, the military style of the activities, the hierarchization, the use of the familiar form of address with the 'leaders', the use of standards, etc., put them closer to the practices of Hitler Youth, emphasizing their marked Fascist character.

The Youth Front and the Feminine Section were, again, charged with organizing sports championships which, at the school level, were held throughout the whole country. For a long time, women participants were limited to the less violent sports: basketball, volleyball and gymnastics; track and field events were long closed to women.

The role that football played during the Francoist period is worthy of special attention, and its impact on daily life cannot be underestimated.

The Royal Spanish Football Federation (RSFF) was governed by Fascists who occupied their positions because they were favoured by the régime, and not because of their administrative capabilities or their knowledge of football. They were neither capable of producing acceptable results, nor of gaining the respect and support of the frustrated clubs. It any case, its functions were strictly limited given that it came under the authority of the National Sports Delegation. During the years that General Moscardó was head of the NSD, the President of the RSFF was replaced at regular intervals, as Moscardó had little patience with men who could not produce a national team capable of beating the world, or who did not show enough enthusiasm in applying to football the Fascist symbols and attitudes of what is called the 'blue period' of the game. Simultaneously there began a 'purge' of football, whereby measures such as cancelling the results of all the games played in the Republican zone during the Civil War were introduced.

The role which football played in the development of Franco's Spain differed over time and can be divided into three different periods. We should bear in mind the length of the period, that periods overlapped, and how conditions, like relations with the outside world, changed with the passing years.

There was an initial period in which, given the ostracism to which Spain was condemned during the 1940s, the national team was hard put to find countries to play. At this time, football was an important element in the hands of the new régime established as a vehicle for Fascist attitudes and propaganda. A good example of this is the image of the two teams which played the first final of the Generalissimo's Cup in 1939, Seville and Racing from El Ferrol; they lined up before the match with their right arms raised in the Fascist salute, enthusiastically singing the *Cara al sol* [Facing the Sun], the Falangist battle hymn, echoed by the crowd which filled the stadium, and which also stood and sang, arms raised.

During this epoch Fascist concepts were applied to the game. The Falange considered it an excellent means of mobilizing the masses under its flag, to reflect the traditional Hispanic values of 'virility and impetuosity', and, above all, to show the world the impressive power and potential of their 'New Spain'. Their aim was to create a Spain in which everyone would practise one sport or another, while the nation's best athletes demonstrated their superiority in international competitions, especially the Olympic Games, thus gaining the admiration of the world. Sport was to be where the masculine Hispanic values, about which the Falange talked so much and so often, 'virility, impetuosity and fury' would be incarnate. The last of these was the most easily applied to football, because, as we have seen, the myth of 'Spanish fury' had existed in the football world since the 1920 Olympic Games.

However, in the hungry Spain of the 1940s, all the yearnings for greatness of the Falange were destined to the most resounding failure. Both in terms of the practice of sport by the general population, and in international competition, like the Olympic Games, the results were pathetic.

After the defeat of the Axis powers in 1945, to a large extent Spain was considered by the rest of the world as the last bastion of Fascism, and thus was subjected to a diplomatic and economic boycott by the United Nations. Franco understood that to free himself from this purgatory, he needed to change the image of his régime, which meant eliminating many of the Falangist symbols of Fascist origin. For example, the salute and the singing before matches were dropped. However, at a structural level the Falangist influence would still take many more years to lose its power; thus the rule that made the presence of two Falangists obligatory on the governing board of every club was maintained until 1967.

The mythology which the press applied to the game continued to be essentially of Fascist origin. The tone adopted by the media was vigorously patriotic and exaggeratedly triumphal.

During the second period, which began in the 1950s, Spain became a country in which a great deal of importance was given to sport, but not in the way that the Falange would have liked. While the few athletic tracks and facilities that did exist were seldom used, the masses swarmed to the impressive new stadia (built by the private football clubs with very little help from the NSD) to admire imported foreign stars.

Football would be useful to the régime to improve its external image abroad. And it was recognized as such by José Solís, who as Ministerial Secretary of the Movement, declared in a speech to the Real Madrid players:

> You have done much more than many of our embassies scattered round the world. People who used to hate us now understand us, thanks to you, because you have pulled down many walls. . . . Your victories constitute a legitimate source of pride for all Spaniards, inside and outside our country. When you go back to the changing rooms at the end of each match, know that all Spaniards are with you and support you, proud of your triumphs which keep the Spanish flag flying so high. [9]

Real Madrid is considered to be the team which most helped the régime to improve its poor image abroad:

> Real Madrid has been, for years, the team which has served the régime best. Real Madrid has proclaimed to the whole continent the importance of a country which has developed with a definite and unavoidable disadvantage with regard to everything European. Our lack of development found in Real Madrid an exception which allowed Spaniards to go abroad 'with their heads held high'. [10]

To judge from the words of Santiago Bernabeu (President of the club from 1943 until his death in 1978) when he replied to a eulogistic speech by José Antonio Elola Olaso during a visit to the Caudillo in his palace of El Pardo in 1960, it would seem that Real Madrid was conscious of its role as ambassador of the régime and the country (both were considered one and the same thing inside and outside Spain) and was proud of it:

> Excellency, the kind words of our National Sports Delegate overwhelm us with satisfaction, because, although humble, our club, and all of us, carry with us our affection and our obligations to our country, and deeply engraved in our conscience is the idea of seeking and finding, at every opportunity, something which will effectively reflect the glory and prestige of Spain. [11]

It would be unfair to state that football was the only sport which helped to improve the foreign image of Francoist Spain. The bullfights (irrespective of the controversy as to whether or not they can be considered a sport) were a powerful tourist attraction. There were also sportsmen like Manuel Santana, mentioned above, or, another tennis player, Manuel Orantes, who were excellent ambassadors of the régime. Basketball also had a great deal of importance in this context: both the national basketball team and the Real Madrid team. However, this corresponds more to a later period, the 1970s.

Undoubtedly, it was football which did most to improve the international image of Francoist Spain. This was achieved in part by the national team, but mainly by Real Madrid. Perhaps it could be argued that the other three main clubs, FC Barcelona, Atlético de Madrid, and Athlétic de Bilbao, also contributed in their frequent trips abroad, and by regularly playing host to foreign teams. However, the fact is that their collective impact on European competitions was minimal compared with that of Real Madrid, and, also, they never played the attractive and exuberant style of football that Madrid did when it played abroad.

Furthermore, the role played by the two clubs, FC Barcelona and Athlétic de Bilbao, together with the Real Sociedad de San Sebastián, was much more important from a political point of view in the context of the problems of regionalism which arose during Franco's dictatorship. These clubs made a series of important political gestures which manifested their opposition to Franco's régime. It is interesting to look at the different 'gestures' of the two regions. While in the Basque country the opposition was more physical than intellectual (above all because of actions taken by ETA), in Catalonia a vast intellectual movement arose against Franco, but there was a remarkable absence of violence. This has been related [12] to the playing style of the different teams. While the characteristic features of the two Basque teams were physical power and aggressiveness, in FC Barcelona they were talent and imagination.

The link between football and regionalism in the Franco era has a very simple *raison d'être*. Because the Basques and Catalans supported the Republican cause in the Civil War, Franco tried systematically to destroy, or at least neutralize, all the institutions which showed even the most remote traces of regionalism or separatism. The Basque and Catalan languages were officially, and at times, brutally, suppressed, being forbidden in schools and in all official institutions. The national flags, the 'ikurriña' [Basque national flag] and the 'senyera' [Catalan national flag] were also prohibited, as were many other regionalist manifestations.

The Basque provinces were officially declared 'traitors' for having opposed the military uprising of 1936, and were later made to pay a high price for this 'treason'. The military and the police behaved like an army of occupation in Catalonia and in the Basque country in the 1940s, and frequently had recourse to brutality when suppressing the most insignificant demonstrations of regionalism or opposition to the centralized régime in Madrid.

In the light of all this, it is not surprising that sport, and particularly football, was the place where regionalism was demonstrated. However, it should be noted that this did not occur until the 1960s, because during the 1940s and 1950s, opposition to Franco's régime was practically non-existent, as the leaders and the great majority of the regionalist militants had either died in the Civil War, or were in exile, or were in prison, where they were tortured and sometimes executed. Those who managed to survive the Civil War and the later purges returned to society, but tried to go about their lives unnoticed, avoiding political activity for many years. [13]

Finally, the third period can be seen as one in which football was used as a 'social drug' or as part of the 'escapist culture'. This aspect, together with its diplomatic and regional importance, was the most important feature of the politicization of football.

Evaristo Acevedo distinguishes three distinct generations, at the mass level, in the Spain of the period we are describing: first, the 'politicized generation', the one which went to war and which, from 1946 onwards, owing to international pressure, began to depoliticize; second, 'the footballized generation' which lasts roughly from 1947, when national 'footballitis' appeared, until 1967 when the easing of censorship on information, brought about by the Press Law, began to reveal the first symptoms of the gradual 'defootballization'; and third the 'protest generation'. [14]

This division is important. The régime used football, but only when football had already established itself as a social phenomenon, from about the 1950s. Before this, its use was unthinkable. In a country with the economic conditions prevalent in Spain after the Civil War, the material assets which the régime possessed did not permit it to promote sports activities to a level at which sport would act as a political 'sleeping pill'. The régime only began to understand the potential of the game for promoting passivity once it had begun to happen, not before. Only with the advent of television in October 1956 was the régime able systematically to increase the country's 'footballitis' or, at least, try to keep it at the current level, and even then, only after television became a popular mass medium. Then it proceeded to do so in an enthusiastic fashion.

This chapter closes with a quote from Raimundo Saporta talking about Real Madrid, in which he explains what, in his opinion, is the link between football and politics:

> Real Madrid is and always has been political. It has always been so powerful because it has served as the backbone of the State. When it was founded in 1902 it honoured Alphonse XIII, then in 1931 it honoured the Republic, and in 1939 General Franco, and now it honours His Majesty Juan Carlos. This is because it is a disciplined club and loyally serves the institution which rules the nation. No further comment on Spanish football, or sport in general, is necessary.

## References

1. For details of the economic situation in this period and its development, cf. Carr, Raymond, (1979) *España 1808–1975*, Ariel, Barcelona, 374 *et seq.*

2.  Borrow, George, *La Biblia en España*.
3.  *The Field*, 28 September 1967.
4.  de los Reyes, Eduardo (1921) *El Ejército y su influencia en la Educaciòn Física Nacional*, Manresa, 66.
5.  March 1902.
6.  Cf. Maluquer, A. (1949) *Historia del Club de Fútbol Barcelona*, Barcelona.
7.  Carr, *op. cit.*, p. 663.
8.  Cazorla Prieto, Luis Mª. (1979) *Deporte y Estado*, Labor, Barcelona, 198.
9.  From the *Real Madrid FC Bulletin*, no. 112, November 1959.
10. Botines, Alex J. (1975) La gran estafa del futbol español, Barcelona, p. 71.
11. From the *Real Madrid FC Bulletin*, no. 128, January 1961.
12. Cf. Shaw, Duncan (1987) *Fútbol y franquismo*, Alianza, Madrid, p. 182.
13. Preston, Paul (1994), *Franco 'Caudillo de España'*, Grillalbo, Barcelona. Vividly describes the terror caused by the 'purges' and their later consequences.
14. Acevedo, Evaristo (1969) *Carta a los celtíberos esposados*, Magisterio Español, Madrid, p. 190–1.

# Chapter 8

# French sport and the emergence of authoritarian regimes, 1919–1939

*Pierre Arnaud*

Shortly after the First World War, sport became a means of gauging the energy and greatness of nations. It was used as an instrument of propaganda, as well as a means of excluding or ostracizing other countries. The so-called democratic states were the first to use sport to these ends. The consequences of the war provided numerous grounds for breaking off sports relations between the winners and the losers.

This was an entirely new situation. Indeed, it is widely held that sport was not used to exert pressure within the field of international relations until the emergence of authoritarian regimes. Italian fascism was born of the march on Rome in 1922, and did not fully develop until after 1925. If sport was to become the glory of fascism, it was not until after this date: the Italian National Olympic Committee (INOC) was not created until 1925, even though Aldo Finzi had laid its foundations as far back as 1923 using the structures of the Italian Olympic Committee, founded in 1906. In fact, the foundations of the fascist policy on sport were laid when the chairmanship of INOC was taken over by Lando Ferretti, who was also editor-in-chief of *La Gazetta dello Sport*. As far as the use of sport in the political and diplomatic strategy of the Nazis was concerned, Hitler was not immediately aware of all the advantages to be gained; it was only after 1933 that they began to use sport as a political vehicle. [1]

Consequently, there is little point in trying to ascertain whether or not sport played a significant role in the relations between states, or if the changes of political regimes and international tension had repercussions in the field of sport after 1925: it is plainly obvious that they did. This chapter aims only to evaluate the extent of its influence, as well as its importance, and the conditions in which it affected the international stage. What is of interest, however, is attempting to pinpoint exactly when sport and international politics can be said to have gone into league together.

Could sport help re-establish ties between the Allies and the defeated nations? Some people considered that sport was (or should have been) autonomous with regard to politics. They believed that sport 'belonged to the athletes', that it had 'nothing to do with politics'. Others believed, however, that sport was inextricably linked to society, and could not avoid being caught up in international tension and disputes. If this was the case, what sort of relationship did the national and international sports authorities have with the state governments just after the First World War?

## The stadium: a new battlefield?

The Joint Allied Games of 1919 marked the resumption of the international sports programme. Organized on the initiative of the USA, only former Allied countries had the right to take part. The aim of these Games was much more to promote the United States in France and to strengthen feelings of fraternity between the Allied countries than symbolically to replace the Berlin Olympic Games, which had been cancelled in 1916 because of the war. [2] Another of its aims was most likely to glorify pacifism and civilization in the face of those who represented barbarism (the defeated nations). However, apart from a few articles in *L'Auto*, *L'Illustration* and *La Vie au Grand Air*, there was little about the event in the press. [3, 4, 5, 6] Seven years later, however, Lucien Dubech spoke quite mockingly about these events: 'In 1919, by a happy coincidence, the rugby final took place on the same day as the Treaty of Versailles was signed. It was such a joyful slaughter that one witness humorously said of the event: "it was the best they could do without resorting to knives and guns".' [7]

The organization of the Antwerp Olympic Games in 1920 provided further evidence of the Allies' belligerent tendencies: the defeated nations were still not authorized to take part. These first incidences of boycott in the history of sport had repercussions: between 1920 and 1924, 84 international events (with the exception of the Olympic Games) pitted French sports teams against foreign opposition, with football, Rugby and athletics accounting for more than 50% of the events. But these events all involved France playing against the Allied countries, mainly the British (41 events, 24 of which were against England) and the Belgians (14 events).

It has been seen that whatever the sport, the organization of international matches was always dependent on foreign policy. The Germans and their allies, along with the neutral countries and the USSR, were all conspicuously absent from the international sports scene. As regards football, the organization of international sports events involving France was subject to exactly the same fluctuations as the Ministry of Foreign Affairs' policy. [8] Until 1924, France's national football team only played against Allied or neutral countries: Belgium, Italy, Switzerland, England, Ireland and Spain. In 1924 it started to play against countries in Central Europe: Hungary in 1924, Austria in 1925, Yugoslavia in 1926, Czechoslovakia in 1928 and then went on a tour of the Balkans in 1932. The first postwar football match between France and Germany took place in 1931, although Franco-German sports relations had actually resumed when Germany was admitted into the League of Nations in 1926, which the newspaper *L'Auto* went out of its way to emphasize on 6 October 1926. The first athletics event involving France, Germany and Switzerland was held on 22 August 1926, with the first Franco-German event being held the following year. The speed with which links were resumed suggests that they had been in preparation for a long time. Sports competitions between the two countries continued until the Anschluss in 1938.

These observations require some explanations: How is it that sport became an instrument used to exert pressure within the field of international relations?

## Sport as an affair of the State

In 1920 the French Government created a Physical Education and Sports Department which was attached to the Ministry of Public Instruction, [9] and which was a response to the desire to promote top level sport as a means of restoring the image of France in the eyes of the rest of the world. This was something of a surprise: Had France not come out of the war basking in the glory of the great turmoil? Did it really need victories on the sports field to add to those on the battlefield?

The French government was, in fact, facing two dangers: German propaganda, which was firmly anti-French, and that of the Allies, which believed that the French nation had been bled dry. Maintaining France's reputation therefore became a prime objective – and sport could help do this. Hence the idea that:

> It is incumbent on the Ministry of Foreign Affairs to handle France's foreign affairs. This means that no political, economic or intellectual action may be initiated or pursued abroad without the intervention of this Ministry. Similarly, it is not permitted to undertake any venture which is outside the control of our political agents [. . .] The numerous tasks for which this service has been created have been divided into four major departments [. . .], one of which is the Tourism and Sports Department . . . [10]

Thus the situation was clear: France's policy on sport was in the hands of the Ministry of Foreign Affairs! The reason why was evident: 'It is also absolutely essential that in competing against countries such as Scandinavia, France does not lose the prestige that has been awarded it by the ultimate sport: war . . .' [11]

The State intended to give financial help to the sports federations so that France's victory on the battlefield could be translated into invincibility on the sports field. A Tourism and Sports Department was set up within the Ministry of Foreign Affairs to promote France's image abroad and to attract foreigners and their money. In 1920 it was attached to the Service des Œuvres Françaises à l'Etranger (Department of French Ventures Abroad), which is an indication of the increasing importance that sport was occupying on the political stage. It should be noted that another organization, the Office National du Tourisme (National Tourism Board), played a similar role in developing winter sports and tourism. [12]

A few months later, when the French athletic delegation was preparing to leave for Antwerp, Gaston Vidal, Director of the Physical Education Department, asserted that our champion athletes will give the best of themselves so as to elevate France's reputation on the sports field to the same standard as that of its reputation in matters intellectual and artistic [. . .] Indeed, sport is no longer a simple affair between individuals, or a modest private venture: it has become a State affair; it is now an official undertaking . . . [13]

Vidal was also Chairman of the USFSA and *député* of the Nièvre district, and because of the latter could be loosely termed the first 'sports minister' to have a real awareness of what this entailed.

Consequently, the State put up 200 000 francs, taken from the Ministry of Foreign Affairs' budget, allocating various amounts to different federations, so that France could be fittingly represented at Antwerp. According to Vidal, this meant that France was the only country in the world which helped its athletes to take part in major international competitors: 'Whether or not France performs well at the Antwerp Olympics, these events will be remembered by every athlete in the country: they will mark the fist step in establishing a close relationship between government and sport.' [14]

## The course of action taken by the Department of French Ventures Abroad (SOFE)

The policy adopted by the SOFE was in keeping with this trend. The publication of its *Note sur la propagande sportive á l'étranger* (Pamphlet on sports propaganda abroad) [15] provides a documented analysis of the awkward situation in which many national and international sports federations found themselves. But the SOFE made sure that it was fully aware of the situation before it took any action:

After the Great War, the various national and international sports federations adopted very different attitudes regarding the way in which sports links should be maintained with the German, Austrian, Hungarian and Bulgarian federations. The international federations crossed more of less all of the national federations of central ex-Empires and of their Allies off their list of members, outlawing all international events between nations, and even (*sic*) between clubs.

The reasoning behind this decision for the Football Associations of England, Scotland, Ireland and Wales was to be found within association football. The Football Association of England resigned from FIFA, having failed to find itself in agreement with the Federation.

Indeed, England wanted to boycott the neutral nations which were attempting to organise international matches against Germany. If, for example, the Swiss Federation agreed to organise a match against Germany, English clubs would be forbidden to play against a Swiss club.

Other international federations left the national federations of neutral nations free to hold events with Germany and Austria, and maintained the same sports relations with them as they had enjoyed prior to the war. A general study of the situation would be simple to carry out.

A summary indicating the broad outlines of the decisions taken by each one of the international federations responsible for governing a sport could be drawn up. Such a summary could provide each of our representatives abroad, and those of the central ex-Empires and their allies, with information about the sports federations of England, Belgium, France and Italy, as well as about the countries which remained neutral during the Great War. [16]

This document also gave an analysis of the conditions in which France could best take advantage of the victories of its sports ambassadors.

French sports victories unquestionably arouse a considerable amount of interest abroad. In the United Kingdom of Great Britain and Northern Ireland, in the self-governing divisions of the British Empire as well as in the United States of America, Georges Carpentier's victory in the world boxing championships, together with Suzanne Lenglen's victory in the world lawn-tennis championships of the All England P.T.C. at Wimbledon in 1919 and 1920 have caused a great sensation. The same could be said of France's win against Ireland in rugby in Dublin in 1920, which was the first win abroad for a French rugby team.

The political newspapers and numerous journals in England and America have related these three recent events in very long, generously illustrated articles.

In similar cases it would be extremely helpful if propagandist films could include a few extracts from major matches in which France has ranked the highest . . . [17]

In short, in 1920, since the various sections of the SOFE could not play at being international sports policemen, they simply set about creating the necessary conditions in which France's reputation could shine throughout the rest of the world. And sport was to play a part in this.

## The main thing is to win!

Although some politicians had reservations [18, 19], for the majority of French people there was no doubting how important it was for France to shine in the major international competitions. The athletes were compared to ambassadors or representatives of French culture and genius in the same way as artists, novelists and couturiers were. Hardly had the SOFE been founded before it, like the major Parisian clubs, was receiving huge numbers of applications for subsidies from official federations. The reason cited was always the same: the travelling and accommodation costs of French athletes who had been invited to compete against American, Spanish, Belgian or Brazilian clubs or federations etc. [20, 21, 22]

A large majority of these subsidies were granted. Only two refusals are noted: one concerned a French officer's trip to Rome for a showjumping event, and the other was a request made by the Union Nationale des Associations Générales des Etudiants de France (National Union of General Student Associations in France) to send an official delegation of student athletes to the Primi Olimpiadi Universitario Italiani. The reasons were clear: using French athletes to serve the fascist propaganda cause was to be avoided, as was any kind of tension not long after the incidents in Turin and Venice, where there had been anti-French protests by Italian students in November 1921. [23, 24, 25]

SOFE propaganda was further helped by its involvement in the setting up of French sports clubs abroad, for example in Romania (the Bucharest sports club, founded in 1922), and even in Germany (in an application for a grant made by the French Sports Union of the Saar to enable them to develop sports fields in Saarbrücken). All these applications for grants were approved!

For the French government and the defenders of sport, victories on the sports field did much more for the image of France than all the political conferences. For Henri Desgranges, sport served the French renaissance. It was both an intimidating weapon and a source of prestige:

> Those of our ministers who know how expensive it is to use commercial, industrial, scientific and artistic missions as a means of spreading French propaganda and influence abroad are no longer in a position to deny that our country can only gain from sending a Carpentier to America, or a Criqui or a Gerbault or a Pivolo. It is also significant that our teams come back triumphant from foreign countries much more often than they used to. Foreigners will judge us on all of our products, and if our couturiers and milliners are hardly ever talked about abroad, then I assure you that they would look upon us as utter half-wits if our teams were to come back beaten 7–0. [a reference to the French football team's defeat against Italy]. [26]

Five years earlier, the joint-allied high commissioners of the Rhineland territories were concerned that 'the Germans can see our obvious inferiority compared to the other Allies . . . if the Rhine Army's sports teams cannot send top rate athletes, then they are better off not taking part at all . . . [27]

Such was the ambassador's suggestion when the issue arose as to whether or not French officers should be sent to Holland or England to take part in showjumping events. [28] And when there was talk of sending Carpentier on a tour of Scandinavia via Berlin, the joint-allied high commissioner of the Rhineland territories remarked that he would 'undoubtedly be an excellent ambassador of our "influence" . . .'. French athletes were only helped by the SOFE if they were certain to win. But not against just any foreign team.

## War and peace, suspicion and exclusion

French athletes could not play against just any team since the list of countries against which they were allowed to play was limited. Shortly after the Antwerp Olympic Games, Géo André, one of the most popular athletes of the period, drew up (possibly quite innocently) a list of countries against which France was likely to compete in athletics events: 'If we look at all the matches which are likely to take place, Britain, Belgium, Sweden, Norway, Denmark, Italy, Switzerland, Spain and Germany are all countries against which we will probably compete. [29]

Those who were in favour of a revival of sports events between France and Germany came up against opposition from both politicians and public opinion; opposition that was all the more strong since many accused the Germans of 'taking part in sports events with a view to murderously preparing the next war of revenge of which they are already dreaming', but defended French participation as a means to a more permanent peace. [30] Many newspapers and journals confirmed this fear: 'Frenchmen staying in Germany cannot fail to be struck by the ardour and enthusiasm with which the youth of Germany carry out their sports training through "patriotic duty".' [31]

Furthermore, there were other causes for concern. Support from French political institutions for the Bolshevik revolution was gaining ground, and its consequences were shaking up the political class and the trade unions. Yet the sports world took no notice. However, the schism which appeared in the Socialist Party during the Tour Congress did have repercussions on the sports world: two rival worker sports federations were created, one affiliated to the Socialist Worker Sport International (SWSI) in Lucerne and the other to Red Sport International (RSI) in Moscow. [32] Both the SWSI and the RSI represented the worker sport movement, but differed slightly in their political outlook, the SWSI being close ideologically to social democracy and socialism, while the RSI were communists. Membership of the two organizations was likewise split, the majority of SWSI members coming from Germany, a country dominated by social-democratic politics, while the largest section of the RSI was from the communist-led Soviet Union (where the RSI had been founded in 1921). Competitive sport between the two organizations did take place, but usually between teams from the main protagonists, Germany and the Soviet Union, and victory was always considered as a success for a political ideology rather than a sporting achievement. (For example, in 1923, when Russia defeated Germany 6–0 at football, 40 000 spectators celebrated a success for the RSI.) In France, on the other hand, no sporting events between the two organizations took place [33]. Meanwhile, some journals continued to denounce the bourgeois sports federations, *Le Sport ouvrier* claiming that the Union of Athlete Workers was under the banner of the RSI. In June 1924, the French Communist Party, supported by the RSI, [34] decided to organize a Workers Olympiad, while violently denouncing the International Olympic Committee's 'sports fascism' which forbade German and Soviet athletes from taking part in the Paris Olympics of 1924. [35] 'The Soviet Russians and the

Germans will be in Pershing. Long live fraternity between French, Czechoslovak, Austrian, Swiss and Belgian worker athletes.' [36] Thus, the French and international worker sport movements, along with the RSI, were responsible for the revival of sports links between the victors and the vanquished of the First World War. [37, 38, 39, 40]

Although the Soviets were unable to take part through not having been able to obtain visas from the French government, the Franco-German rift *was* being mended through the intermediary of sport, as a photograph taken from *L'Avant-Garde* (the organ of the French Young Communists) showed. It comes as no great surprise that the Germans organized the first Worker Olympic Games in Frankfurt in 1925, under the auspices of the SWSI, whereas the RSI did not hold its first sports event until 1928 with the Moscow Spartakiad. [41, 42]

Furthermore, the issue of the Soviets participating in international sports competitions was about more than just their relationship with France. The French government had its political reasons for refusing them visas, but it is also quite clear that the USSR had always refused to join the International Olympic Committee (IOC). It therefore excluded itself from Olympic events by virtue of its willingness to fight bourgeois and capitalist sport. But if the USSR had wanted to take part in the Olympic Games of 1924, how would the IOC, the French Olympic Committee, and the French government have reacted?

With the advent of fascism, sport took on a whole new aspect. Those athletes who espoused the communist revolution, along with the leaders of the French Communist Party, signalled the danger very early on. At the end of 1923, *Le Sport ouvrier* denounced the fascist candidates and their Christian leaders who were a threat to the worker sports organizations. [43] When the threat became more real, the paper published an article entitled 'Préparons-nous à la lutte contre le fascisme!' ('Let us prepare for the struggle against fascism!'):

> Worker athletes, rise, all of you, against the fascist cause! This is the resolution of the RSI's Third Congress against bourgeois political activism. With the slogan 'Bolshevism justifies fascism', militant capitalism is trying to use the lower middle classes to do here what Mussolini succeeded in doing in Italy, thanks to the proletariat's lack of preparation and the betrayal of the socialist leaders. We will allow neither Millerand nor Blum nor Renaudel to do this [. . . ] The bourgeoisie has understood the important role that young people will play in the imminent struggle, and subsequently, a new organisation, *les Jeunesse patriotes* [the Patriotic Youth Movement] has been formed. A few weeks ago it made a nationalist appeal [Pierre Taittinger's initiative in November 1924, from the League of Patriots led by Colonel de Castelnau. A few months later, Georges Valois, a former member of Action Française, launched 'le Faisceau', the first French fascist movement, inspired by the Italian model under Mussolini] that blatantly sought to boost its popularity: 'tomorrow, when the communists and the foreign troublemakers believe themselves masters of this country in chaos, we must ensure that they find

themselves at the mercy of our youth movements.' The bourgeoisie is counting heavily on the support of bourgeois sports organisations [. . .] because
sport has eliminated people's readiness to criticise and more importantly has
wiped out their feeling of discipline. [. . .] Every Sunday, General Castelnau
inspects several thousand bourgeois athletes who are all preparing for the revolutionary 'blood bath' [. . .] The struggle against fascism is an integral part
of the class struggle. [44]

As for the Catholics, their initiatives were less ostentatious, but fulfilled the same
objectives: to use sport as a means of promoting values and beliefs. [45] What is
more, Pope Pius X had given his moral support to Pierre de Coubertin in 1903 for
the organization of a Rome Olympics. [46] After the First World War, various
attempts to re-establish international sports events were thwarted by Mussolini. An
international competition which was supposed to be held in Rome in 1926 was
cancelled and even the FASCI announced its dissolution the following year. [47]
Consequently, all international Catholic 'games' thereafter took place without the
Italians and, after 1935, without the Germans (the German Catholic Federation
having been dissolved by Hitler).
    These debates, which were reported by the activist journals (in France, mainly
those of the worker sport press, and for the Catholics, the journal *Les Jeunes*; in Italy,
mainly *L'Osservatore Romano*), failed to illicit any kind of response in the sporting
national press. *L'Auto* made no mention of them, and *L'Echo des sports*, *La Vie au grand
air* and *Le Miroir des Sports* continued faithfully to report and chronicle official sports
events, while mainstream sports journalists chose simply to ignore the consequences
of the war as far as international relations were concerned. Germany was still considered to be the enemy, but the debate was limited to questions which were raised
by the possibility of its participation in the 1924 Olympics.

## The question of Germany or the illusions of pacifism

There were those, however, who were convinced that sport could bridge the gap
between countries and enable them to come to an understanding. The League of
Nations, for example, in 1920 received a communication from the IOC which indicated that in the IOC's opinion the first international merger since the war had
been attempted by the athletes at the 1920 Olympic Games: because the Games
were a courteous and pacific gathering of sporting nations. The League counted a
considerable number of well-known athletes among its members' delegates (including the Norwegian explorer Nansen), but even they must have been surprised, as
well as the rest of the sporting world, when Scandinavian delegates proposed that
the question of international sport should be added to the League's agenda. [48]
This was followed immediately by a suggestion from Andre Glarner, a journalist
from *Le Miroir des sports*, that the Olympic Games of 1924 should be organized by
the League of Nations! However, Gaston Vidal was sceptical: 'The responsibility

of organising sports events should remain that of the athletes. [. . .] but we could consider making the IOC part of the League of Nations.' [49] This, by the same token, would have enabled the over-aristocratic IOC to be re-formed and would have stood Paris in good stead to host the next Olympics! Vidal clearly, had inherited de Coubertin's ability to play to the gallery.

Nevertheless, it was not easy for French national teams to face their German counterparts without provoking a great deal of discussion and debate, and some federations even refused to take part if Germany was competing. For example, French car manufacturers abandoned the idea of taking part in the Targa Florio in Italy in 1921 because the Germans and the Czechoslovaks would be there. This was a huge risk, since they knew that winning a major racing grand prix could have very positive effects on the French economy. They hesitated again later that year over taking part in the French Automobile Club Grand Prix, an event with an international reputation, which in previous years had served to boost the French car industry abroad.

It is not certain whether the Germans would have accepted an invitation to the Antwerp Games as readily as they did to the Paris Games of 1924, especially since a few days after the signing of the Armistice (22 November 1918) the French National Sports Council forbade the sports federations affiliated to it from organizing or taking part in international events in which Germans, Austrians, Hungarians, Bulgarians or Turks were participating. [50] And almost one year later, Vidal even considered maintaining official sports relations only with states which had been admitted into the League of Nations. [51] In 1924 the IOC finally adopted the same stance and, somewhat belatedly, forbade Germany from taking part in the Olympic Games in Paris. [52]

Indeed, the whole of French thinking on this matter was inspired by the English who, shortly after the end of the First World War, had proposed forbidding countries which had emerged victorious from the war from competing against neutral or defeated countries. 'England was obliging France to follow suit, much in the same way that a barge follows a tug . . .' [53, 54]

And not only France followed suit. For example, in 1921 at a meeting which included the England Football Association Selection Committee, all the British national federations, as well as those of Belgium, France, Spain, Denmark and Norway, it was agreed not to 'play matches against associations of the central Empires'. [55]

But not all the international federations took the same view. In August 1920, at the Congress of the International Cyclists Union, the decision was taken to 'leave every country free to do as it sees fit with respect to the central powers'. [56] And at its thirty-seventh Congress in 1923, it admitted Austria, Hungary and Poland into the world championships.

Politicians, on the other hand, had to be more pragmatic and cautiously avoided all Franco-German incidents on French soil. Pierre de Coubertin could not do anything about this, but asserted that: 'Although the French government considers it unwise for the German flag to fly over the Colombes Stadium, this is not necessarily representative of public opinion'. [57]

As far as the sports press was concerned, opinions differed. For example in September 1922 *L'Echo des sports* committed itself to oppose any immediate revival of sports events involving their traditional enemy. [58] On the other hand, M. Pfefferkorn, an athlete-journalist of great renown, was not totally opposed to allowing the Germans to take part in events, believing that the Olympic spirit would grow from it. After all the Olympic Games were held outside of the traditional sports fixture calendar, and provided an opportunity for sports links which might then open the door for a gradual revival of links with Germany. The most ardent pacifists even saw the beginnings of *détente*. But the ultimate argument for the most optimistic was that Germany did not stand much chance against France's athletes:

> To sum up, let us accept the decision that has led to the Germans referring to our Olympic Games as a 'carcass' (one newspaper has even talked about 'the headless Olympics'). But I do believe, quite honestly, that they would have ranked below us [. . .] Let us keep a watch on ourselves, so that in four years . . . when we next face them . . . [59]

There was unquestionably a wide current of opinion which was opposed to any official revival of Franco-German sports relations. This was hardly surprising, given that people were still talking about the nature of the reparations demanded from Germany and the fact that the French Army was occupying the Ruhr! Furthermore, internationally, French sport in general was at a modest stage of development so there was little to boast about: some people were even very pleased that the Germans had been excluded. Their presence could have served to injure national pride even more! A defeat at the hands of the Germans would have had a most disastrous effect. And nobody could afford to run such a risk. The watchwords of the day were 'caution', 'suspicion' and 'opposition', but it was clear that they only targeted Germany. Austria, Bulgaria and Turkey – all countries absent from the Antwerp Games – were admitted to the Paris Games.

## Events held 'in secret' . . .

This cautious politico-sports stance was followed until the beginning of the 1920s and in some cases quite hard-line positions were adopted. For instance, when the French club Gallia refused to take part in a football match against the Swiss club La Chaux de Fonds, which had recently played against a German club, its line of thinking was, 'the friends of my enemies are also my enemies'. For a while, at least, the British example was being enforced in France.

However, a few international federations adopted their own policy. The professional cycling world championships were held in Berlin in July and August 1920, at the same time as the amateur world championships and the Olympics were taking place in Antwerp. The International Marathon in Turin pitted French athletes against German athletes in October 1922. [60] There were many other examples of attempts to bring France and Germany closer together through sport. In January 1920, the French lightweight André Dumas, who dealt in cars in Austria, secured a contract for a serious of four fights. Through his influence, other French boxers travelled to Germany from 1922 onwards, interested in the rewards that were available. Furthermore, the Austrian Charles Weinert defeated the Frenchman Journée in a boxing event held in the USA in June 1921, even though during its session of 17 March 1921 the French Boxing Federation had forbidden contact with boxers of the central Empires until further notice. This astonished *L'Auto*: 'Hasn't all contact with Germans been banned? Unless, of course, it's to go and beat them up, and even then . . . !' [61]

However, the return of German boxers to French soil was heralded on 10 May 1922 for a Franco-German match between Bretonnel and Czirson. There were even boxing bouts between the English and the Germans in 1924![62] Even though there were no official football matches between national teams, a few French and German clubs competed unofficially against each other, the French Club and Le Borussia, for example. [63]

Politically, there appeared also to be a difference of opinion. In September 1922, just as the situation in the Ruhr was becoming more serious, *Le Miroir des sports* commented, 'the authorities of occupied countries in the Rhineland understand that in certain circumstances sport could positively serve France's foreign policy'. [64] Whereas, one month later, a circular sent out by Prime Minister Poincaré to all French agents abroad 'made it clear that German artists and athletes are banned from coming to France'. [65] However, these stipulations cannot have been enforced, since the journalist acknowledged that in car racing, aviation and cycling, German and Frenchmen had already competed together.

## . . . and events held in occupied territories

It was obviously tempting to try to win the Germans over on their soil. In a note dated 4 December 1919, the joint allied high commissioner set out the conditions in which the people of the Rhineland could 'be guided towards seeing things from the French point of view'. [66] Published in a local newspaper, *Le Rhin Illustré*, the note read,

> the Rhineland people's artistic tendencies are being flattered, their interest in French business is being aroused, and they are being reminded of their Latin origins and the not so very far distant time when they would have had French nationality [. . .] With this in mind, there are good grounds for considering the use of a new means of propaganda – a more moderate and realistic means.

Sport (taking into consideration sports events held in Rhineland and the allied countries as well as in Germany) appeared in the 'light propaganda' section of the newspaper, alongside drama, music, literature, fashion, fine arts, hunting and fishing. As the delegate at the High Commission (at the Meisenhein Club) wrote:

'spreading propaganda is a long-drawn-out affair which requires tenacity. While varying the techniques used, you must always come back to the same idea . . .' [67]

In reality, this propaganda had some negative effects. The Rhineland population were urged to oppose any kind of official revival of sports links between Germany and France and were told that any scheme designed to win them over was only encouraging people to go against the general consensus. As a result, the creation of the Civil Sports Group in Mayence and Wiesbaden in September 1921 served to turn sport into a means of spreading French propaganda. This group organized sports events in aid of German disaster victims in November 1921; however, it still met with opposition and not everyone would agree to participate. Their excuse was amusing: such events had been banned by the French sports federations. But others did take part and events took place quite frequently since 'The case of the German athletes', *L'Auto*'s front page article of 17 May 1924, examined the possibility of a return to normal a few days before the opening of the Olympic Games. Furthermore, at around the same time, 'the football associations of Scotland, Ireland and Wales seceded and agreed to break the order that forbade UK clubs from taking part in matches against former enemy powers'. [68] Was it possible for the sports movement to continue resisting government injunctions without abandoning its main purpose?

However, it would seem that the reasons behind these discreet, not to say clandestine, revivals were far more economic than political:

> A few months ago, the French and German newspapers declared that relations had been revived between French and German athletes and that football and tennis matches have already been played between athletes from both countries. It is likely that, given the fact that the value of the French Franc is favourable for the German athletes, the following winter would see them invading the tennis courts of the Côte d'Azur.

## National prestige and the first incidents

Politicians ran a huge risk in declaring that sport had become an affair of the State and had to serve as a means of enhancing the image of France abroad. They risked laying themselves open to bitter disappointment. The first doubts appeared in 1921. After a few good or at least respectable performances for the French football and Rugby teams in 1920 and the beginning of 1921, boxer Georges Carpentier's defeat against Jack Dempsey (2 July 1921), and then Suzanne Lenglen's first defeat at Forest Hills in the US Tennis Championships seemed to herald a crisis in French sport. [69] One cannot simply say that these numerous defeats were due to so many would-be French champions having been killed in the war. [70] Should one conclude that France was particularly touchy on points of honour? All evidence points to this – the SOFE never hid the fact that French athletes were welcome to perform abroad, but only if they could be more or less guaranteed to win. It is therefore understandable that France's defeats turned into serious diplomatic incidents. Sport and politics were already creating bizarre alliances.

The first sports 'incidents' were unquestionably the result of political tension. Mussolini's march on Rome in October 1922, followed by his accession to power in November concentrated the surge in fascist ideology and culminated with a succession of violent incidents. This was the start of an increase in nationalist and chauvinist tendencies, together with a proliferation of measures intended to humiliate foreigners, especially French athletes. At the same time, the occupation of the Ruhr at the beginning of 1923 exacerbated francophobia in Germany, and helped to revive national socialism. The part played by the English, who were opposed to the occupation, made it far from easy to establish links between the French and German governments.

This was the situation on 26 May 1923, when the prestigious French fencer, Gaudin, competed against Sassone, a renowned Italian fencing teacher at a gala match held in Rome:

> Even though this event should only have been, even in the eyes of those who organised it, a purely academic spectacle with no winner or loser, the public cheered the Italian champion, carrying him in triumph as though he had won the tournament, only granting Gaudin a little polite applause – in spite of the perfection of his performance and his obviously superior skill. The Italian national anthem was played at the end of the event: nobody played the Marseillaise, and nobody even requested it. The next day, the *Giornale di Roma* praised the superiority of the Italian fencing school and celebrated Sassone's 'easy victory' over Gaudin – whose refinement and chivalrous style they did, however, acknowledge.

A diplomatic incident was avoided, however, and French honour was restored when:

> An official note clarified the situation. Two days later most Roman newspapers and the *Corriere della Sera* were recalling [. . .] how the French champion had shown himself to be what he truly was: 'a master'. The *Giornale di Roma* was sorry for the 'improper' fashion in which our champion was welcomed [. . .] which was evidence that the Italian public did not yet have the necessary sports awareness to be able to watch international matches objectively.

All the same, French national pride had been tarnished: 'It is in everybody's best interest to take these collective scruples into consideration before French teams or champions are ever allowed to take part in sports events held in Italy again.' [71]

This did not stop Henri Desgranges from applauding the Italian Bottecchia's victory in the 1924 Tour de France: 'Italian friends! We value your victory, it is an opportunity for us to tell you how much we like you.' [72] As for the Germans, they seemed quite eager to revive sports relations with France; initially extending invitations – albeit reticently – to renowned French athletes. The French Ministry of Foreign Affairs, however, was reluctant. As a result, an invitation extended to Georges Carpentier was declined.

> German opinion is still too easily stirred up by nationalist feeling for M. Carpentier's safety to be guaranteed. If the former champion were to appear at a sports meeting, he would probably receive a warm welcome. But as the planned meeting would be given a lot of publicity, it would be easy for a few extreme right-wing newspapers or associations to organise hostile protests that the Sport Palace management would be powerless to prevent. Such a campaign might even be encouraged in certain sports milieux which were annoyed by the exclusion of the Germans from the Olympic Games.
>
> I must add that we should not overestimate the ways in which victorious displays of even individual strength are likely to help French influence in Germany. [73]

But the major sports coup for France following the war was being granted the right to host the Olympic Games. A few months before they opened, a number of countries had officially or unofficially, revived sporting links with Germany and the central empires, and changes taking place throughout the political community seemed to be encouraging *détente*: the Left Coalition's victory in the presidential elections of 1924, preceded by the election of a pacifist Labour government in England in January, but above all the failure of Hitler's putsch in November 1923 and Lenin's death in January 1924. In addition, it was hoped that the Dawes plan, which was voted at the London conference in August 1924, would ease the strained relations between the former allied countries and the defeated nations. But the organization of the Games had been decided upon well before any rumblings of détente were felt.

## The possibility of peace at the Colombes Stadium

One of the most important issues that the SOFE had to tackle concerned the position of the French government regarding the Paris Olympics of 1924. The severe diatribe launched against Pierre de Coubertin was a clear indication that the person responsible for reviving the Olympic Games had not always been that enthusiastic about holding them in Paris:

> The Olympic Games [. . .] are a powerful means of spreading French sports propaganda abroad [. . .] It would therefore be desirable in all respects for France to be chosen to host them. This would be of high moral benefit for its initiatives throughout the world. Pierre de Coubertin seems undecided as to whether or not he should assist the activities of the various unanimously

agreed French federations within the French Olympic Committee in their application to organise the Games. [74]

A few acerbic remarks referring to the ambiguous relations that the IOC had with the national and international sports federations supported this accusation. Vidal and Albert Milhaud, leader of the SOFE, did not appreciate the unpatriotic activities of de Coubertin, believing that nothing would 'have a worse effect on French influence abroad'. [75]

In 1920, the government started to put pressure on de Coubertin to ensure that the Games would be held in France, relying on his good will and hopeful that he was not sensitive to criticism. Although the history books indicate that he had always been an ardent supporter of the Games being held in France, the Archives of the SOFE tell a different story: [76, 77]

> M. de Coubertin has let himself be guided by considerations of self-esteem rather than an awareness of national benefit [. . .] It would perhaps be desirable for the agreement to be re-established between the uncompromising, aristocratic Committee and the essentially democratically orientated federations and for a type of 'constitution' to sanction this agreement. As far as holding the 8th Olympiad in Paris is concerned, a matter discussed in a letter from the Department to M. de Margerie dated 12 August 1919, I think that M. de Coubertin, following the incidents described in the aforementioned letter by M. Jaunez, has used his influence to make sure the Games are *not* hosted by France, and has furthermore encountered little opposition from the Committee of which he is the chairman: with the result that, all in all, we should be pleased that the decision over this issue has been postponed and referred to the Lausanne Congress to be held in early 1921. [78]

De Coubertin did change his mind, however, and on 21 June 1921 the Lausanne Congress of the IOC awarded the Summer Games to Paris and the Winter Games to Chamonix. [79] It was decided that all countries should be invited despite the fact that a large proportion of public opinion (which included war veterans) and the vast majority of politicians were still opposed to any of the former enemy countries taking part. The Scandinavian countries are generally credited with having intended to boycott the Games, but a dispatch from M. Delavaud, France's minister in Stockholm, exposes a surprising current of opinion:

> Most Swedish newspapers are praising the International Olympic Executive Committee's decision to open up the next Games in Paris to athletes of all countries including Germany. This news will be well-received by the sports milieux of all the neutral countries, especially by Sweden. There is a significant difference between the Antwerp 'Victory' Games of 1920, in which the neutral countries seem to have participated reluctantly and those of 1924, which will be genuine 'Games of Peace'. Suddenly, all the criticism directed

at France' equivocation regarding preparations for the next Games has evaporated . . . [80]

Such information should have caused quite a commotion in the corridors of power. However, there is no evidence of a response from Poincaré, nor any information which could confirm the Swedish position. It can be confirmed that the Secretary General of the French Olympic Committee sent a list of 54 countries which stood a good chance of being invited to Jean Giraudoux, Director of SOFE on 17 February 1923. Germany, Austria, Russia, Hungary and Bulgaria were included on this list, but it was modified on orders from the Ministry of Foreign Affairs and the Head of Government, [81] resulting in the French Olympic Committee cautiously stating 'the invitations to Germany, Austria, Bulgaria, Hungary and Turkey are awaiting confirmation'. [82] The same happened in Chamonix for the Winter Games, although Austria *was*, in fact, invited since it had been admitted into the League of Nations. [83] The French Olympic Committee did not follow the French National Sports Council's recommendations of November 1918, instead, it kept the door open for these countries to participate while at the same time expressing its reservations. This allowed the foreign policy makers to come to a decision.

Granting France permission to host the VIIIth Olympic Games sparked a huge anti-Olympic spirit campaign – especially in Germany – as well as a number of attempts to boycott them. Albéric Neton, France's Consul General in Hamburg, informed Poincaré of the smear campaign being conducted by the German press: 'We should have expected this. In their fever of jealousy and denigration, the Germans are trying to belittle the Olympic Games that France is readying itself to celebrate – without them . . .'

An article from the 28 October 1923 edition of the German newspaper *Fremdenblatt* reads as follows:

> The Olympic Games are blighted by a peculiar twist of fate. Created in the spirit of a demonstration of international sport rather than as an imitation of the former Olympics, these modern events were inspired by the idea that every people, every race, every part of the Earth would send their best athletes to them [. . .] It cannot be denied that since the Stockholm Games of 1912, there has been a certain harmony missing from the Games, a harmony without which the Olympics are merely a caricature. The 1916 Olympics, which should have been held in Berlin, did not take place because of the Great War. The Antwerp Olympics of 1920 sadly involved only a dramatically reduced number of countries. There is some danger of the Paris Games of 1924 being a mere parody of an Olympiad, since the exclusion of Germany alone has already detracted from the international aspect of the event.

The German journalist went on to explain at length that the Scandinavian countries were preparing a counter-Olympiad known as the 'Olympiad of the North', as a mark of protest. It was to be held on the occasion of the three hundredth anniversary of the town of Christiana, the Germans would be invited. 'This intention to isolate France has met with a very enthusiastic response from the neighbouring countries, and it is very possible [. . .] that the Paris Olympics will be reduced to a mere sports fair for the former allied countries [. . .] [84]

Using their exclusion as a pretext, the Germans encouraged the Danes, the Finns and the Austrians to refuse to take part. This resulted in

> the Finnish newspaper *Svenska Pressen* (run by a German Jew) publishing a long article in which it detailed the reasons why Finland should not participate in the Paris Games. As was the case four years ago, Germany has not been invited [. . .] This exclusion has quite naturally outraged the pro-German newspaper. The playing of sport, which should be a courteous affair, has become a political pawn and a means of adding to the feelings of injustice and hatred directed at countries which lost the war . . . [85]

As far as Russia – one of the countries likely to be invited – was concerned, the invitation was not forthcoming owing to an order given by the Council of Ministers: 'It is my duty to inform you that the Council of Ministers before which I submitted your request has not judged this invitation appropriate.' [86]

No serious incidents occurred during the Olympic Games – neither in Paris nor in Chamonix. The only thing worth mentioning was

> the very bad impression created by the incidents which took place at the rugby-football match [. . .] The *Washington Post* has summed up the information it received as follows: 'American people were beaten, the flag was booed [. . .] the American team's win has caused wild chaos, and growling and mewing drowned out the sound of the American national anthem'. [87]

Such behaviour was also deplored by Gaston Bénac of *L'Auto*: 'the crowds at the Colombes Stadium are giving the foreign correspondents the impression that they are a community which does not know how to accept defeat.' [88]

## Games of victory or Games of peace?

The sudden intrusion of sport into government strategy in 1919 was an entirely new phenomenon in the history of international relations. As far as sport was concerned, the five years following the signing of the Armistice were unquestionably marked by two problems: Olympic spirit and anti-German feeling. The Joint Allied Games in Paris and the Olympic Games in Antwerp were both Victory Games, as Delavaud, France's Minister in Stockholm, liked to call them, insofar as they instituted the first ever boycott in the history of sport. The situation was a peculiar one which had been left over from the war. While internationalism, as well as the pacifism which was the basis behind the Olympic and sporting spirit were being betrayed, the democratic states were being set up as guardians of both the athletes and international politics. Sport, even Olympic sport, would not be able to avoid political arbitration – even though the Treaty of Versailles disregarded it. It was at this time that sport became an instrument of propaganda and a means of exerting diplomatic pressure. Is it any surprise that, a few years later, the total-itarian states would remember the lesson that the democratic states had taught them?

The leaders of the national and international sports federations, like those of the IOC, had made a series of political choices. They could have made others, but it was obviously unthinkable for them to envisage German athletes competing in Belgium, England or France. Consequently, no olive branches were seen at the Colombes Stadium, and this policy of excluding certain countries from sports events was merely the expression of a line of thinking initiated by the English through their sports federations. The institutional and ideological dynamics of the political arena and the sporting world seemed to fit in with the prospect of change which had been brought about mainly by the democratic states. The boycotts which had been initiated by the international policy builders of the allied countries were to have serious consequences for the future of international sport and would definitely cast doubts on the sport's so-called apolitical qualities.

However, in resigning as chairman of the IOC, Pierre de Coubertin divulged a few secrets which betrayed his disillusions. As a defender of the sporting spirit in the purest aristocratic tradition, he regretted that the English had been the first to break the sacrosanct rule that only amateur athletes should compete in the Olympics. As an ardent sports propagandist, he could only rejoice at seeing sport beginning to be played by members of all social classes. He had reservations, how-ever: 'What is important is that the bourgeois youth and the proletarian youth both partake of the same joys of physical training; whether or not they actually play each other is of only incidental importance at the moment.' [89] Although he was worried and disappointed by the upsurge of sports nationalism, he nonetheless remained optimistic: 'Despite a few disillusions which dashed my greatest hopes in an instant, I still believe in the pacific and moralistic qualities of sport. Out on the sports field it ceases to be a question of political or social friends and enemies. All that remains are men playing sport.'

Does this show a lack of clear-headedness? The visionary qualities with which Pierre de Coubertin was often credited were seen to be very limited in this instance, and remained so from 1921 onwards.

## Gently, but not too gently . . .

The end of 1924 saw the beginning of a new era: Franco–German relations became less volatile and France recognized the USSR. French troops left the Ruhr in July 1925, and a few months later the Locarno Pact initiated a period of peace – illustrated by Germany's admission into the League of Nations (8 September 1926). Peace seemed to have won the day, and was celebrated by the award of a joint Nobel peace Price to the Frenchman A. Briand and his German counterpart G. Streseman.

These political and diplomatic conditions made it possible for international sports events to be revived between the allied countries and their former enemies. Numerous newspapers expressed their delight. [90] Furthermore, an official delegate was sent from Germany to Paris to speed up the process. [91] The FINA (International Federation of Amateur Swimming) Congress of 1925 readmitted the German Swimming Federation, which made it possible for records set by German swimmers to be ratified. In fact, records set by the German champion Rademacher were ratified when they were set abroad, but not when they were set in Germany. University exchanges enabled German students to come to France and French federations took it upon themselves to call for competitions to be organized in Paris and Berlin. Georges Carpentier was even given permission to referee boxing matches in Germany. Other federations followed suit and by 1927 Franco–German sports links had been properly revived. Furthermore, events were being heralded through diplomatic channels as early as 1926. [92] Clubs and athletes competing in a private capacity were the first to be sent to compete in Germany (Red Star competed in both Berlin and Hamburg). Pierre de Margerie, France's ambassador in Berlin, saw this as an indication of the meagre respect that people had for formalities and prestige. [93] Although initially reluctant, the Germans quickly understood that these events enabled them to assert their superiority, even in the field of architecture. [94] Reintegrated into the alliance of nations, they set up their first cycling Tour of Germany in 1931.

It seemed as though everybody wanted to do away with the hypocrisy of banning everything while at the same time defying those bans: the Lausanne Conference at the end of 1925 brought together the leaders of the Swiss Athletics Federation with their French and German counterparts 'with a view to discussing the basis of an agreement on which would be founded the revival of international athletics relations between France and Germany.' [95] The Conference decided that the first Franco–German athletics meeting would be held on either 18 or 20 August 1926 in Switzerland. From then on, nothing stood in the way of the 'revival': the first Franco–German Rugby match took place on 19 April 1927 in Paris, followed on 23 August 1927 by the first athletics meeting. The first swimming and water-polo events were held a year later. However, football – the most popular sport on both sides of the Rhine – had to wait longer: although the French national Rugby team played against Austria in 1926 and Hungary in 1927, it was not until 17 March 1931 that it faced Germany's national team at the Colombes Stadium. According to *Le Miroir des Sports* 55 000 spectators watched the match, 15 000 of which were Germans.

These events raised an unexpected problem: it was traditional for countries' national anthems to be played by military bands. In 1927, many letters expressed embarrassment: 'Must our French military bands play the national anthems of the countries with which we were at war? The Minister of Foreign Affairs did not have any qualms about what should be done: I do not think we should pursue this line.

This way we avoid our military bands having to play the *Deutschland über alles* in public.' [96]

Hitler's coming to power revived the question over national anthems. Should the *Deutschland über alles* be played in 1934, or *Horst Wessellied*, the German national-socialist anthem? As a general rule, the Ministry of Foreign Affairs decided every time on the *Deutschland über alles*, although he did allow it to be played by a military band. It was a question of honour just as much as a question of politics, which led to the circulation of an official note:

> The Ministry of War frequently receives requests for the national anthems of participating countries to be played by military bands at international sports events [. . .] Such requests are not without their problems: there are occasions when it is awkward for certain national anthems to be played in barracks or in public by military bands. Consequently, there have been times when you considered it appropriate to play the *Deutschland über alles* and other times when you considered it inappropriate, depending on the nature of the circumstances. On the other hand, it is customary for the national anthem of the USSR to be requested from time to time. This anthem is of a politically extremist nature. However, refusing to play it might be interpreted as retaliation [. . .] Adopting an unchanging line of conduct is the only way to avoid this tendentious interpretation.

The offices of the Ministry of Foreign Affairs replied quite unequivocally:

> The following provisions will be applied in future [. . .]
>
> 1°)   There will be no military bands at events in which Germany and the USSR participate. The organisers will be entirely free to enlist the help of civilian bands.
>
> 2°)   For all other ceremonies, the involvement of military bands is authorised, but only for important events and on condition that they are presided over by a member of the government [. . .] [97]

However, the matter had not been resolved. These provisions were rejected by the Minister of Foreign Affairs who had quite clearly not been consulted: 'The German national anthem has the same melody as that of Austria. I do not think that it will be easy to prevent it from being played by our military bands.' [98] In fact, on 11 January 1937, permission was granted for the Austrian national anthem, *Sei Gesegnet ohne Ende*, to be played at the France–Austria match, 'because it is slower than the German national anthem(!)'.

Six months later, the question of national anthems came up again when France were due to play Portugal at football. The position that Portugal had adopted over the situation in Spain gave rise to fears of an adverse public reaction. But nothing came of it: General Salazar, Portugal's dictator president, did not send his team to France, fearing 'hostile protests from the French public'. [99, 100, 101]

The copious correspondence concerning the question of national anthems is evidence of the prudent and often contradictory position adopted by the French government. The objective was to avoid all provocation or feelings of indignation on the part of the public. But this objective had to be reconsidered for each individual situation: each decision had to be made according to circumstance. This line of thinking was implemented at least until the end of 1938. [102] (There is, in fact, no correspondence pertaining to this matter after July 1938.)

The first France v. Germany football match (March 1931) was of course as much a source of apprehension as it was of excitement. The event of the year is what all the French and foreign newspapers called it, causing a world-wide sensation. [103, 104, 105, 106] The match was broadcast on the radio, and France's victory elicited much praise from the German press. However, the match was marked yet again by a number of incidents relating to the playing of the national anthems and by criticism from a number of German journalists who disputed the French victory (the only goal was an own goal scored by a German defender: the German coach was dismissed). Jules Rimet, Chairman of the French Federation of Association Football and of FIFA spoke of the passion that this match had sparked, stressing in particular the peacemaking role of sport. L'Humanité labelled the match a masquerade orchestrated by the bourgeois federations. [107]

Matches between France and Italy, however, scarcely aroused any comment. France's crippling defeat in Bologna can only be explained by Italy's excellent training and the decisive role that the fascist state played in the promotion of sport. [108] Outside the communist press, nobody talked much about Il Duce's sports policy – unless it was to praise its positive effects.

Overall, international sport seemed to be getting back to normal. There was a crisis which Rugby underwent in 1931, but this was due to reasons completely independent of politics: the British rugby unions broke off their relations with France on 13 February, accusing the French players of brutality, crooked amateurism and failure to respect the rules of the game. The 'affair' caused a great deal of commotion, and kept the sports press busy for quite some time. [109] More seriously, the issue gave rise to a split within the French Rugby Federation, and the Parliamentary Under-Secretary of State for physical education volunteered to mediate.

## From Rome to Berlin

Journalists, politicians and sports event organizers were far more preoccupied by the poor results and the repeated defeats of French teams than they were by Hitler's rise to power. For example, the national football team's win against Belgium in 1930 was the first overseas victory since the Antwerp Olympic Games! This statistic incited France to take an interest in Italy's results (starting in 1927) and later Germany's (starting in 1934). The analysis quickly became political – many people saw an obvious link between State intervention and sports results. [110, 111, 112, 113] Having a strong, centralized state was seen to be the only way of guaranteeing a prestige policy on sport. Certain people wasted no time in asserting that Mussolini was a great athlete, details of his ventures having been effectively relayed across Europe by groups of fascist academics. [114] Several enquiries were subsequently carried out by journalists so that they could give their readers an idea of how sport was organized in Germany, Italy and 'Soviet country'. [115, 116]

But these investigations gave rise to another question: given the logic of performance and record-setting – which resulted in an increasingly large amount of time being set aside for training – were not some of these athletes professionals, having become athletes of the State? With its amateur status, French sport presented itself as a victim. This theme recurred tirelessly at every international event, particularly at the Olympics (the Los Angeles Summer Games of 1932, and the Winter Games of Garmish-Partenkirchen in 1936): France was a laboratory of pure sport and of sports honesty, and so the 'black sheep' (identified as the Germans, the Italians and the Americans [117, 118]) had to be disqualified. Furthermore, this issue of amateurism resulted in the great French champion Jules Ladoumégue being disqualified for life in the 1930s and in the status of professional footballers having to be ratified!

The communist newspapers immediately accused the authoritarian states of using sport to propagandist ends: 'In Germany, fascism has found a good home for its development in the sports movement. And even in France, the National Union of War Veterans (a clearly fascist organisation) is increasingly in favour of setting up sports clubs.' [119] Meanwhile the communists themselves called for anti-fascist groups to rally together.

These issues rapidly paled into the background behind the consequences that international politics had for sport. In Italy, Mussolini, who was keen to develop his colonial policy, was seeking – for supposedly humanitarian reasons – to annex Ethiopia, the last independent territory in Africa. The Italian troops started their manoeuvres in the autumn of 1935 and occupied Addis Ababa in May 1936. The situation became critical and the League of Nations voted to impose economic sanctions against Italy (which were never enforced). However, this was enough for Mussolini, who gave the order for all sports links between Italian national teams and the countries which had supported sanctions against Italy to be suspended. Consequently, the Italian cycling team was unable to take part in the Tour de France of 1936, and all football matches and athletic events were cancelled. This decision did not meet with any opposition within Italy, since the Italian National Olympic Committee was under the direct supervision of the Fascist Party, and the twelve Italian Olympic Federations were under the leadership of men who had been very sympathetic to fascist ideology since 1935. In France, the Head of Government and the Minister of Foreign Affairs stated quite tersely 'in principle, Italy will not take part in any sports event organised by "sanctionist" countries'. [120, 121] After the cancellation by the Portuguese football team, followed by the refusal of Italian cyclists to take part in the 1936 Tour de France, and the withdrawal of an Italian football team in April 1937, sports columnists concluded: 'Sport has been defeated by politics.' [122]

As for the situation in Germany, the Hitler regime was more cunning. In 1934, French athletes were still given a warm and courteous welcome on arriving in Germany.

> On entering the stadium, the French athletes, led by Padou, the popular water-polo team captain, were heartily applauded. The French flag was the first to be hoisted and the 1,000 spectators stood up and saluted them in the Hitler manner. They maintained the salute while the orchestra played the French national anthem. [123]

As a rule, French journalists and athletes were easily affected by these displays of friendship and were fascinated by the German spectators' enthusiasm. A truly sporty people!

François-Poncet, the French ambassador in Berlin, was not, however, fooled by this masquerade. In 1934, he informed Louis Barthou, the Minister of Foreign Affairs, of the way in which Germany's victories were being flaunted by the national-socialist government.

> The press itself is paying tribute to Hitler and his regime by considering these victories to be a positive testament to the effects of policy change, as well as a means of propaganda capable of heightening faith in the regime. [. . .] Since the rise to power of national-socialism, Dr Goebbels' propaganda has worked to give the German people back their faith both in themselves and in the destiny of their country. Every week, newspaper articles and cinema newsreels document their champions' success [. . .] Public opinion is getting drunk on this success, and the fanaticism that people are endeavouring to spread throughout the various sectors of the population is being fed by it. The public has gone back to believing that Germany absolutely must be the best at everything. They are once again believing in the natural superiority of the German people, this sometimes unbearable vanity and this taste for hegemony which was a feature of Germany under Wilhelm II. [124]

He also noted that in 1936,

> all the German newspapers announced and enthusiastically celebrated the boxer Max Schmelling's victory over his black opponent, Joe Louis. For the press and the public, this represented a two-fold victory for the Third Reich: a victory for German sport over American sport and a victory for the white race over the black race. [125]

The organization of the Berlin Olympics in 1936 quickly gave rise to questions. In 1934, *L'Auto* expressed its concern over the Aryan issue and made a point of mentioning the measures that Germany had taken to allay the fears of the USA. [126] But for all that, the election of a Popular Front government did not prevent French athletes from going to Berlin and Garmish-Partenkirchen. [127, 128]

While the right-wing press claimed that the Games had been distorted, [129, 130] the communists stated that the Games had been exploited by Hitler's regime: free sport is dead in Germany. Or else they presented them as a caricature: *L'Humanité* published 'Civilisation and Fascist Olympics', an article in three parts about the popular games of Barcelona. [131] In short, everybody felt as though they had been cheated – albeit a little belatedly. However, such feelings did not stop the German and Italian footballers being welcomed in Paris for the 1938 World Cup.

## Munich – a major sporting city

The Germans were particularly good at intensifying their plan of seduction. Even the relations between the French Consul in Munich and the Minister of Foreign Affairs emphasized the popular success of the Franco–German sports events during the Anschluss. [132] All the reports suggest that the French were given a warm and hearty welcome on their arrival in Germany, whether they were there for the International Congress of the Catholic Youth Movement in Ljublijana, in which gymnasts from the Fédération Gymnastique et Sportive des Patronages de France (Gymnastic and Sports Federation of French Youth Clubs) were taking part, or for the international regattas in Frankfurt. Neither the SOFE nor the Minister of Foreign Affairs saw any problem in Franco–German sports events being continued. [133] This was August 1938. What was even more surprising was that in September and October 1938, when international tension was at its highest and the reservists were being recalled (24 September), sports events were taking place as usual. And the press praised the friendly way in which the French women's basketball team had been welcomed to the European championships in Rome. [134] Generally speaking, there were few 'incidents', the only ones of note were the Italian anti-fascist attacks on Italian athletes during an event held at the Italian Drancy Stadium in Paris, but these were minor. [135]

In September 1938, France's women athletics team was supposed to compete in the European championships in Vienna: the Minister of Foreign Affairs expressed extreme reservations. He considered that, given the circumstances, it was only prudent to send the team to Vienna if they could be guaranteed to give an excellent performance. [136] The same arguments prevailed when the French football team had to go to Naples on 4 December 1938. In winning the football World Cup in Paris, the horse-riding Grand Prix and the Tour de France, Italy had undeniably become a major sporting nation. It was also the case, according to the Minister of Foreign Affairs, that the Italians were convinced of their superiority on the sports field. Consequently, they had to be 'set straight . . .' [137] A number of unfortunate incidents took place during this match, but the official match report disappeared. [138] The press was deeply disturbed by the explosive atmosphere which had marked Italy's victory. Never had they witnessed such an excess of fanaticism, such an absence of the most basic rules of common courtesy, kindness and just plain sportsmanship. [139, 140]

On the other hand, the Italians themselves were renowned for 'crying off' when they were not sure of victory. They thus withdrew from the France–Italy athletics meeting of 13 June 1939 – in curious circumstances. An eleven-page report relating the history behind this last-minute withdrawal, alleges that the Italians were afraid of losing after the defeat of their boxer Turiello against Marcel Cerdan. The Italian government allegedly feared pro-French rallies from the Italian spectators. [141]

But these circumstances were quickly forgotten and the Minister of Foreign Affairs gave his approval to all the national team's international fixtures from February 1939 onwards. The facts would appear to justify this approval: 'Wherever they go, the French are lavishly welcomed.' [142] However, the situation was to change dramatically in April 1939. The FFR resigned itself to cancelling the France–Germany match of 30 April 1939 owing to the procrastination of the authorities. One week later it was the Interior Minister's turn to ban a football match between France and Germany. Hitler ordered the German athletes not to compete against France on French territory as long as the French authorities could not guarantee that the matches would take place. He did, however, extend an invitation to French athletes to compete in Germany! [143] French journalists were up in arms: 'sport is not politics, and there have never been any anti-German protests in French stadiums.' [144]

Events at the beginning of July 1939 illustrated the hypocritical nature of nations. While the French and the English wondered if they were going to be able to renew their Rugby rivalry, the French national athletics team refused to go to Italy, but went to Munich to hear what Hitler had to tell them! [145]

Jean Fusil was a member of that French team. bBearing in mind that this took place ten months after the Munich agreements were signed (29 and 30 September), and only two months before war was declared and troops were mobilized, his account of the situation makes interesting reading. According to him, the Germans welcomed the French team amicably and warmly. The event took place quite harmoniously – he saw no signs of aggression in the crowds, in the officials or in the athletes and 'nothing to indicate that the war was not far off'. [146, 147] These opinions were confirmed by the press, which expressed delight at the ovation with which France's only victory (that of J.F. Brisson in the 110 metres hurdles) was met. 'In welcoming the French national team to the stadium in such a fraternal way, the Germans have shown everybody how enthusiastic about sport they are and how keen they are to maintain the excellent sports relations that we have always enjoyed together . . .' [148]

Why did the Minister of Foreign Affairs authorize the sending of a team to compete in Germany, when he had forbidden the selection of athletes who were doing military service, consequently weakening that team? 'It is a total mystery', clamoured the journalists in unison! [149, 150] The event should have been held in France, but the government made it clear that it was unable to assume responsibility for the organization and security. Could it be that the French did not want to lose face? If so, their reasoning backfired. Hitler had been very shrewd. Inviting the French athletes to Germany – where both organization and security *could* be guaranteed – was a major propaganda coup. Add to this bitter defeat, and all the exercise succeeded in doing was highlighting the decline of the French nation! [151]

Undeterred by what happened to the athletes, the French were still prepared to send a team to compete in the international cycling championships. It was only on 25 August 1939, nine days before war was declared, that they decided not to: 'The UVF [Cycling Union of France] is afraid that the partial mobilisation will prevent France from being able to put up a dignified fight in the international cycling championships . . .' [152]

## Conclusions

Were the French naïve? The right-wing press continued to believe that sport could flourish without recourse to politics. [153] The left-wing press, particularly the communists, argued that sport was being exploited by politics and authoritarian regimes. Sports officials stuck to what they believed – that sport should remain independent of nationalist and political unrest, that sport belonged to the athletes. Some still claimed that French defeats were simply an illustration of the nation's decline and its political leaders' incompetence. 'The State is losing interest in sport, unlike the totalitarian countries where sport is a national institution, a demonstration of regenerative racism, an instrument of propaganda.' [154] Thus, in order to improve, France would have to follow the German and Italian models.

What conclusions can be drawn today? It is highly probable that democracy protected France, its people and its athletes from the nationalist drifts of sport, as Pierre Marie emphasized in 1934. According to him, the bourgeois federations, military preparation federations and the Catholic Federation

> would be the first to join a dictatorship if one were established in our country. In Germany and elsewhere, athletes were by no means the last to acquiesce to dictatorship, to give in, right arms outstretched as a sign of adoration to the Emperors without crowns. It would seem that these federations were already prepared for the consequences of coups d'Etat, ready to have walk-on parts in the stadiums and processions that would acclaim the new regime [. . .] In countries where nationalism is triumphing, athletes have quickly, and with only a few rare exceptions, sided with the favourites. What would happen to French sport if nationalism became predominant in France and its athletes reacted in the same way? You do not have to be a genius to know that French athletes would rally to the rulers of the hour. [155]

## Sources

### *Specialised journals and newspapers of the period.*

*L'Ami des sports* (1931–32). Major weekly providing sports-related information and opinion. Low circulation. Right-wing extremist newspaper, founded by perfumer François Coty (in the same tradition as his other paper *L'Ami du peuple*) to attract sympathizers from among the worker youth movement. The editor-in-chief was Frantz Reichel, the *éminence grise* of Pierre de Coubertin.

*L'Auto* (1919–39). The main sports newspaper of the period. As a general rule it only provided an 'orthodox' vision of sport, simply publishing results and details of forthcoming events. There was little in the way of bias that might have fuelled debate, except regarding sports policy under the Third Republic. High circulation (even higher during the Tour de France), but reduced after 1930: 164 000. *L'Echo des sports* became its main rival in 1930.

*L'Echo des sports* (1919–39). Sports information newspaper which did not, however, have any basic articles concerning major international problems of the era.

*Le Miroir des sports* (1920–39). Weekly journal (bi-weekly during the Tour de France) which expressed the apolitical nature of sport in quite broad terms. Richly illustrated, it is probably the most valuable source of information, providing much detailed information on the development of sport in the interwar period. However, it was somewhat closed to so-called 'contact' sports, and expressed the point of view of the official federations through its prominent journalists. Having been very successful (200 000 copies in 1922), its circulation dropped after 1930, hitting 80 000 in 1939.

*Sport* (established in 1934) by *L'Humanité*.

*Le Sport ouvrier* (established in 1924).

### *Daily newspapers and general publications of the period*

*Gringoire* (1928–39). Extreme right-wing newspaper. No articles about sport, apart for a few reports during the Olympic Games of 1936. Very high circulation: 500 000 copies in 1939.

*Je suis partout.* Right-wing newspaper. A few surveys carried out in the 1930s. Sympathetic to Hitler and Mussolini. Nothing about sport, except for two articles published during the Olympic Games of 1936. 45 000 copies in 1939.

*L'Aube* (1932–39). Conservative Catholic revue. Nothing about sport, apart from match results published without comment in small boxes. Low circulation.

*L'Echo de Paris* (1920–39). Right-wing, conservative. Founded in 1884. Very little about sport – the sports section was less than a page long. 100 000 copies in 1939.

*L'Excelsior* (1920–39). Little or nothing about sport, except for a few articles with an educational slant written by sports and medical experts. 132 000 copies in 1939.

*L'Humanité.* Little about bourgeois sport, apart from criticism of it compared to various initiatives taken by the national and international worker sport federations. Uninterested in sport in general. It unquestionably grew more than any other daily during the interwar period: 170 000 copies in 1930, rising to more that 350 000 in 1939. The Olympic Games of 1936 were the subject of very few articles (a small feature). In 1924 the paper started to report on sports events organized by the Fédération Sportive de Travail (Worker Sports Federation), and after 1934, it started to pay closer attention to sport.

*L'Illustration* (1919–39).

*L'Intransigeant.* Founded in 1880. Conservative right-wing. It included quite a large number of sports sections which grew after 1925. Very successful in the 1920s. It organized a number of sports events (*le cross de l'Intransigeant*) and did not hide its sympathies for German and Italian achievements (Summer and Winter Olympic Games). It was behind the creation of *Match* in 1936. Circulation: 135 000 copies in 1939.

*L'Œuvre.* Created in 1902, major radical newspaper. Little reference to sport. 236 000 copies in 1939. Opposed to fascism.

*Paris-Soir.* Created in 1923, apparently the only daily with a large sports section, sometimes as long as three or four pages. But little in the way of polemical comment or fundamental articles. Very successful, with a circulation of some 1 740 000 copies in 1939, and often more.

## References

1. Arnaud, P. and Wahl, A. (1993) *Sport et relations internationales pendant l'entre-deux-guerres*, CNRS-PPSH, Lyon.
2. Cf. Spivak, M. (1983) Education physique, sport et nationalisme en France, du second Empire au Front populaire; un aspect original de la défense nationale, State Thesis, Université de Paris I – Sorbonne. State Thesis 4. Cf. p. 940.
3. Cf. *L'Auto*, the first half of July 1919.
4. Cf. *Illustration*, 28 June 1919.
5. Cf. *L'Illustration*, 12 July 1919.
6. Cf. *La Vie au Grand Air*, 15 July 1919.
7. Dubech, L. (1931) *Où va le sport?*, A. Redier, Paris.
8. Braud, D. (1984) Le sport français entre les deux guerres. *Relations internationales* (38).
9. Decree of 20 January 1920.
10. A report to the Chamber of Deputies concerning the budget of the Ministry of Foreign Affairs, for 1920, *Journal Officiel de la République Française* (Government publication) (820), 28 April 1920.
11. Ibid. The reporter was J. Noblemaire.
12. Arnaud, P. and Terret, T. (1993) *Le Rêve blanc, Olympisme et sports d'hiver*, Presses Universitaires de Bourdeaux, Lyon.

13. *Le Miroir des sports*, 29 July 1920.
14. Ibid.
15. Arnaud and Wahl, *op. cit.*
16. Diplomatic Archives of Nantes, SOFE, no. 85.
17. Ibid.
18. Spivak, M. (1984) Prestige national et sport. *Relations Internationales* (38).
19. Braun, *op. cit.*
20. Diplomatic Archives of Nantes, SOFE, no. 85 (1920–1922).
21. Ibid., no. 89 (1921–1924).
22. Ibid., no. 93, (1922–1927).
23. Ibid., no. 85, a letter from the Head of Government, Minister of Foreign Affairs, to the Minister of State Education, dated 16 March 1922.
24. Cf. Milza P. (1987) *Le Fascisme Italien et la presse française*, Edit. Complexe, Paris, p. 73–4.
25. Arnaud, P. (in press) Naissance d'une Fédération: enjeux de pouvoirs autour du sport scolaire et universitaire, in Comité des Travaux Historiques et scientifiques (CTHS), *Histoire des jeux et des sports*, Ministère de l'Education Nationale, Paris.
26. *L'Auto*, 18 August 1925.
27. National Archives, AJ9/6311. A letter dated 6 July 1920.
28. Diplomatic Archives of Nantes, SOFE, no. 85, in correspondence dating from 1 to 29 March 1923.
29. *Le Miroir des sports*, 10 February 1921.
30. Ibid., 3 March 1921. Comments by José Germain, chairman of the Association of Fighting Writers.
31. Le sport 'ersatz' du service militaire en Allemagne. *Le Miroir des sports*, 16 June 1921.
32. Cf. Arnaud, P., (1994) *Les origines du sport ouvrier en Europe*, L'Harmattan, Paris.
33. *Le Sport ouvrier* (4), 20 September 1923.
34. Ibid., (12), 26 January 1924.
35. Ibid., (21), 7 June 1924.
36. Ibid., (23), 5 July 1924.
37. *L'Humanité*, 12 July 1924.
38. Ibid., 13 July 1924.
39. Ibid., 15 July 1924.
40. Ibid., 16 July 1924.
41. Riordan, J. (1991) *Sport, politics and communism*, Manchester University Press, Manchester and New York.
42. Cf. Arnaud (1994) *op. cit.*
43. *Le Sport ouvrier* (5), 5 October 1923.
44. Ibid., (30), 25 December 1924. Article by R. Savin.
45. Dumons, B. and Pollett, G. (1992) Eglises chrétiennes et sport international dans la première moitié du XX$^{ieme}$ siècle, in CTHS, *Jeux et sport dans l'histoire*, Ministère de l'Education Nationale, Paris.
46. *Les Jeunes* (journal), 1 April and 14 October 1905. The Sports and Cultural Federation Archives of France.
47. Cf. Dumons and Pollet, *op. cit.*, p. 216.
48. *Le Miroir sports*, 30 December 1920.
49. Ibid., 27 January 1921.
50. *Le Gymnaste*, 1 February 1919, p. 308.
51. *L'Auto*, 12 September 1919.

52. *L'Echo des sports*, 9 April 1924.
53. *La Vie au grand air*, 20 May 1920, p. 39.
54. *Note sur la propaganda sportive à l'étranger* (1920) SOFE, extracts in Arnaud and Wahl, *op. cit.*
55. *L'Auto*, 6 July 1921.
56. *Le Miroir des sports*, 12 August 1920.
57. Quoted in Spivak, *op. cit.*, p. 1163.
58. *L'Echo des sports*, 7 September 1922.
59. *L'Auto*, 1 May 1924.
60. *L'Echo des sports*, 3 October 1922. The journalist referred to the first handshake between French and German athletes.
61. *L'Auto*, 24 June 1921.
62. Ibid., 8 January 1924.
63. *Le Miroir des sports*, 3 June 1925.
64. Ibid., 7 September 1922.
65. *L'Auto*, 17 May 1924.
66. National Archives, AJ9/6323.
67. Ibid., 6324.
68. *L'Auto*, 27 April 1924.
69. *Le Miroir des sports*, 21 July 1921. An article by André Glarner.
70. The period of weakness in French sport. *Le Miroir des sports*, 25 August 1921.
71. Diplomatic Archives of Nantes, SOFE, no. 89, confidential. An unsigned letter dated 9 June 1923.
72. *L'Auto*, 21 July 1924.
73. Diplomatic Archives of Nantes, SOFE, no. 93, reply to a telegram sent by the French Ambassador in Berlin, 6 March 1924. It concerned an exhibition match in which Carpentier would compete against an Englishman!
74. Ibid., no. 85, *op. cit.*
75. Arnaud and Wahl, *op. cit.*, for details of this line of argument.
76. Müller, N. and Schantz O. (1986) *Pierre de Coubertin, textes choisis*, 3 vols, Hildesheim, Zurich and New York.
77. See also, Callebat, L. (1988) *Pierre de Coubertin*, Fayard, Paris.
78. Diplomatic Archives of Nantes, SOFE, no. 85, an unsigned note sent to M. Milhaud, 6 September 1920.
79. Arnaud and Terret, *op. cit.*
80. Diplomatic Archives of Nantes, SOFE, no. 90, a letter dated 12 June 1922 to Poincaré, Head of Government and Minister of Foreign Affairs.
81. Ibid., *op. cit.*
82. Ibid., a letter from the secretary general of the French Olympic Committee to Jean Giraudoux, dated 17 February 1923.
83. Ibid., undated note to the Head of Government, Minister of Foreign Affairs.
84. Ibid., a letter dated 26 October 1923.
85. Ibid., a copy of a letter, dated 26 November 1923, from M. de Coppet, Finland's Minister for France, to His Excellency M. Poincaré, Head of Government and Minister of Foreign Affairs.
86. Ibid., an undated letter from the director of the SOFE to Count de Clary, Chairman of the French Olympic Committee.
87. Ibid., a letter dated 20 May 1924 from France's Ambassador in the US to Poincaré

about the anti-American incidents which occurred at the Olympic Games.
88. *L'Auto*, 19 May 1924.
89. *Le Miroir des sports*, 24 November 1921.
90. *L'Auto*, 12 August 1926, an article by Géo André.
91. Ibid., 6 October 1926.
92. Ministry of Foreign Affairs, Paris, Diplomatic Archives, Europe, 1918–1929 – Germany – 602.
93. Ibid., letter dated 29 January 1929.
94. Ibid. letter dated 5 August 1929 from P. Margerie to A. Briand, Head of Government and Minister of Foreign Affairs on the occasion of the three-way athletics match between the Stade Français, the Charlottenburg Sports Club and the Swedish club Göta Stockholm.
95. Ibid., Germany 603, letter dated 16 December 1925 from the French Consul at Lausanne to the Head of Government and Minister of Foreign Affairs, Paris.
96. Ibid., weightlifting event, the Wagram hall in Paris. Correspondence from 29 June to 5 October 1927.
97. Ibid., Series C. Administration. 1908–1940. C2 – Interior, 270, letter dated 3 May 1935 from General Maurin to the Minister of War, forwarded to the Minister of Foreign Affairs (marked "SECRET").
98. Ibid., letter dated 3 June.
99. Ibid., a letter dated 23 November 1936 from the Minister of National Defence and War to the Minister of Foreign Affairs.
100. Ibid., letters from the Chairman of the French Federation of Association Football.
101. *L'Intransigeant*, 25 November 1936.
102. Ministry of Foreign Affairs, Paris, Diplomatic Archives, Series C. Administration. 1908–1940. C2 – Interior, 270.
103. *Paris-Soir Sportif*, 17 March 1931.
104. *L'Auto*, 16 March 1931.
105. Ibid., 17 March 1931.
106. *Le Miroir des sports*, 17 March 1931.
107. *L'Humanité*, 16 March 1931.
108. *Le Miroir des sports*, 3 February 1931.
109. Various issues of *L'Auto*, *Le Miroir des sports* etc. for 1931.
110. *L'Auto*, 14 February 1936.
111. Ibid., 15 February 1936.
112. Ibid., 18 February 1936.
113. *Le Figaro*, 14 August 1936.
114. *L'Auto*, 1 June 1932. Statement made by Dr Chappert, chairman of the University Sports Office.
115. *Le Miroir des sports*, starting in September 1927.
116. *L'Auto*, a series of articles starting 7 August 1934.
117. Ibid., 3 September 1932, an article by Jacques Goddet.
118. Ibid., 17 September on the militarization of German sport.
119. Red Sport International's great day of 1 July 1934. *L'Humanité*, 19 June 1934.
120. Diplomatic Archives of Nantes, SOFE, box 459, 1933–1939.
121. Cf. *L'Auto*, 31 January 1936 concerning a possible revival of Franco–Italian sports links which would begin with cycling.
122. Ibid., 9 April 1937.

123. Diplomatic Archives of Nantes, SOFE, box 59, 1933–1939, a letter from the French General Consul in Dresden, 27 June 1934 to the Minister of Foreign Affairs.
124. Ibid., box 460, 1934–1939, letter from François-Poncet dated 6 June 1934.
125. Ibid., a letter dated 21 June 1936.
126. *L'Auto*, 16 August 1934.
127. Brohm, J.M. (1983) *1936, Les jeux Olympiques de Berlin*, Ed. Complexe, Brussels.
128. Bourgois, C. (1981) *Le Mythe olympique*, L'Harmattan, Paris.
129. *Les jeux défigurés. L'Auto*, 18 August.
130. A la recherche de l'olympiade perdu (The Quest for the Lost Olympics). *Le Matin*, 18 August 1936.
131. *L'Humanité*, 2, 6 and 18 August 1936.
132. Diplomatic Archives of Nantes, F 17 – 14460, Foreign Affairs, international events. Report dated 30 March 1938 by J. Bourdeillette, French Consul in Frankfurt to Paul Boncour, Minister of Foreign Affairs concerning the France–Germany Rugby match of 27 March 1938 at Frankfurt. The French lost the match, to everybody's surprise. Cf. also the note from the Minister of Foreign Affairs to the Minister of Public Health.
133. Ibid., SOFE, letters from the Minister of Foreign Affairs to the Minister of Education dated 28 April, 4 July and 26 August 1938.
134. Ibid., a letter dated 19 October 1938.
135. Diplomatic Archives of Nantes, SOFE, box 458, 1932–1935.
136. Ibid., letter dated 6 September 1938.
137. Ibid., a long letter dated 24 November 1938 from the Minister of Foreign Affair to the Minister of Education and to the French Consul in Naples.
138. Ibid., a letter dated 14 December 1938 from Jean Zay, Minister of Education to the Minister of Foreign Affairs.
139. *Le Miroir des sports*, 6 December 1938.
140. Ibid., 13 December 1938.
141. Diplomatic Archives of Nantes, SOFE, box 458, 1932–1935, a report dated 18 June 1939.
142. Ibid., letters dated 2 February and 5 and 6 March.
143. Diplomatic Archives of Nantes, SOFE, box 460, a letter dated 25 April 1939.
144. *Le Miroir des sports*, 18 April 1939.
145. *L'Auto*, 4 July 1939.
146. Interview with Jean Fusil, August 1989.
147. Cf. interview with James Couttet who had had the same impressions at Garmish-Patenkirchen in 1936. Interview conducted in June 1991.
148. *Le Miroir des sports*, 4 July 1939.
149. Ibid., 2 May 1939.
150. Ibid., 30 June 1939.
151. Ibid., 11 July 1939.
152. *L'Auto*, 25 August 1939.
153. *Le Figaro*, 14 August 1939.
154. Commets s'en sortir. *Le Miroir des sports*, 9 September 1938. Article by Gabriel Hanot.
155. Marie, P. (1934) *Pour le sport ouvrier*, Lib. Populaire, Paris.

# Chapter 9

# Italian sport and international relations under fascism*

*Angela Teja*

Sporting activity under fascism was regulated by the State and was a way of controlling citizens during their leisure time, in their private life and in their social relations. Controlling sport enabled the regime to study and manipulate young people and their skills. At the same time, sport was a means of promoting and spreading fascist ideology at home and abroad.

Such conclusions, however, were not arrived at straightaway. In fact, at its outset the Fascist government regarded sport mainly from an educational rather than a competitive standpoint. The story of sports policy under fascism can be divided into three phases. The first, from the inception of the regime of the 1920s, saw sport more as a physical activity; in the second phase, up to the end of the 1930s, the regime recognized sport as a powerful vehicle of political propaganda. For this reason, from the 1930s on, athletes were very well trained and participated whenever possible in international sports events. In the third phase, in the late 1930s, there was a gradual move from sports skills to military skills on the physical education curriculum, following the pattern of other totalitarian states where militarization had begun to affect physical activity. Thus, military games were introduced into the World University Championships, held in Vienna in 1939.

## The golden age of physical education

In the early days of fascism, the Italian government was greatly concerned with problems relating to the physical education of the younger generation, problems which it considered necessary to overcome if it was to create a powerful new nation capable of supporting its policy. It decided, therefore, that young people were to be physically strong, well formed in their character and experienced in military skills. [1] Physical education was therefore used to create a 'New Person', understood by the State as a sort of 'Soldier-Citizen', yet one who would safeguard the nation's health and physical integrity. Thus, two organizations, the school and the Milizia Volontaria per la Sicurezza Nazionale (MVSN – Voluntary Militia for

---

* This work was concluded on 30 June 1995.

National Security), an organization established on 14 January 1923 for the sports and paramilitary training of young people aged 18 to 21, as well as postmilitary training, were entrusted with the physical education of all citizens. [2, 3] State medical organizations were also enlisted to play an important role.

Fascism had the opportunity to resolve serious social postwar problems in Italy caused by the economic and social crisis. On the one hand, the first objective was to strengthen popular accord; on the other, it was important to organize youth education according to the new principles. Guiseppe Gentile, in 1923, understood the importance of school and promoted its reform, assigning physical education and sport to the Ente Nazionale per l'Educazione Fisica (ENEF – National Institute for Physical Education), which had been established by Law D.R. No. 864, 15 March 1923.

After this, all pupils had to follow PE courses at local societies of gymnastics and sport, chosen by the ENEF; they could not attend school unless they were officially members of an authorized sports club. Much that had been achieved through the law promoted by De Sanctis in 1878, however, was soon ruined. The most proficient teachers of PE were obliged to retire after 20 years in order to give way to younger trainers who could run and jump with the children – to urge them towards a more active life and self-esteem. PE training colleges in Turin, Rome and Naples were closed; the new trend was to train personnel on short courses.

School gyms were handed over to the management of sports clubs and were taken out of local authority control. Many doubled as a classroom, and wide groups of children practised their physical activity with the same teacher. This way of organizing and method of instruction was soon realized to be a mistake, however, when it became apparent that detaching physical from intellectual and ethical education could damage an individual's whole personality. The effort to avoid such damage was often to change the ENEF management.

The ENEF was initially directed by Professor Franzoni, who was also head of a high school in Milan. He organized a programme based on three periods: first, development and training, the so-called pre-sporting period for children aged from 10 to 14; second, the so-called sporting or applied period, for children from 14 to 16; and, third, the so-called sporting military period, for 16–18-year-olds. The latter was immediately criticized since its activities did not correspond to health and rationality criteria. Overall, the programme was criticized mainly because it did not produce educational results. Under the auspices of the Direttorio of the Fascio of Milan, a group of PE teachers wrote in a document published in Milan:

> Simply reading this programme shows that it is about 'sport', it does not deal with 'physical education'. It ignores the basic hygiene criteria and the laws of child development . . . Sport, therefore, and not physical education. Yet at school we deal with education, and sport is not education. Hygienists and teachers agree that sport is not an educational activity at all. From Baumann to Pagliani, to Sclavo in Italy, from Lagrange to Demeny and Tissié in

France . . . And in Britain, experts propose systematic physical activity, and prescribe Swedish gymnastics for the army, navy and even the pupils at Eton. [4]

Subsequently the ENEF was managed by a Commissioner, Gino Salvi, who was professor of anatomy at the University of Naples. He reinstated teams of 30–40 pupils, divided into four age groups: 10–12, who engaged in activities based on play and the use of small pieces of equipment; 12–14, who did hygienic-therapeutic exercises developed in Sweden; 14–16, who undertook non-competitive agility, flexibility and balance exercises, as competition was considered harmful during puberty; and 17–18, who practised sports and paramilitary activities.

Such a programme shows that physical activity was organized from a medical standpoint. Nonetheless, it seemed that the ENEF had not yet found the right formula. In 1926 General Grazioli became its Director; and he soon asked Giuseppe Monti (1861–1938), the major Italian gymnastics specialist who was Director of the Physical Education Institute in Turin, to rebuild a Higher Institute of Physical Education in Bologna, linked to the Medical Faculty. Monti introduced 'sports exercises' such as rowing, tennis, skating, cycling, etc., but stayed for only two years.

The pressure on the ENEF to organize physical activity for schoolchildren, or even for private sports clubs and military purposes, was immense, but it lacked a central body of technical experts and so was doomed to failure. Grazioli tried to maintain the Institution's activities with the aid of Renato Ricci (1896–1956) [5] of the Opera Nazionale Balilla (ONB – the National Youth Association which had been established by Law No. 2247, 3 April 1926); but at the end of 1927 the ENEF was disbanded by order of Decree No. 2341, 20 November 1927, and the organization of physical education of young people was handed over to the ONB. [6]

## Party control

Until the end of 1926, PE and sport were controlled by the National Fascist Party (PNF). *Foglio d'ordini* No. 16, 4 December 1926, following the circular of 30 November issued by Party HQ and signed by Ricci, set out the norms for the new avant-gardist organization: '[. . .] the young Italian will be first a Balilla, then an Avant-gardist. He will follow military service. Then, the young fascist can come back to Party activity, both as a fascist and as a soldier.' Sport was submitted to PNF control for the following reasons:

Though all Italian young people would be fascists, the world of sport should not be submitted to the 'Littorio' (fascism), mainly because sport has an influence not only on physical development, but also on moral and political functions and it is linked to economic interests that should be followed and controlled. [7]

Thus, on this occasion, the term 'sport' was linked to 'physical education' in the general context of youth education.

As regards physical, ethical, religious, political, hygienic and military education of the younger generation, the ONB, while a more complex organization, took care only of basic physical activities without reference to other institutions. The key maxim of the ONB was 'Libro e moschetto' (book and musket), which suggested taking care of both the spirit and the body. The way in which the ONB organized the 'Pupilla del Regime' (pupil of the regime) was generally accepted as being the best way and received great support. Its emphasis was on military education; the first technical and disciplinary rules were proposed by the Head of the Government through an agreement with the War Minister and the Captain of the Milizia Volontaria per la Sicurezza Nazionale. The President of the ONB had to be an officer in the military, at least a Consul General of the MVSN. [8]

Young people were also involved; they were called *Balilla* (14–16), or *Avanguardisti (16–18)* according to their age. From 1929, there were also the *Piccole* and *Giovani Italiane* (small and young Italian girls) for young females, and for small children under eight, the *Figli della Lupa* (Sons of the Wolf).

## Rejection of competitive sport

The ONB became much more educationally orientated when Renato Ricci was made Under-Secretary of Physical Education by the Education Minister. [9, 10] In a letter written in May 1929 by Ricci to the President of the Council of Ministers (PCM), who had requested information about the ONB for the French scholar Professor Mericlen of the University of Nancy, the basic characteristics of the method of education used by the ONB are defined:

> The system of physical education organized by the ONB Presidency has the following basic characteristics: education and general training until 18. Two main periods can be delineated: up to 14 the focus is on general physical activity for recreational-hygienic and physiological purposes, and from 14 onwards, the focus is on sports activity for hygienic-physiological and recreational purposes.
> There is no specialization [. . .]
> Special rules for competition are proposed by ONB. [11]

Renato Ricci understood clearly the regime's demands on controlling and influencing young people, as well as the need to get them used to discipline, to reinforcing the race, and to training for military exercise. The ONB could respond to such demands, but, in terms of sport, it was unable to promote a competitive spirit. It did not aim for sports results, its purpose was more the ideal, recreational and educational meaning of sport. The sports facilities at its disposal were suitable for ONB championships (such as those to celebrate 24 May: each year there was the 'Festa Ginnastica Nazionale' (National Gymnastics Celebration), where every elementary and middle Italian school put on a special performance made up of the same physical exercises. At the same time of year, there were events and the Littorio national competition, as well as the 'Coppa del Duce' (the Duce Cup) and the 'Ludi Juveniles' for sports disciplines in which the preliminary heats were followed by the ONB provincial committee, but they were certainly unsuitable for international competitions. At the Accademia femminile di Educazione Fisica di Orvieto (Orvieto Female PE Academy), the athletic track was 313 metres long, and the swimming pool 20 metres long, deliberately to avoid Olympic dimensions.

An interview published in *Il Popolo d'Italia* on 25 March 1925, reads:

> As regards the Balilla, they do not practise any sport other than gymnastics, following the most suitable method for children. As regards the Avangardisti, their psycho-physical development has to be taken into consideration. In any case, they can practise sport only after the age of 16, and after developing a mature fibre system necessary to overcome the effort required to perform physical exercise; otherwise, they may damage the physical development of the race. Young people must understand – and some teachers too – that sport is the application of muscle development, obtained after a specific education with certain exercises.

In a speech delivered at the opening ceremony for the Higher Institute of Sport and Gymnastics (which was to become the Male Academy of Physical Education of Rome), on 5 February 1928, Professor Versari, Dean of the Medical Faculty and also Director of the School, underlined how the school should put less emphasis on sports activity. He advocated instead the scientific culture of physical education. [12]

Sport as a competitive activity was condemned by some medical doctors because such effort could damage the physical development of young people. However, such condemnation was due to moral motivation: too often sports events were exploited for profit. For this reason, there were people who advocated the 'nationalization' of sport, by means of effective laws, thereby making it a 'gymnasium of physical education and strength training so as to enable our race to conquer all', while keeping sporting activity as healthy leisure activity. [13]

In this period, Italian athletes did not achieve worthwhile results in any international competition. The athletes, in fact, did not train enough because of the policy to increase physical activities rather than to produce a sporting elite. This was due to the organizing institution: the National Olympic Committee (CONI) was still to be restored. Hence the poor Italian performances in international sports competitions.

Women's involvement in sport was particularly low until the end of the 1930s. Sport was seen as demanding physical activity, and also as harmful to the female procreative system, where it was thought to have a negative influence on the reproductive organs, and the hormonal balance. All the ONB medical doctors and specialists in sports medicine (the Sports Medicine Federation came into being in

1929) were asked about women and sport. The general consensus was 'The Duce orders us not to Americanise women . . . Some sports activities do have a strong influence on the personality. The environment of honour, of satisfaction, of awards and suchlike do not nourish modesty, meditation, or docility of the bride and mother.' [14]

Scientific activity was highly developed in this period, especially in the biomedical field. From this medical viewpoint it is easy to understand why the female team was excluded from participation in the Los Angeles Olympic Games. But, apart from this episode, women's participation in sports events was gradually accepted.

At a *Gran Consiglio* meeting of 16 October 1930, the CONI president was made responsible for a study of female sports activity, with the assistance of medical doctors, in order to fix the limits, and also to safeguard women's principal role in society, that of motherhood. After this decision, the ONB doctors as well as those of the Federation of Sports Medicine (FIMS) started to examine all the potential harmful effects of some sport disciplines on women, as well as research into the most suitable sports activities. Generally speaking, sportswomen were widely distrusted by the public.

On many occasions, the need to organize sport for women was quite urgent. International competition were regarded as a means of emancipating women from their habitual role – in spite of the *Gran Consiglio*. The general consensus was that Italian women should not follow what was happening in other countries, since their physical characteristics were different from those of foreign women. Consequently, the Federation of Track and Field Athletics prevented female athletes from appearing at international meetings. Only in 1936, with the results attained by Italian female athletes Valla and Testoni, did the regime back down.

From the perspective of sport for all, a new discipline was created, the 'volata'. It was invented by Augusto Turati, an important figure in fascism. He was the Secretary of the PNF and a member of the board of CONI from the end of 1928 to 1930 as well as member of parliament and an under-secretary of state. Apart from being highly regarded as a politician, he was well known in the world of sport until 1930, when he fell into disgrace and had to give up politics. This 'most Italian game', as defined by Lando Ferretti, could be played without special training, and was a sort of Rugby and soccer mixed together. It became the favoured game of the regime because it instilled discipline into a warrior mentality. [15] The 'volata' was played for only a few years by the Opera Nazionale Dopolavoro (National Leisure and Recreation Association).

The sports directors, in this first phase of the regime's sports policy, were against competition. This created difficult relations between the ONB, the clubs, and the sports federations. The ONB asked the owners and managers of gymnasia and sports facilities to allow people to use them only for a few hours each day. Renato Ricci struggled against CONI and individual federations to avert the trend towards the creation of 'champions'. In 1932, he tried to merge the Italian Gymnastics Federation into the ONB, because it was linked to the largest number of clubs in the country, and its objectives were contrary to those of the *Balilla*. [16] The Federation promoted championships where athletes under 18 were involved. However, it was able to see through the ONB's proposal of cooperation and integration and rejected it.

School competitions followed special hygienic and educational criteria, which had been imposed on ONB policy by Eugenio Ferrauto (1888–1976), Head of the Central Service of Physical Education and Sport and close collaborator with Ricci. He advocated PE as a valid means of character formation and safeguarding health. In his programme, he addressed the *Balilla, Avangardisti,* and *Piccole and Giovani Italiane* to whom he stressed the physical and ethical education of young people through physical activities. Ferrauto later organized the Programmi della Gioventù Italiana del Littorio (Programmes of Littorio Italian Youth), when it replaced the ONB. His Quaderni reflect the same aims apart from the political changes.

In 1927, the regime dismantled the sports clubs of the Federazione delle Associazioni Sportive Cattoliche Italiane (FASCI – Federation of Catholic Italian Sports Associations) as well as those of the YMCA, creating other organizations such as the ONB. In 1928, even the Boy Scout movement was disbanded because it was considered 'a grotesque foreign imitation' [17] Clearly, the presence of two organizations dealing with young people of the same age group was impractical. *Balilla* and the Scouts risked meeting on the same days to practise similar activities. In 1929, camps, and the annual camp known as 'Campo Dux' were created: fascism would never leave its children to any other organizations.

In 1927, the first World University Championships was organized and Italy was very successful. This success was repeated in several international contests, including the World University Championships held in Paris in 1928 when the crowd were hostile. In this period, many anti-fascist refugees built up a strong movement, and generally the public was against Italian athletes. Even if it was often possible for representatives of the two factions to meet, very seldom were the competitions held without incident. During this period, fascist political relations with France were ambiguous and conflicting; on the one hand, France was seen as the most important country in Europe from a political standpoint so it had to be prevented from becoming too powerful, on the other, it was the only country that could prevent Germany from becoming the most powerful nation in Europe; so it had to be supported. In 1930, Augusto Turati was very much concerned about the anti-fascist movement in Paris. For this reason he wrote a 'highly confidential' circular warning the Secretary of GUF to prevent university athletes from coming into contact with anti-fascist propaganda. [18]

## The 'Carta dello sport'

The 'Carta dello sport' (sports charter) established on 30 December 1928 was the first sign of a change from the strictly educational purposes of the sports organizations towards a more competitive sport. The ONB was still responsible for the physical education of 6–14-year-olds, and with the 14–17 age group we find the concept of sport very close to physical education. However, only the clubs and the organizations included in CONI were responsible for sport, even if the ONB could arrange competitions. It was impossible to become a sports club member without joining the Opera Nazionale Balilla. Military training and competitions were organized by the MVSN. The OND organized sports activities for workers and took control of the Federazione Bocce (Federation of Bowls) and the Federazione Tamburello (Federation of Tamburin). The Italian Touring Federation – dealing with cycling and hiking activities – also came into being. The GUF had to cooperate with the federations, while they were to increase the number of competitions and promote participation.

The regime used the charter to try to bring order to events that were becoming more and more popular. Sport had an uncertain start, owing to the interference of school, PE and military training, as well as the official trend towards gymnastics. Yet, sports disciplines were widespread which meant that the regime had to evaluate their social importance.

The first youth organization to point out the importance of competitive sport was the GUF, founded in 1920. University students achieved good results both in national and international competitions, mainly in the first four World University Championships held respectively in Rome (1927), Paris (1928), Darmstadt (1930) and Turin (1931). Sports training of university students was very thorough; each year students could participate in the 'Littoriali', contests among universities. They could also take part in the 'Agonali', contests among students of the same faculty. The 'Littoriali' were so popular that, afterwards, other competitions on the same pattern, called 'Littoriali della Cultural dell'Arte', were organized. [19]

The regime began to emphasize competitive sport activities and at the same time, 'constitutionalize' fascism. In other words, it was establishing sports organizations along centrally planned lines. In fact, the complex structure of CONI reflects fascist organization. Fascism also wanted to coordinate CONI from the PNF headquarters. Among the famous sports directors of the period we find either people deeply involved in sport or fascist leaders involved in sport. For example, Leandro Arpinati, the CONI President in the early 1930s, was also 'Podestà, (Mayor) of Bologna, and Under-Secretary of Home Affairs; the Marquis Ridolfi, the most popular person in track and field and President of the sports club 'Assi Giglio Rosso' of Florence, was also Mayor of Florence; Puccio Pucci, CONI President during the Social Republic of Salò, was well known as the *Moschettiere* of the Duce, a sort of bodyguard; and Aldo Finzi, CONI President between 1923 and 1924, and Turati fencer and sports administrator, who was also CONI Commissioner from 1928 to 1930, was a well-known co-worker of the Ministry of Home Affairs.

This process began in 1925 when the PNF influenced the nomination for CONI presidency and the direction taken by the various federations. The regime was trying to control all the sports organizations through a sports policy which would have radically changed its initial position against sport.

The number of federations increased, and the regime was aware that it had to discipline them at central level. During this period, the CONI structure was reorganized. This lasted until 1942. A special law institutionalized the 'Federation of Federations', the largest body forming a sports monopoly.

The crucial years for this new organization were 1926 and 1927, when CONI was slowly taking shape. In *Foglio d'ordini* No. 16, 4 December 1926, signed by Turati, CONI came under the PNF, and President Lando Ferretti had to follow its directives, keeping always in touch with the appropriate office in Palazzo Littorio, the party HQ.

In 1927 CONI gained a new charter, which was not planned by the Olympic Committee General Assembly, but by the Party Secretary. This caused the following changes: there would no longer be an election system for directive posts; the various administrators had to be appointed by Mussolini after being proposed by the Party Secretary. The board was made up of the following members: the President, the presidents of the various federations, some Party representatives, the representatives of organizations such as GUF and the ONB, the representatives of some ministries (e.g. the Finance Ministry – to check the budget). Finally, the Provincial Fascist Federation was set up as a means of approving the administrators of the sports clubs, increasing sports propaganda, and creating new facilities. This Federation was an appendix of the PFN. [20] In 1929, the process of sport centralization was complete, and all the federations were housed in Rome. At this time, the project for organizing the 1936 Olympic Games began. On the one hand, the Games were considered important for enlightening the nation, its athletes and its politics. On the other, Italy would show its organizational ability. In the words of Luigi Ferrario, in *La Gazzetta dello Sport*: 'Organizing the Olympic Games obviously shows the power as well as the Nation's maturity [. . .] It is a sign of civilization, it is a conquest for admiring the country which organizes the Games.' [21] In this project, Rome was to be transformed into the 'imperial' capital. The sports sites would all be vastly improved and the architect Piacentini was asked to design the 'Città dello sport' (City of sport).

In a brochure published by CONI for the Olympic Games, Rome is presented as follows:

> Here is *Roma Olimpiaca* designed by the Fascist régime to allow the most important sports event in the world to enjoy the very best sports facilities. The sculptors of Olympism, above all the members of the International Olympic Committee, could see that nothing was neglected to provide the *Urbe* with the optimal multifunctional Olympic facilities. [22]

The brochure also provided information on Rome's history, the climate (what was most appropriate for Olympic events), sightseeing, hotels, etc. It described the Foro Mussolini and the Olympic Stadium. For gymnastics, a theatre was to be built at the foot of Monte Mario. 'He wanted to recreate a sort of Olimpia, with the idea of preserving physical strength in eternity through the bronze statues of Italian champions.' [23]

The 1936 Olympic Games were, however, held in Berlin. Rome then presented its bid for the next Games (due to be held in 1940).

## Change of direction

In the meantime, the athletes were to behave abroad as 'bishops' of Italian politics, following a strict discipline imposed by fascist Italy. This term was used by Turati when he addressed students going to Paris in 1928 for the World University Championships. He recommended that they behave themselves so as to avoid any incident 'against the Party and Fascist Italy'. [24] Later that year, Lando Ferretti, CONI President for three years, wished the athletes going to the Amsterdam Olympics every success in winning as many medals as possible and to gain 'their rightful place in the world thanks to fascism'. [25]

From now on, throughout the 1930s, competitive sport replaced the recreational-educational physical activity of Renato Ricci. This was due to the increasing frequency of sports events: at an international level, there were many international contests, a number of sports disciplines came into existence, and there were now world as well as European championships, not to mention the Olympic Games. The regime decided that Italian athletes should take part in competition and attain the results necessary to demonstrate their superiority over opponents.

This change of direction followed fascist imperialist policy. After 1929, the end of the first political phase, when foreign policy came second to domestic policy, the regime was strong and relatively popular. Sport was then a tool to promote abroad, demonstrating the viable training methods of Italian athletes, their capacity for athletic effort, and the superiority of their race. A gold medal in any discipline at the Olympic Games, or in the Tour de France, was more important than a thousand diplomatic acts, inasmuch as to celebrate victory meant to celebrate Italy and fascism.

Athletes were defined as 'blue ambassadors'; they had to 'display glorious actions in sports struggles against the strongest representatives of other races in the world'. On the other hand, they knew that the government was providing them with all help and support; but the highest award was the praise of the Duce. [26]

Sport had officially been recognized and was now being appreciated and enhanced in all its aspects.

A new phase in sport policy commenced with the important role assigned to the Federation of Sports Medicine. It proposed medical control over every sports activity through a compulsory medical, the *visita medica di orientamento* (medical examination for vocational purpose) for all club members, in order to decide whether they were fit for sport. [27] Turati, a member of the CONI board and 'Commissario' of FIMS (the Italian Sports Medicine Federation), prescribed regular medical examinations for elite or amateur athletes.

These decisions brought athletes under control and a new approach to sport. Ultimately, sport was considered a healthy activity for the individual. Medical research had a very important role to play, and, once sport was free from age-old fears, its potentials could be developed.

Augusto Turati became a member of the International Olympic Committee (IOC) in 1930, a sign of the recognition of Italian sport abroad. Italy was open to Olympism, to international rules, to competition against other countries.

Turati encouraged students through GUF to attain the best possible results, just as American, British and German students did. [28] He was sure that GUF was heading in the right direction, and he considered that the students will be 'fearsome competitors'. It is noteworthy that Roberto Maltini, GUF Secretary, planned to give permission to take part in competitions abroad only to 'reliable subscribers' of GUF, in order to prevent students, once abroad, from 'forgetting their fascist duties'. [29]

In 1930, Iti Bacci was appointed Commissioner of CONI, while Starace passed to the OND and left the 'Militia'. It was a difficult period for all sports institutions: Turati left the sport and political scene altogether; CONI started to change into what would become the only sports institution in the country.

Leanadro Arpinati supported this change. When he was CONI President (1931–33), he helped to effect many changes in both CONI and sports policy. In a speech to the Chamber of Deputies on 18 March 1933, as Under-Secretary of Home Affairs as well as CONI President, he said that sport could not damage young people at all. The fighting spirit is within the human soul, and pushes the young boy to repeat thousands of times the same sports performance in order to gain a good result. This is the only way to become a champion; 'the sentinel in international competitions represents the nation, holds high the flag and his country's prestige'. [30, 31]

Young people were advised to become sports club members so that they too might follow in the footsteps of the Italian Olympic team which had done so well at the Los Angeles Games in 1932. This was the regime's greatest achievement. Olympic champions represented national honour, they were a means of gaining prestige in the world. After Los Angeles , the *Popolo d'Italia* wrote: 'The new Italian man won . . . Our athletes competed courageously against all comers.' [32]

The victorious team became known as 'Mussolini's boys', and the Duce sent them a good luck telegram before the competition. Referring to the bronze medal won by Ugo Frigerio in the 50 kilometres walk, Mussolini wrote:

> Sports achievements . . . increase the prestige of the nation and allow men to struggle in open competition. In this way, however, physical strength is measured as well as the nation's moral values . . . Marching, walking, are they not the expression of fascist dynamism? [33]

## Sport and diplomacy

In many cases a sports event was a means for the regime to reinforce relations with other countries. For example, the soccer match between Juventus and Marseille was a way of keeping on good terms with the French: although an Italian victory would be 'a wonderful factor in political and sports propaganda' among the many Italians living in Marseille. [34] And in December 1932, according to the Italian Consul in Nice, the tour Milan–Turin–Nice cycling race would once again be a means of 'reinforcing, even in a limited way, the relations between the two nations'. [35]

Yet the political struggle against Italian athletes was soon fought in countries opposed to the fascist regime. There were many incidents in Prague during the soccer match between Slavia and Juventus which were repeated when the teams met in Turin. On 16 July 1932 the President of the Council of Ministers asked Mussolini to stop all sports events for a while. [36] In fact, very serious incidents took place in Prague accompanied by sharp invectives 'against Italy and the Duce', and players were seriously injured. The Italian Ambassador in Belgrade wrote: 'Sports criteria, cups, championships are all very well, but sometimes the nation's reputation comes before a sports event.' [37]

The Czechoslovak complaints reflected the cool relationship between the two countries. Politically, Italy was closer to Germany, while Czechoslovakia, Yugoslavia, and Romania signed an agreement with France against Germany. Italy was against the presence of France in Eastern Europe, and it was, therefore, opposed to this agreement. However, Zanetti, CONI Secretary, had committed Italy to play in a football tournament in Czechoslovakia and not to take part would be dishonourable. [38] Sport therefore tried to go beyond politics, but this happened only on rare occasions. Sport in Italy was a creature of fascism, and strictly dependent on it.

Italy participated in the Fourteenth Congress of the International Student Federation in Riga in August 1932. Here it was decided to hold the World Winter Student Games in 1933 in Cortina and the World University Student Games in Turin. Also two Italians were appointed to the Federation board: Mr Poli, who was consul of the Militia, became Federation Vice-President, and Mr Gardini became Treasurer. However, Italy gained a very important position in university sport by persuading the Federation to locate its permanent office in Rome, in the Palazzo Littorio.

A memorandum from GUF to the PCM in August 1932 stressed that the mission of university students was to promote their national political position abroad through 'foreign scholars in order to give foreigners a better knowledge of fascism and to promote it'. [39] The *Corriere di Napoli* on 18 August 1932, underlined that the Federation was eager for Italy to play a prominent part, and the meeting ended with the song *Giovinezza*, sung by all participants. The congress was followed by considerable student activity. Baltic students came to Rome 'to visit the Duce'; German Hitlerites invited 500 Italian students to visit Berlin for a soccer match; French students invited Italians in Nice in 1933 to celebrate the *sorella majorie* (elder sister). [40]

GUF confirmed its status within the International Student Federation when it had to mediate between the Federation and the German Student Association which wanted to take part in the University Student Games in Turin in 1933. The German Association, in fact, was no longer in the Federation because of the Czechoslovak complaints about the incidents in Darmstadt and in Brussels. All German students were in the Deutsche Studentschaft, even those in the old German regions, such as Poland, Czechoslovakia, Danzig, and Austria. This caused problems. However, the organizing committee of the Turin Games was able to overcome the difficulties through diplomacy. According to Poli, the Vice-Secretary of GUF, 'sport is beyond politics and is related to comradeship'. [41] There was a special agreement to permit Austrian students to be members of the same association as the Germans – they wore the same uniform, but in the event of victory either the German or the Austrian flag would be used. It was forbidden to refer to the problem of Danzig. Consequently, the Deutsche Studentschaft was accepted back into the World Student Federation so that they could take part in the Turin Games. Poli wrote to Goebbels in May 1933: 'The university fascists, after Hitler's election, and in respect to the excellent relations recently confirmed between fascism and national socialism, would like the German comrades to take part in the Turin Games.' [42]

At the meeting of the IOC in June 1933, in Vienna, all the Italian delegates attended – General Montù, Earl Thaon di Ravel, Earl Alberto Bonacossa, CONI Secretary General Vaccaro, and Consul Poli from GUF – because the focus was on Italy. Baillet Latour and the American delegate William May Garland were presented with an award by the King of Italy, proposed by the Head of Government, and Consul Poli invited the IOC President to attend the World University Games in Turin. While this was taking place news reached the meeting of the signing of the Mussolini-engineered four-power non-aggression pact in Monaco. An interview with Earl Bonacossa in *La Gazzetta dello Sport*, gives an insight into the climate in Vienna after the news was announced: 'We felt happy and proud when at the most important phase of our work the radio, newspapers, telephone and telegraph sent the news of the agreement in the Four Power Pact by its creator, the holy Duce.' [43]

Many international sports congresses were now taking place. In 1933 the International Congress of Sports Medicine was held in Turin. Although Italy was not a member of the International Association of Sports Medicine in France, a note for the PCM Prime Minister in August 1933 stated that many foreign delegates would have to 'pay homage' to Italy. General Vaccaro, in a letter to the PCM, made the point that the World University Games could be a wonderful occasion to remind 'the Italian leadership of medical care'. [44] The Games would be one of the major events used to promote fascism for the 'Rivoluzione Fascista' (Fascist Revolution) held every ten years. [45]

## Role of the mass media

The sporting press, initially disliked by the regime because of its opposition, was re-evaluated and introduced into the wider political project; after all, the press had an important role to play in the regime's propaganda. [46, 47] Mussolini was very often depicted in the press as the bearer of new sports values. There are pictures of him horse-riding, fencing, skiing and flying, or even driving a racing car. He was never afraid to display his body. In fact, he believed that a healthy and strong body was testimony to great effort. He therefore gave instructions to Starace that all the *gerarchi* (fascist chiefs) should keep fit through physical activity. [48]

The picture of Starace passing through a hoop after a vault is still remembered in Italy. The image reflects fascist thought, which required efficient, physically active leaders because: 'Without setting an example there is no right or chance of having command'. [49] The nation had to be prepared in the event of a sudden war, not unprepared as it had been prior to the First World War.

The press was a helpful tool for the sports administration. Corruption and conflict among local powers were increasing, and they endangered the spread of the educational and moral values of sport among the younger generation. The promotion of so-called minor sports (athletics, swimming, skating) could be contrasted to the exasperated search for champions in other disciplines. An examination of the language used to report on sport and sports events in 1930s newspapers, such as *Il Littoriale, Lo Sport Fascista, Il Guerin Sportivo, Il Tifone*, makes interesting reading. There was a tendency to use Italian words with very few foreign words. They were prone to xenophobia. [50] Apart from literature on this subject, the regime was eager to follow the public's suggestions to avoid the use of foreign vocabulary. [51, 52] Many letters testify to this in the Italian State Archives. [53]

Mussolini used the radio as a means of political propaganda. In 1932 a draft law on the radio was presented to Parliament. The proposal was to create an Ente Autonomo Radiorurale (Autonomous Radio Rural Body) with a network link to radio in elementary school, as an aid to teaching. Even physical exercises were broadcast by radio. *L'Educazione fisio-psichica*, in October 1932, wrote: 'Our country shows boldness and modernity for all Italians and the teachers who will certainly make a contribution.' [54]

The songs of the girls attending the Orvieto Academy, directed by Cortiglioni, were broadcast by radio. Instructions for physical exercise was given by Mario Gotta (1907–93), the most eminent figure in physical education in postwar Italy. He obtained a first diploma at the Academy of Physical Education in Rome, then a qualification in law, and he was Head of the Central Service of GIL. In the postwar period he worked in the reconstruction of PE and sport. He was also President of the Federation of Gymnastics. In 1932, the Ente Italiano Audizione Radiofoniche (EIAR) was responsible for the radio broadcast of the Giro d'Italia (the Tour of Italy cycle race). The mass media acquired importance for the diffusion of ideas and the strengthening of consensus.

## Sport and champions

The newspapers above all created wonderful myths around athletes. When it was hard to follow a sports event, the newspapers could easily create myths about the famous champions.

Sport was emerging into a show, divorcing itself from its previous educational aspects. This was also a means of concealing the economic and political problems of society. In fact, sport was the real tool for establishing agreement among social classes. Sport was widespread among the public at large.

The fascists developed a double-track policy – that is, sport considered simultaneously as both an educational and a competitive medium. The latter aimed for achievements and high performance; it was an attempt to enhance the combative instinct in men. Emilio Servadio, author of the section on 'sport' in the *Italian Encyclopedia Trecanni*, maintained that 'competitive sport had a latent combative instinct which, if it was transformed into something else, would be seriously harmful for the society'. [55] Even Futurism showed that sport as a peaceful pastime was a 'healthy and necessary instinct', though that instinct was combative and competitive. [56, 57, 58]

The cult of Olympism was born. CONI had the most important position in sports policy in Italy and abroad; it had a fundamental role in the organization of international sports events, as well as in controlling the activities of all the federations, sports clubs, and the various associations. On the CONI Board were some IOC members. From 1934, a representative of the Ministry of Foreign Affairs attended the General Council. Sport was finally recognized as a vital element in foreign policy. Fascism actually used sport to enhance relations with friendly countries, as well as to resolve some political problems arising with other nations. The reports to the PCM on sports events were often written by Italian ambassadors abroad. [59]

Some CONI sports members were also appointed to posts abroad. For example, the Cycling Federation appointed a member to safeguard the athletes participating in international competitions and to submit them to 'strict discipline to perfect their performance'. [60] In reality, the aim was to check on opponents and to seek the best performance from Italian athletes.

From 1933, the CONI President was also PNF Secretary: 'State Sport' had now become 'Party Sport' (Royal Decree Ministry, no. 1456, 17 November 1933). The General Council was instituted on 5 October 1933, but had only an advisory role. An office for the promotion of CONI activity was established when a number of federation offices amalgamated, and Raniero Nicolai, Olympic poet in Antwerp (1920), and a refined scholar who published works on olympism and sport, apart from many collections of poems, became its Director. It also had an advisory role, but was subordinate and directly responsible to the CONI General Council. It wrote the CONI bulletins, checked the federation bulletins and was in touch with journalists. According to the appropriate article, 'the office interprets the CONI presidential directions, keeps the public informed and organises news without contradictions'. [61] The Propaganda and Press Office was already established through the *Regolamento* of 1936. It was also decided that the Office would have an archive for federation announcements, a photo archive, a sports film library, a special office for statistics; the CONI library stored a collection of plans and designs of the most important facilities. From the Report of the General Council of CONI, November 1935, we know that the Office organized weekly radio broadcasts in Eastern Africa, the Mediterranean, and North and South America 'in order to clarify the sports activities of CONI and its moral and political functions'. [62]

In 1934, CONI organized two awards: the Medaglie al valore atletico (medal for athletic merit) and the Stelle al merito sportivo (star shape pins for sporting merit). They were intended for athletes, federation presidents, military bodies, and institutions that had special functions abroad. [63] Mussolini himself made the award following the proposal of the CONI President. From 1935, the winner of a Medaglie al valore atletico received free life insurance into the bargain. [64] All this was meant as a testimony to an 'imaginary continuity . . . between the athlete and the future and to underline that sports diffusion was linked to the demographic policy of the country'. [65]

A decree of February 1934 established CONI as an institution under the PNF. As a result, CONI received government funding, which enabled it to build up its membership, bringing it into conflict with other organizations which faced a loss of large numbers of young people. The conflicts came to an end when CONI monopolized Italian sport.

In June 1934 Italy won the soccer World Cup in Rome. This served to cement further the relations between the Italian public and Mussolini, and to enhance fascism. Later that year, Mussolini made his famous speech *Agli atleti d'Italia* (To Italian Athletes) in the Via dei Trionfi. The athletes walked behind Mussolini with arms outstretched. A part of that speech can be read in the CONI brochure. 'You must be brave, chivalrous and tenacious. Remember when you compete abroad, your muscles and spirit bear the honour and prestige of the Nation.' [66]

Also in 1934, the Cassa Interna di Previdenza (CIP – Domestic Social Security) was set up in order to provide athletes with medical care for injuries. This is a good example of how the citizen's well-being was catered for under fascism. Another is the Opera Nazionale Maternità e Infanzia (National Institution for Motherhood and Childhood).

The CONI Sports Facilities Commission continued its work (its first meeting was in June 1933), examining all projects for new sports facilities (stadiums, swimming pools, etc.) according to the rules and norms 'without wasteful expense from a poor economy'. [67] The dimensions of all newly built facilities allowed for athletes to train under the best conditions. [68] There was an evident conflict between the ideas that the regime had and those the ONB had for the construction of facilities. The regime maintained that every sports facility could be exploited 'as a powerful means of promoting political ideas' and, thus, it should be exploited. [69]

Vast stadiums were built: the 'Mussolini' stadium in Turin was built in 1933 for the World University Games, the 'Littoriale' in Bologna, the stadium 'della Vittoria' in Bari, the 'Berta' in Florence, the 'Edda Ciano Mussolini' in Livorno, the 'XXVIII Ottobre' in L'Aquila, and finally the 'Città dello Sport' (City of Sport) in Rome. The latter was opened in 1932, although building work had begun in 1928. These seven stadiums were a 'sign of a fascist will to work and achieve power'. [70]

In 1934, the IOC presented the OND with an 'Olympic Cup' in recognition of its promotion of recreational activity. [71] In an article in the *La Gazzetta dello Sport* the American delegate in proposing the award said: 'We are proud of this official recognition of the Duce's recreational activity admirably led by S.E. Starace, Secretary of the Party and President of CONI.' [72]

After the war in Ethiopia in 1935, foreign policy and sports policy changed. On the one hand, Italian champions were celebrated (personalities like Learco Guerra, Primo Carnera, Gino Bartali), on the other, opponents were carefully chosen.

In the pseudo-autarky policy, the *Premio di importazione* was over, since nothing could be imported, so any sports equipment not produced domestically had to be imported from countries not subject to sanctions.

The press also pointed out that Italy under fascism would not yield to sanctions, so that Italian sport 'takes punches, responds, and does not disarm'. [73] *Lo sport fascista*, December 1935, stated: 'the fascist sports answer to sanctions is Taruffi-Rondine reaching the fastest speed of 244,869 km per hour.' No comment is needed. 'We will march straight on' – the motto of all Italians, athletes or not. [74]

If sport expressed 'comradeship, solidarity, mutual support, sincere relationships, chivalry', as Emilio Colombo wrote in *La Gazzetta dello Sport*, it would be impossible to establish sporting relations with an enemy that exhibited none of these in trying to reduce Italy to famine. Italy, therefore, had to choose really friendly nations with which to compete; the athletes should not suffer, so competitions with countries uninvolved in sanctions were arranged. This is why Italy did not take part in the World Athletics Championships held in Budapest in 1935.

The CONI General Council decided on 7 November 1935:

> Even in sport, Italy can manage on its own. Italy prefers the sincerity of foreign friends. Italian sport must develop international relations with other countries [. . .] Nevertheless, such a strong policy of sanctions is trying to destroy Italy's vitality in sports relations. Fascist Italy should offer friendship only to the most worthwhile people. Although we aim to avoid damage to sports activity, we are aware of giving up normal international relations to which our athletes have become accustomed. Such relations, in fact, are a sign of effective friendship among peoples, and they cannot be maintained when international friendship is manipulated by insidious and unfair interests. [75]

At the Olympic Games in Berlin, Italian athletes were successful with a very good team that had been trained with a view to amazing the world. The Olympics were a window through which Italian sport could show an image of harmony and national unity. Victory not only meant much stronger internal cohesion to stimulate national pride, but also that Italy could overcome sanctions.

Italy obtained impressive results in Berlin, even better than it had in Los Angeles. After this, however, performance declined. In 1938, at the soccer World Cup, the Italian team, though successful, ran into sharp opposition from anti-fascist and French refugees. [76] The previous year, in Vienna, the same kind of harassment occurred. In August 1937, when the GUF was invited to take part in the World Student Championships, students played only in soccer and fencing events, 'owing to a friendly gesture from the Organising Committee', and they did not take part in the Congress. The Student Federation administrators, though neutral, could argue that it was because they felt opposed to 'politically subversive trends'. [77] Starace wrote to the Minister of Foreign Affairs (Medici del Vascello) on 27 December 1937, and forced the GUF to resign from the World Student Federation. This decision reflected Italian political events during that period. In 1937, moreover, Italy ceased to be a member of the League of Nations.

## New trends in sports policy

Disagreement grew between Ricci and the regime regarding the new sports policy, and, in 1937, the ONB changed its name to the Gioventù Italiana del Littorio (GIL – Italian Youth of Littorio), under the PNF's control. [78] This change came through the interference of the Party. In 1933, a letter from Ricci (prot. 17295, 13 April 1933), insisted on his position towards educational and formative sport, but he was against competitive sport. He was strongly against certain gymnastics exercises introduced into competition of the Società varesina. As he put it, such exercises did not seem to have a firm and useful aim, they did not even fit in with the discipline chosen.

The regime's interests shifted from gymnastic activities to sports and military activities – which had always permeated the educational programmes of the younger generation. After the Ethiopian adventure and the Italian intervention on Franco's side in Spain, Italy found a new ally – Hitler. In February 1937, Mussolini became increasingly impressed with German might and joined the Anti-Comintern Pact with Japan and Germany. From 1 February, Italian troops adopted the typical German goose-step. Signals of war were heard, and the GIL increased the physical, and above all, the military training of young people. [79]

Renato Ricci gave up youth education to be involved in other activities: he could no longer take part in developing a sports policy which was definitely changing direction. Since Starace was elected CONI President, Ricci had felt awkward with this new situation. Starace was Ricci's adversary; and, as soon as he adopted the presidency, he declared that sport should be controlled only by sports technicians and the federations. He condemned whoever considered youth organizations 'as his own property', adding that we clearly detect this about Ricci. He then went on to say that these people were forgetting that they should be 'at the service of the régime for the honour of Italian sport'. [80]

After Ricci was dismissed, GIL was led by Starace. He talked to the Duce about the need for both unity and change in sports policy in order for Italy to become a popular nation in the world of sport. He was able to persuade Mussolini on various points to side with him against Ricci; maintained that the *Balilla* and the *Avangardisi* followed Ricci's orders too rigidly, and that the *accademisti* (Academy members) praised his name more than that of the Duce.

In this climate, the youth organization, which was more successful than the others, was abandoned to allow the growth of a more respectful and malleable body under Party directions. At the same time, GIL was the only organization for spotting potential sports talent; CONI signed several agreements with GIL with this in mind. This new policy of CONI towards GIL is shown in the 1939 Charter. In Article 2, one of the aims of the institution is to dictate technical directions to the organizations dealing with sport (i.e. GIL, GUF and OND).

Sport was defined as the 'crown of physical education'. [81] This was a way of conveying nationalist propaganda. Sport was intended to defend Italian prestige in international competition and achieve successful results; the new Italy showing itself as the best sporting race.

Fascist policy was well received abroad, as well as its sporting administration. From 1929 onwards, Germany had tried to emulate this organizational system, as did Yugoslavia. [82] In January 1923, the Bulgarian Olympic Committee abolished its old charter and adopted a new one, similar to that of CONI. [83]

The success of Italian athletes alerted a foreign audience, and many foreign delegates arrived in Italy to study the structure of the sports organizations. The academies of physical education were studied by scholars from all over the world. However, what was more remarkable was the vast number that were members of sports organizations. While the OND had two million members, the ONB, in 1936, had five million and more than five thousand facilities. Every Italian citizen of whatever age group could practice a physical activity from early childhood, passing from school to university, to recreational centres to the militia. Italy was indeed a model to emulate.

In 1939, with a new Charter changed by Royal Decree (no. 3) on 23 January 1940, CONI started to assume exclusive ownership and control of Italian sport. This process reached a decisive point with the constitution law (law no. 426, 16 February 1942). Article 11 of the previous Charter was changed through the *Foglio di disposizioni* no. 38, 26 December 1939. According to the new arrangements, the office of CONI President and that of PNF Secretary became separate positions again, although the CONI President still came under Party control. The President of CONI was designated by the Prime Minister (Head of Government) and proposed by the Party Secretary. [84] The National Council was made up of the federation presidents designated by the PNF Secretary and proposed by the CONI President and the sport-related ministries (National Education, War, Finance, etc.). Thus CONI was rigidly connected to the PNF.

Another point to emphasize is that officials with an important role in the world of sport were included in the framework of CONI. The Federation of Timekeepers, for example, in 1942 came under CONI jurisdiction. Thus records set by Italian athletes would now be officially recognized because they had been monitored by officials working under international rules and regulations.

CONI's central role in sports policy gave it a wide remit; its peripheral organization was enhanced through the creation of a provincial committee and local *Fasci di combattimento* (combative fascists). The presidents of the various provincial committees were appointed by the CONI President and the PNF Secretary. [85]

Among the Party directions to the Olympic Committee was that the Committee was to 'manage chosen forces of fascist sport in order to confirm the spiritual valour in national and international competition as well as the physical value and brilliant fighting skill of Mussolini's Italians'. When the PNF Secretary changed from Starace to Muti, the CONI President changed as well. Perhaps this was due to the increase of power of the Party Secretary. In fact, in 1937 (Royal Decree 11 January 1937 no. 4) the office of Party Secretary was amalgamated with that of State Secretary, which meant that with an increased workload, the officeholder would have less time to spend on developing sport. Therefore, the direction of sport was delegated to politically involved people. The first CONI President elected according to the new rules was Rino Parenti, assigned to the OND in 1940. The last was Raffaello Manganiello, who remained until the downfall of fascism in 1943. [86]

Among a dozen 'Olympic' federations there were six presidents who were also deputies, and four 'trusties' of the regime; in non-Olympic federations there were three presidents who were deputies, a Consul, a General Consul, and a *Primo Seniore* (Prime senior). All the presidents were in the political ranks of the PNF. The 'constitutionalization' of fascism in sport was at an end.

In January 1933, the *Carta della scuola* (School Reform) by Minister Bottai enlarged the role of GIL in school-related physical education, while CONI was responsible for Italian sport.

The disintegration of fascism had already begun when Italy won its second soccer World Cup in 1938. Mussolini's support for Hitler over the Anschluss of Austria in March 1938 had done fascism no favours abroad, and when he declared war on France and Britain in 1940 fascism was all but finished. The regime's propaganda addressed new ideas, such as Empire and Race. Meanwhile, the role of sport was diminishing.

The law of 1942 set CONI in a wider framework: it began to focus on more ambitious achievements, like the coordination and control of sports activity *whenever and wherever practical* (Art. No. 2, paragraph 2).

## The final exaltation of political sport

The final influence of the regime on sports policy was to entrust CONI with the planning of a vast sports exhibition in 1942 to celebrate the first twenty years of fascism in Italy. Bottai had submitted the original programme to Mussolini in 1935, and he had presented it officially in the *Campidoglio* (City hall) in October 1936. The International Exhibition Bureau had already accepted the Italian proposal for an international exhibition to be held in 1941. Legislation measures laying out clear guidelines for the programme followed, and a General Commissioner was appointed. At the end of 1936 and 1937 a provisional programme was presented stating that in the second session, in the *Città delle nazioni* (City of Nations), an international exhibition would be held. The exhibition had previously been called *Olimpiade delle civilà* (civil Olympics) and, when the war started, it was changed to *Esposizione della pace* (peace exhibition). [87]

CONI's role was to emphasize the results achieved by the various athletes in their respective sports disciplines. [88] A session called 'Records and International victories' was also arranged. Puccio Pucci, Secretary of the Committee, announced the construction of a model of a city of sport provided with the most up-to-date facilities. Along with Pucci, the CONI President, first Rino Parenti, then Raffaello Manganiello and nine federation presidents were involved in the Organizing Commission.

In the session 'Records and International victories' (there were other sessions: Eugenics of sport; Development of sports facilities; Sport practice; Materials, Equipment), Enrioc Luciani explained that it was intended to celebrate the sports success of Italian athletes, compared to those of other nations. The list of the athletes would be given with their respective performance, and pictures would show the various triumphs set against an enthusiastic audience, 'mainly foreign'. [89]

This would be the last act of fascist sports policy implemented by the vast propaganda machine created by the regime before war intervened.

At a national level sport survived; its organization was due to the PNF in northern Italy and in the Social Republic of Salò. Rome was responsible for organizing some sports and, at the end of the war, Giulio Onesti was appointed Commissioner for this part of the programme. [90]

But the rebuilding of sport in postwar Italy opens a new chapter in the history of national sport as an expression of civilization and of unique educational values for the younger generation. The political exploitation of sport was over; Italy now faced the construction of a new sporting civilization.

## References

1. De Felice, R. (1973) Mussolini il duce, I., *Gli anni del consenso 1929–1936*, Einaudi, Torino, pp. 50–1.
2. Ulzega, M.P. and Teja, A. (1993) *L'addestramento ginnico-militare nell'Esercito Italiano (1861–1945)*, Stato Maggiore dell'Esercito, Rome, p. 32.
3. Teja, A. (1993) L'instruction à la guerre dans l'éducation physique et le sport en Italie de l'Etat liberal à la fin du fascisme: le combat comme idéologie, in Renson, R., Gonzales Aja, T., Andrieu, G., Lämmer, M., Park, R (eds), *Actas del Congreso Internacional ISHPES 1991. las Palmas de Gran Canaria 31 / V-6 / VI.1991*, INEF, Madrid, pp. 282–92.
4. Partito Nazionale Fascista, (PNF) (1924) Gruppo di competenza per l'educazione fisica. Relazione sulla prima applicazione della riforma dell'educazione fisica nelle Scuole medie. *L'Educazione fisio-psichica*. **VI**(2) (1924) pp. 1–12.
5. Setta, S. (1986) *Renato Ricci*, Il Mulino, Bologna.
6. Di Donato, M. (1984) *Storia dell'educazione fisica e sportiva. Indirizzi fondamentali*, Studium, Roma, pp. 190–2.
7. L'educazione fisica e lo sport inquadrati. *L'educazione fisio-psichica*, **VIII**(4) p. 57.
8. Teja, *op. cit.*, pp. 286–8.
9. Di Donato, *op cit.*, p. 191.
10. Ferrara, P. (1992) *L'Italia in palestra*, La Meridiana, Roma, p. 228.
11. Letter from Renato Ricci No. 25982/A7, 10 May 1929 to the Council of Ministers President, in Archivio Centrale dello Stato (ACS), *PCM – gabinetto (gab.), 1928–1930*, f. 15.2–3, no. 6525.

12. PNF (1928) La Scuola Superiore ginnico-sportiva inaugurata dal Duce. *L'educazione fisio-psichica*, **IX** (5), pp. 73–4.
13. Morgagni, M., Discipliniamo lo sport. *L'educazione fisio-psichica*, **X** (4) (1929) pp. 53–4.
14. Preve, B., Ave Caesar . . . *L'educazione fisio-psichica*, **IX** (9) (1928) pp 144–8.
15. CONI-EIAR (1938) *Cronache radiofoniche dello sport, anni XIV e XV dell'era fascista*, Arti Grafiche Trinacria, Roma, p. 119.
16. Le deliberazioni prese ieri nella seduta del Congresso del CONI. *Il Littoriale*, 20 May 1932, p. 6.
17. Guglielmotti, U., A noi giovani. *Roma fascista*, 1 April 1928, quoted in Fabrizio, F. (1976) *Sport e fascismo. La politica sportiva del regime 1924–1936*. Guaraldi, Rimini-Firenze, p. 35.
18. Circular GUF No. 10, 27 January 1930, in ACS, *PNF – Direttorio Nazionale Segreteria GUF*, b.46, f.619 Circolari GUF 1930'.
19. Zangrandi, R. (1962) *Lungo viaggio attraverso il fascismo*, Feltrinelli, Roma, pp. 381–7 e 637–713. It includes a list of the winners of the 'Littorriali della Cultura e dell'Arte'.
20. Marani Toro, I and A. (1977) *Storia degli ordinamenti sportivi*, Giuffré, Milan, pp. 222–4.
21. Ferrario, L., Puntare su Roma per i giochi del 1936. *La Gazzetta dello Sport*, 12 June 1930.
22. ENIT-CONI (1939) *Roma olimpiaca*, F. Capriotti, Roma tip, p. 1.
23. Ibid., p. 45.
24. Gli studenti italiani a Parigi. Precise disposizioni di S.E. Turati. *Il Popolo d'Italia*, 7 August 1928 quoted in Fabrizio, *op. cit.*, p. 26.
25. Ferretti, L. (1928) *Il libro dello sport*, Libreria del Littorio, Roma-Milano, p. 228.
26. Storica celebrazione. *La Gazzetta dello sport*, 28–29 October 1933.
27. La Federazione del Medici Sportivi. Le proposte del Comitato Tecnico e le disposizioni dell'on Turati. *L'Educazione Fisio-psichica*, **XI** (3), (1929), p. 36.
28. Circular No. 51 prot. 715/y 17 September 1930, in (ACS), *PNF Direttorio Nazionale, Segreteria GUF* b.46–f.619 'Circolari GUF 1930.
29. Circular No. 53, 18 September 1930, Ibid.
30. *Leandro Arpinati illustrò alle Camera il preciso concetto dello sport fascista: creare dalla massa il campione, alfiere della Patria nel mondo* (Leandro Arpinati showed to the Chamber the concept of fascist sport: creating a champion from the masses, a bishop of the country in the world). *La Gazzetta dello Sport*, 19 March 1933.
31. Lo sport e Arpinati. *Lo Sport fascista* **VI** (4), (1933) pp,. 9–1.
32. Lo spirito della nuova Italia e gli atleti di Mussolini. *Il Popolo d'Italia*, 10 September 1932 quoted in Fabrizio *op. cit.*, p. 60.
33. Mussolini, B., Marciare in nome d'Italia, in Susmel, E. and D. (eds), *Opera omnia*. Sansoni Firenze-Roma, 1951–63, vol. XXV, pp. 237–8.
34. Note for the Head of Government, Presidency of the Council of Ministries, 20 December 1932, in ACS, *PCM – gab., 1931–1933*, f.114–3, no. 7607 'Marsiglia (Francia). Incontro di calcio italo-francese genn. o marzo 1933)'.
35. Note for the Head of Government, 26 December 1932, in ACS, *PCM - gab., 1931–1933*, f. 14–3, no. 7595 'Corsa ciclistica Milano–Torino–Nizza'.
36. In ACS, *PCM - gab., 1931–1933*, f.114–3, no. 6102 'Partita di calcio Italo-Cecoslovacca a Praga Incidenti'.
37. Telexpress no. 221125/132, 9 July 1932, ibid.
38. Letter prot. No. 6924, 22 September 1932 for PCM, in ACS, ibid.
39. In ACS, *PNF Direttorio Nazionale segreteria dei GUF*, b. 1, f.5 'Conferenza internazionale degli studenti – Delegazione italiana'.
40. Ibid.

41. Ibid.
42. Ibid.
43. Colombo, E., Lo sport italiano nel mondo. Conversando con Alberto Sonacossa sul congresso del CIO. *La Gazzetta dello Sport*, 13 June 1933.
44. Both letters are in ACS, *PCM - gab.*, 1931–1933, f.14–3, No. 8365 'Torino'. Convegno internazionale di medicina sportiva, 6–8 September 1933
45. Letter of the Ministry for Home Affairs, General Direction of Public Health, prot. 20173.c.280/02250, 17 July 1933 to PCM, in ACS, idem.
46. De Grazia, V. (1981) *Consenso e Cultura di massa nell'Italia fascista*, Laterza, Roma-Bari; and the extensive bibliography.
47. Del Buono, O. (1971) (a cura di), *Eia, eia, alalà. La Stampa italiana sotto il fascismo 19190043*, Feltrinelli, Milano.
48. *Foglio di disposizioni* No. 1083, 7 June 1938.
49. Ferretti, L., Gerachi atleti. *Lo sport fascista*, **12** (8) (1939), p. 10.
50. Fabrizio, *op. cit.*, pp. 161–5.
51. Morelli, P. (1933), *Il barbaro dominio*, Hoepli, Milano.
52. Bianchi, A.G. (1926) *Evviva lo sport*, Istituto Educativo Italiano, Milano.
53. ACS, *PCM - gab.*, 1934–1936, f.3, 2–2, No. 5488, dott. Francesco Buttaro: *'Per sostituzione parola* 'Sportman' *in* 'Juvenludo'. (Prof. Francesco Buttaro asked the President of the Council of Ministers in 1935 to use 'juvenludo' instead of 'sportsman' (*sic*).
54. La radio nella scuola e gli insegnanti. *L'Educazione fisio-psichica*, **XIV** (1) (1932), p. 12.
55. Servadio, E. (1936), 'Sport', in *Enciclopedia Italiana Treccani*, Roma, vol. 32, p. 416.
56. Corra, B., Fascismo e sport. *Il Popolo d'italia*, 2 April 1924.
57. Ferrara, *op. cit.*, pp. 195–202, for relations between futurism and sport.
58. Brunamontiwi, G., Il movimento aggressivo molla del futurismo. In *Lo Sport italiano*, **1** (12) (1994), pp. 140–3.
59. Extensive documentation may be found in the State Archives in Rome.
60. *Lo sport in regime fascista 28 ottobre 1922–28*, October 1935, special issue of *Lo sport fascista*, Rome 1035, pp. 51–2.
61. *Annuario Italiano dello Sport* (Italian Sports Year-book), CONI, Roma, 1936, pp. 115–16.
62. Ibid., p. 120.
63. *Foglio d'ordini* No. 117, 20 December 1934.
64. *Foglio d'ordini* No. 138, 20 June 1935.
65. *Annuario Italiano dello Sport*, p. 1080.
66. Mussolini, B. (1940) *Scritti e Discorsi*, vol. VIII, Hoepli, Milano, pp. 141–2.
67. Alassio, A. (1934) Lo sport nello stato fascista. Regio Istituto Superiore di Scienze economiche e Commercial of the University of Genoa – Istituto Superiore di Scienze Economiche e Commerciali. Degree thesis. p. 36.
68. Ibid., pp. 36–7.
69. Ibid., p. 36.
70. Otto stadi italiani segno della volontà di lavoro e di potenza della Patria fascista saranno teatro domani degli ottavi di finale del più grande torneo del mondo. *La Gazzetta dello Sport*, 27 May 1934.
71. Ferretti, L. (1951) *Lo Sport*, l'Arnia, Rome, p. 206.
72. La coppa olimpica per il 1934 assegnata dal CIO all'opera Nazionale Dopolavoro. *La Gazzetta dello Sport*, 10–11 June 1933.
73. Colombo, E., *Lo sport incassa, risponde e non disarma. La Gazzetta dello Sport*, 8 November 1935.

74. La squadra italiana parte par Garmish. *Il Popolo d'Italia*, 18 January 1936, quoted in Fabrizio, *op. cit.*, p. 67.

75. Cronache radiofoniche dello sport, CONI ed., in *Annuario italiano dello Sport*, p. 123.

76. Papa, A. and Panico, G. (1993) *Storia sociale del calcio in Italia*, Ill Mulino, Venezia, p. 197.

77. Lettera del Vicesegretario dei GUF Mezzasoma all PCM, 2 August 1937, in ACS, *PCM-gab.*, 1937–1939, f. 14–4, No. 1838 'Parigi. Giuochi Universitari internazionali – agosto 1937. XV'

78. ACS, *PGM - gab.*, 1931–1933, f. 14–3, No. 8270 'Varese. XVI Concorso Ginnastico Federale Internazionale organizzato dalla Società Varesina di ginnastica e scherma 8.9.10 settembre 1933'.

79. Teja, *op. cit.*, p. 289–90.

80. Le direttive del CONI tracciate dall'on. Achille Starace nella riunione dei rappresentanti delle Federazioni. *La Gazzetta dello Sport*, 6 October 1933.

81. CONI-EIAR (1938) *Contributo dell'Italia alla storia dello sport*, CONI, Roma, p. 13.

82. Kruger, A., Fasci e croci uncinate. *Lancillotto e Nausica*, **VIII** (1–2) (1991), p. 95.

83. La riunione del Comitato Olimpico Bulgaro e la proposta di modificare lo statuo attuale copiando lo statuto del CONI Italiano. *La Gazzetta dello Sport*, 4 January 1933.

84. Letter of the Political Secretary of PNF No. 1/664, 6 December 1940, signed by Alessandri, in ACS, *PCM - gab.*, 1940–1943, f.3 2/5 368, s.f. 1–2 'Comitato Olimpico Nazionale'.

85. Marani toro, *op. cit.* pp. 227–8

86. *Foglio di disposizioni* No. 38, 26 December 1939, signed by Ettore Muti.

87. Exhibition Catalogue *E 42, L'Esposizione universale di Roma. Utopia e scenario del regime*, organized by the State Archives, in April–May 1987.

88. Letter from the Exhibition Organizers, Office for Foreign Participation, sums up relations with CONI, 9 November 1940, in ACS, *EU 42*, b. 989. f. 9768, s.f.6 ins. 3 'Servizio Organizzazione Mostra. Mostra dello Sport'.

89. Lineamenti programmatici per il settore nazionale della Mostra Internazionale dello sport. Memorandum 20 April 1942, in ACS, *EC 42*, b. 989, f. 9768 s.f.6, ins. 5, pp. 7–8.

90. De Juliis, T., Il CONI dalla tragedia della guerra all'inizio della ricostruzione, 25 July 1946. *Lo sport italiano*, (11) (1994) (insert), for a recent article on the history of the structure of CONI and sport in Italy.

# Chapter 10

# The Belgian Catholic gymnastic movement in its international context, 1908–1940

*Jan Tolleneer**

Je vous bénis parce que vous fuyez l'oisiveté , parce que dans ces concours fraternels et amicaux, de quelques pays que vous soyez venues, vous provoquez une sainte émulation que vous pouvez porter sur le terrain de la vertu.

Mais je vous recommande la modération, parce que c'est en elle que résiste proprement la vertu, parce que vous ne pouvez vous faire du tort à vous mêmes, parce que vous ne pouvez pas négliger vos études et vos devoirs religieux. Sans un solide fondement de piété, vous ne pourrez conserver les sentiments de votre foi. [1]

(I bless you because you flee from idleness, because, from whatever country you come to participate in these friendly and fraternal contests, you encourage a moral rivalry which you can carry over into the wider sphere of virtue.

But I recommend moderation to you because there will you find true virtue, because you must not harm yourselves, because you must not neglect your studies and your religious duties. Without a solid foundation of piety, you cannot retain your real faith.)

Thus spoke the Pope to a vast assembly of Catholic gymnasts who had gathered in Rome in 1908 to celebrate the fiftieth anniversary of the ordination of Pius X as a priest. His message was predictably both supportive and cautionary, encouraging Catholic youth to take healthy exercise whilst warning against an excessive worship of sport for its own sake. Among the participants listening to him were athletes from fifteen French gymnastic clubs and seventeen in Belgium. The relatively high proportion of Belgians was significant. For it was in Belgium that a particularly lively enthusiasm for Catholic gymnastics and international collaboration was to be found. In these early years the relationship between French and Belgian Catholic gymnasts was close and played an important part in the negotiations leading to the formation of the first international Catholic gymnastic organization in 1911. Hence the first part of this article looks at the international context largely in terms of Franco-Belgian relations. However, after the First World War attention

* The author wishes to thank Richard Holt for his help in discussing and translating the text.

shifted towards closer relations between western and central Europe. In the Belgian case this led to a special interest in the Orel movement in Czechoslovakia and it is this aspect which is explored in the second half of the chapter.

## Before the First World War

The Fédération Belge Catholique de Gymnastique (FBCG) was founded as early as 1892, some ten years before its French national counterpart. [2] From around the turn of the century there were regular contacts between French and Belgian Catholic gymnasts. On the occasion of the twelfth national FBCG festival in 1903 in the city of Tournai, close to the French border, a number of French clubs were present. A Belgian report of the festival stated that Monsieur Michaux, the President of the Fédération Gymnastique et Sportive des Patronages de France (FGSPF) 'présente les sociétés de France á leurs soeurs Belges et offre, au nom des 20,000 gymnastes français, le salut de la paix et de la fraternité. La Belgique, a repondu M. Delrue, rend la salut á la nation soeur. Que ce jour de fête scelle leur amitié. "Vive la France! Vive la Belgique!" Ce cri est répété avec enthousiasme par tous les gymnastes présents.' [3] ('presented the French participating clubs to their Belgian sister clubs and extended his greetings of peace and fraternity in the name of 20 000 French Catholic gymnasts. [For the Belgians, Monsieur Delrue President of the Belgian organizing committee] replied, sealing the friendship of the two countries with a cry of "Vive La France! Vive la Belgique!" – a cry that was taken up with enthusiasm by all those gymnasts present.'). The ensuing speeches made reference to the friendly role of France after the foundation of the Belgian state and Belgium's sympathy for France in the Franco-Prussian War of 1870–1.[4] However, despite this Franco-Belgian friendship, Belgium was a neutral state and this probably made it easier for the FBCG to act as a focus for the formation of a wider Catholic federation.

The first decade of the 20th century was very active as far as the growth of Catholic gymnastics was concerned, climaxing in the international meeting in Rome in 1908. This event galvanized the enthusiasm of the large Belgian contingent. Here was a vision of what Catholic gymnastics might be: a great international force, a focus for youth and a source of regeneration in an increasingly secular world. This was an era of internationalism – of the Olympic Movement, for example, and the Scout movement, which began in the same year as the great Catholic gathering in Rome. As John Hoberman has recently noted, there was a large and little studied growth of international organizations of all kinds around the turn of the century. [5] Alongside this Utopian self-image, there co-existed a strong male-dominated nationalism which urged reconciliation of class conflict and political stability. Hence, just as the Scouts and the Olympians sought royal patronage and aristocratic support, so the new Catholic gymnasts naturally looked to the Pope. In 1908 their hopes were fulfilled, which explains the ecstatic tone of Belgian reporting of the meeting in Rome: Sa Sainteté s'avança pour bénir une derrière fois les gymnastes; ceux-ci s'agenouillèrent en un silence solennel. Mais tout à coup des rangs de cette jeunesse s'élevèrent des acclamations enthousiastes, les chapeaux s'agitèrent dans l'air et, comme sur un signal donné, tous les participants se précipitèrent vers la tribune de Pie X et, en un transport de joie, tendirent les bras vers Lui, pendant que les cris 'Vive Pie X' et 'Vive Sa Sainteté' s'échappèrent de centaines de jeunes poitrines. Pleurant d'émotion en présence de tant d'attachement filial le Saint Père se retourna à plusieurs reprises . . . [6]:

> His Holiness came forward a last time to bless the gymnasts, who knelt in solemn silence. But suddenly the lines of the young stood up, cheering wildly, hats thrown in the air and, as if given a signal, converged on the Papal platform, joyfully extending their arms to him, hundreds of young hearts shouting 'Long Live Pius X!', 'Long Live His Holiness!' Weeping with emotion at such filial feeling, the Holy Father turned to them several times . . .

It was through the preparation of this gathering that the idea for a more permanent organization came into being. Reflecting on the success of the gymnastic festival in Rome, the Board of the FBCG noted that 'nous voudrions voir organiser momentanément quelque chose de plus pratique avec les pays voisins. Un mouvement fédéral sérieux se dessine dans les Pays-Bas et se manifeste dans la Prusse Rhénane catholique. On connaît l'organisation française et l'association catholique des sociétés du Nord de la France. Ces deux organismes sont tout disposés à nous aider pour conclure cette nouvelle entente.' [7] ('We would now like to organize something more practical amongst neighbouring countries. A significant federal movement is underway in the Netherlands and the Prussian Catholic Rhineland. We also know the French organization and the Catholic association of clubs in the north of France.') The Belgians saw an opportunity to co-ordinate these developments, remarking that there was 'a disposition to help across the border'.

France seemed an especially promising partner for Belgium. Both were characterized by a strong tradition of Catholicism. [8] In the last decades of the 19th century the Catholic Church and the entire Catholic community in both countries encountered powerful opposition from both Liberals and Socialists. From 1897, which was an important year from an anticlerical point of view both in France and in Belgium, there was a concerted effort to break Church power, especially by changing the national education system. The counter-reaction of the Catholics took similar forms on both sides of the border. An important element in this was the gradual creation of all kinds of socio-cultural activities and organizations, amongst them gymnastic clubs. In depicting these developments from the perspective of international Catholic relations, several key issues arise. Can one, for example, compare the forms of nationalism and militarism in both countries? Did the federations work in the same ideological and political context? Did they learn from each other as far as their physical activities and the federation's structure were concerned?

In the tense period before the First World War physical exercises and group discipline were dominated by the idea of patriotism and preparation for military service. Strength, self-control and group consciousness were indispensable not only for external national defence but also to defend the Catholic Church against its secular enemies. Catholics took a hard line against the more manifest forms of anticlericalism, with included rivalry and criticism of the non-Catholic gymnastic world. In both countries the Catholic Gymnastic Federation was a direct 'political' answer to the so-called 'neutral' organizations. The official Belgian gymnastic federation, the Fédération Belge de Gymnastique, was presided over by Nicolaas Jan Cupérus, who was a close friend of Charles Cazalet, the chairman of the Union des Sociétés de Gymnastique de France (USGF) [9] The Catholic national bodies were in many ways copies of these non-Catholic national bodies. They performed the same kinds of gymnastic exercises and were structured in the same way on national, regional and local levels.

What applied to the national level also applied at the international level. For Cupérus also presided over the Fédération Européenne de Gymnastique (what was later to become Fédération Internationale de Gymnastique). It was this body which provided both the example and the rationale for the foundation of the Union Internationale des Oeuvres Catholiques d'Education Physique in 1911 (the UIOCEP or what came to be known after the Second World War as the Fédération Internationale Catholique d'Education Physique or FICEP). Both France and Belgium played a major role in the foundation and the long history of this international federation, the first vice-presidents of which were Baron de Diedonné from Belgium and Dr Michaux from France. [10]

In Belgium the clerical–anticlerical confrontation did not come to a head in quite the same way as in France. The hard-line liberal government of Prime Minister Frère-Orban lasted only from 1879 to 1884. This government's educational reform caused an 'acute' struggle, a real battle between Belgian clericals and anticlericals, but after five years the Catholics regained their political power and monopolized the government until the First World War. Hence the Catholic Church in Belgium operated in a broadly favourable political context in the late 19th and early 20th centuries, whereas the French Catholics were more or less permanently excluded from power until the First World War. French Catholics working through socio-cultural and youth organizations like the gymnastic clubs found their energies fully absorbed by internal conflicts, especially after the separation of Church and State in 1905. [11] Their Belgian counterparts, however, were in a more established position and could take the time to develop a wider European dimension and cooperate with the wishes of the Papacy in promoting Catholic youth work through physical culture. Catholic cultural life was rich and lively in Belgium amongst adults as well as the young. Youth sections, in fact, formed only a minority in the FBCG at that time. Apart from a number of patronages or youth groups, there was a wide variety of organizations such as the so-called 'Cercles Catholiques' et 'Gardes Catholiques' ('Catholic Circles' and the 'Catholic Guards') which taken together created a powerful network or *pillier* (pillar) to use the useful term developed by Belgian and Dutch historians and sociologists to explain the development of self-contained social worlds – the Catholic, the Liberal and the Socialist. Without leaving the *pillier* organizations like the Catholic, gymnasts could also develop more independent structures based upon specific activities. The *pillier* provided both the opportunities for wider international contacts and the freedom to adapt themselves to this end. [12]

However, the Catholic *pillier* could not isolate itself from the diplomatic and military realities of the age. Belgian Catholics had a divided duty. On the one hand there was the need to promote international contacts and a common structure to take advantage of the great strengths of the Church in terms of its established organization and patronage. Hence the significance of the international assembly of gymnasts in Rome and the setting up of a coordinating body afterwards to bring Catholic gymnasts together from all over Europe which led to the founding in 1911 of the UIOCEP. On the other hand there was the inescapable fact that Catholics no longer belonged to a supranational Christendom as in the Middle Ages but were members of rival nations with strong and conflicting interests. This is what largely determined the pattern of international contacts before the First World War as far as the Belgian Catholic gymnasts were concerned. It was not simply a matter of language that brought the French and the Belgians together. After all, despite the official predominance of French, more than half of Belgium was Dutch-speaking. It was rather that Belgium and France were liberal democracies with open borders facing the threat of a new German Reich based upon an authoritarian control of parliament by the monarchy and the army. Moreover, this was a Protestant state. German Catholics were a large but isolated minority. They were no longer persecuted, as in the days of Bismarck, and had parliamentary representation through the Centre Party, but they had never gained the position of influence in Germany that their numbers warranted.

Hence both Belgium and France had a common interest in drawing closer together before 1914. The French Catholics were strongly nationalist. Their movement and its state counterpart were partly founded on the wave of 'Revanche' that spread through France after the loss of Alsace-Lorraine. [13] In the Catholic camp this chauvinism mingled with a religious militancy. The defence of the fatherland was always bracketed together with the defence of religion. Youth had to be prepared physically and morally. This explains the success of the Catholic gymnastics and sports clubs, especially in regions such as Lorraine where tension increased from day to day. In this respect one can also easily understand the role played by Jeanne d'Arc as a symbol of the defence of France on the one hand and the defence of religion on the other.

French militancy also spread to the FBCG whose journal *Belgica* published several texts written by Paul Michaux, or themes such as the improvement of race and the reinforcement of 'God and the Fatherland'. [14] Yet in Belgium, where the threat to the Church and to the integrity of the national territory was perceived as less immediate than in France, patriotism took milder forms in keeping with the official statute of neutrality of 1839. Belgian Catholic patriotism had a somewhat more romantic character than the fiercely militant French, contenting itself largely with flags, songs and speeches. In addition, the divisions within Belgium between the linguistic communities weakened the force of a more cohesive state nationalism. [15]

As the international situation grew more tense before 1914, the more 'neutral' patriotism that had formerly held sway was increasingly overtaken by a real sense of alarm. Despite their religious status as subjects of Rome, the Catholics – ironically in many ways rather like the members of the socialist Second International – began to put the defence of the nation above all else. Under a Catholic dominated government the Belgium law on military service was changed in 1909 and in 1913. As a result a growing number of young men had to serve in the army and the requirements for preparation for military service expanded. A 'union sacrée' was in the process of taking shape as both the State as well as the Catholic gymnastic federations took on the task of the physical and moral preparation of youth for war. The Belgian federation not only dealt with gymnastics but also with weapons exercises. This was even reflected in the federation's official name at that time: the Fédération Nationale des Sociétés Catholiques de Gymnastique et d'Armes de Belgique. However, the weapons exercises were limited to discipline and drill exercises. Unlike the French Catholics, the Belgians never put real shooting or fencing competitions into their programme. Nor did the Belgians agree to incorporate modern sports selectively as the French did. French Catholics simply could not afford to take the purist line followed in Belgium where sports like football and athletics were still looked upon as dangerous foreign innovations. The French had to capture the young to ensure both internal and external security and were prepared to make compromises to do so. Hence in Belgium a separate Catholic sports body came into existence in 1906. [16]

With the outbreak of the First World War, the life of the FBCG was severely disrupted. During the occupation, the publication of *Belgica* was abandoned and regional and national festivals were not held. Local gymnastic activities continued, but at a restricted level because many members had left to join the army at the front in that small section of Belgium held by the allies around Ypres. A number of them, who were taken as prisoners of war, stayed in contact with those who were left at home under German occupation. A remarkable collection of letters written by these Catholic gymnasts, which are part of the FBCG archives now kept at the University of Leuven, show how activity was sustained during the most difficult circumstances. The correspondence, for example, of Léon Rosier of Kessel-lo, who was to become a key figure in Catholic gymnastics in the 1930s, revealed a great effort to sustain a social and cultural life at local level, of which organizing gymnastics was an important part. Rosier not only took a major role in running local Catholic youth clubs but also became the secretary of the football club and stage manager of the drama society. Contacts such as these help explain the speed with which a full programme of events resumed after the war and the anti-German tone which was expressed in them.

## Interwar relations with Germany

The first meeting of the UIOCEP after the war took place in Paris in 1920 from 8 to 10 August, a few days before the opening of the VII Olympiad at Antwerp. At this meeting it was decided to exclude from UIOCEP all those who had taken up arms against the allies, [17] a decision supported not only by the anti-German sentiment of France and Belgium, on whose soil Germany had chosen to fight the war, but also by countries such as Italy, which had suffered heavy casualties on the Austrian front. Here the Catholic international gymnastic community chose to follow the line taken by the IOC, which had given the Games to Belgium in 1920 partly as a reward for the suffering of the Belgian people under German occupation and had excluded Germany and its allies from participation. Belgian gymnasts participated in the Antwerp Olympics despite the critical attitude to sport they had formerly displayed and which continued to play an important part in the movement between the wars.

These Olympics were no mere sporting event; they were an expression of national thanksgiving and rebirth for the entire international community. [18] There was a significant Catholic presence and an opening mass was conducted by Cardinal Mercier, the leader of Belgium's Catholics, who addressed athletes and gymnasts alike, praising the role of physical culture, shorn of fanaticism, as a wise preparation both for the rigours of war and the need of peace. In a thinly veiled attack on Germany, Mercier, who had been a vocal supporter of gymnastics as well as sport in general, expressed the hope that 'l'athlétisme ne soit pas la traduction brutale, orgueilleuse de la conception Nietschéene de la vie' ('Athleticism does not have to follow a Nietzchean conception of life where brutality and arrogance reign.'). Giving thanks for the victory of the allies, he added: 'Nous ne sommes pas, Dieu merci, des sauvages, nous nous piquons de civiliser ceux qui le sont restes.' [19] ('We are not savages, thank God, and pride ourselves on civilizing those who remain so.') As the Cardinal, the King of Belgium, Pierre de Coubertin (the founder of the modern Olympics) and other dignitaries followed by the participants and the spectators entered the Olympic stadium, they were confronted by a large statue of a Belgian soldier throwing a grenade and the date of 11 November 1918 inscribed beneath. [20]

Hosting the Olympic Games, however, offered only a brief respite from the more important issue facing the country – reconstruction after the war. Belgium, like the rest of Europe, was suffering from social and economic deprivation – life was financially difficult; transport especially was expensive and hard to find – which could be countered only by finding a new political balance. Universal male suffrage, introduced in 1919, had produced a striking shift of opinion to the left and this had put Catholics on their guard politically, but somewhat paradoxically, [21] partly as a result of this heightened climate of anticlericalism and partly as a general European reaction to the privations of war. Catholic gymnastics like other sports and physical culture clubs enjoyed extremely rapid growth. The annual report of 1921, when they held their first postwar national gathering at Spa, [22] listed only 106 local societies with a total of 4200 adult members and 4000 youth members, but the following year 64 new clubs were either formed or re-formed and had applied to affiliate. [23, 24]

As the immediate postwar period passed, the intense anti-German sentiment of Belgian gymnasts and the UIOCEP began to weaken. Germany was taking steps towards democracy and had accepted, albeit reluctantly, the duty to fulfil the demands of the Treaty of Versailles. After the occupation of the Ruhr and the collapse of the German economy in 1924, there was a broad international effort to support conciliation through the mutual guarantee of frontiers at Locarno and a tentative move was made to accept Germany back into the community of nations. Germany was admitted to the League of Nations in 1926, and allowed to re-enter Olympic competition in 1928. Similarly, in 1927, German Catholics were re-admitted to an international gymnastic movement over which Belgium continued to exercise considerable administrative influence. [25, 26, 27] In terms of gymnastic technique there was a sharp decline in military-style exercises and army influence, and a greater willingness to accept different approaches, including the Swedish gymnastics of Ling. The UIOCEP, in fact, dropped the words 'for military preparation' from its official title in 1924.

The acceptance of Germany was not easy, however, as Belgium had been occupied for almost all of the war, with serious loss of life and property. In particular, the anti-German sentiment of the Belgian President of the UIOCEP, Felix Van de Kerckhove, who had been elected in 1920 just before the Olympic Games, proved unacceptable for an international Catholic organization, [28] and when the journal *Belgica* published several of his speeches which were strongly patriotic [29] he had no alternative but to resign his UIOCEP post. With the apparent democratization of Germany under the Weimar Republic, such attitudes were incompatible with the wider interest of Rome in promoting good relations within the 'Catholic family'. It is interesting to note that this relatively uncritical attitude of Germany continued after the advent of Hitler and the 'integration' of the Catholic sports movement into the Nazi system. Fear of communism and the imperatives of Belgian neutrality meant that Belgian Catholic gymnasts were very reluctant to speak out against Germany: indeed, there was a deafening silence on the subject of the German threat to peace. Even in 1938, when the rise of an expansionist Nazi state was quite evident, the only comment that the Belgian Catholics would make was that it was with regret that we saw 'the (Catholic) federations disappeared recently in Germany, Italy and Austria as a result of their dissolution by the authoritarian governments'. [30] This was one of the rare acknowledgements of the international difficulties of Catholics under fascism and even then it appeared only as an explanation of the reduced list of member countries. There was no further political comment. Why was this? The challenge from Germany in the later 1930s was even more dangerous than before the First World War. But the circumstances had changed and the situation was complex. The Catholic attitude to Germany was determined partly by the fact that they, like the fascists, were intensely anti-communist and partly by the general Belgian policy of neutrality. Furthermore, the strength of nationalist feeling among certain Flemish Catholic gymnasts, which had already manifested itself in the creation of a separate federation, meant that it would not have been possible to take a strong line against Germany without causing internal divisions. To keep the Belgian Catholic gymnasts together and united, it was necessary to keep a low profile.

## Belgium and Orel

For most of the interwar period as far as international contacts were concerned, the Belgians seemed more interested in the new successor states, in particular Czechoslovakia, than in Germany. Before the war Czech nationalism and desire for independence from the Habsburg empire had been powerfully displayed in the Sokol (falcon) movement, a gymnastic body founded as early as 1862 and which had 120 000 members by 1914. However, it was a newer Catholic counterpart of Sokol, Orel (eagle), founded in 1902, that began to attract attention in Belgium. Before the First World War, Orel with only 12 000 members was not widely known, but after the war the readers of *Belgica* were confronted with astonishing photographs of gymnastic events and mass displays by the Orel gymnasts. In 1922 Orel affiliated to the UIOCEP and asked it to become patron of the *Orelsky Slet* (Orel festival), a competition to be held in Brno later that year. The federation agreed and made the festival a recognized event and an official competition. It was this festival in particular, which caught Belgian attention. Never before had they seen such room for 120 000 spectators and a field area of 130 000 sq.m. where 10 000 children could be involved and 10 000 adult gymnasts could compete. There were colourful processions in the streets of Brno with male and female gymnasts in national costumes. [31, 32, 33] This rapid growth of Czech Catholic gymnastics painted a hopeful picture for French and Belgian activists. It coincided with the papal launch of Catholic Action, an offensive against the evils of modern society, which in a wide variety of forms involving men and women, young and old, was to place far greater stress than before on initiative from the laity. [34] Catholic Action strived for a rich, sociable life so as to be able to resist the temptations of a modern popular culture epitomized by American cinema, secularism, consumerism and a general trend towards permissiveness which was evident in, for example, the image of the 'new woman'. Orel, as we shall see, was able to offer Belgian gymnasts an example of how solid Catholic values could be combined with a more dynamic attitude to change, integrating, for example, the full Holy Mass into its ceremonies on the one hand and accepting the participation of women on the other.

Alongside Yugoslavia, Czechoslovakia started to play a major role in the General Assembly of the UIOCEP, sometimes coming into conflict with senior Belgian figures. These newcomers had all kinds of suggestions and remarks which were sometimes critical of established policy. For example, a particular problem here concerned the place of women. From 1927 onwards there were tense and difficult discussions concerning what form female gymnastics should take and their place in the wider Catholic world stemming from the different conceptions of the place of gender in gymnastics. Enjoying flourishing female sections itself, Orel could not accept that female gymnasts were excluded from international competition by the central Church authorities who were notoriously conservative in these matters.

The FBCG found itself involved in the controversy. Catholic gymnasts in Belgium had been slower than their progressive Czech counterparts in coming to terms with female gymnastics. It was not until after the First World War that female divisions of existing clubs or new clubs specifically for women began to appear. The term used in Belgium for women's gymnastics was 'damsels' to stress the pure, serious and dignified image they wished to present. Women were not integrated into the existing structure but set up their own organizing body in 1923, the Association Régionale Catholique de Gymnastiques des demoiselles d'Anvers which ten years later took the lead in forming the Fédération Catholique de Gymnastique des demoiselles de Belgique. However, this movement did not take off in Belgium until after the Second World War and during the interwar years never succeeded in attracting more than a thousand members. There was no proper link and no collaboration between the male and female associations in Belgium. Hence it was not surprising to find that the Belgian male officials active in UIOCEP were particularly unsympathetic to the dynamic growth of Catholic women's gymnastics in Czechoslovakia. In fact, the Ganda club of Ghent, a leading Catholic gymnastic club, which had attended the Orel festivals and was impressed by the Czech model, was expelled from the FBCG for being too active in promoting women's events.

It was not just in this area that the dynamism of Orel posed problems for the Belgians. Orel had grown enormously and claimed around 170 000 members by the late 1930s. [35] The suppression of separate Catholic sporting and gymnastic bodies in Italy and Germany with the advent of fascist corporatism under Mussolini and Hitler meant that Orel became proportionately more important in the international movement. This, at least, is the impression which comes from reading the coverage of foreign gymnastics in the Catholic gymnastic press in Belgium between the wars.

Orel took up much of the time spent by Belgian officials on international business, not just the gender issue but on other technical and administrative matters too. Not surprisingly, a crucial issue was its demand for better integration of Slav gymnasts in the international federation. Orel resented the fact that the UIOCEP tended to organize UIOCEP meetings in Paris; it wanted these meetings to be held from time to time in its own country or, if not, in a more central location in Europe. It also criticized UIOCEP for pretending to be an international and open-minded federation, but in reality failing to take proper initiatives to attract federations not just from eastern Europe but from other continents, too. Why, for example, was there no proper contact with American Catholics, who had taken the gymnastic traditions of central Europe and developed them actively in the New World? Orel had a sister body in Chicago formed by Czech migrants and there was clearly scope for action to bring more clubs together and spread the word. [36]

Orel was also a promoter of the introduction of new activities and new sports into the UIOCEP; an initiative that posed a real problem for the Belgians who had been strong advocates of keeping sports out of gymnastics and had carried on that policy despite the enormous success of sports like football in the 1920s. For all these differences, however, there were important similarities between the two countries. Both were relatively small states bordering Germany, which after 1933 became an extremely dangerous neighbour. Both were trapped between the need to appease Germany to avoid war and the desire to oppose her. Both in the end required the support of the international community to defend them. In the Czech case, this was not forthcoming; in the Belgian, it came too late to be effective. Moreover both countries had a similar *pillier* structure reflected in gymnastics. In Czechoslovakia through Sokol, Orel and the Czechoslovak Workers' Gymnastic Units which in turn were affiliated respectively to the secular Fédération Internationale de Gymnastique (FIG), UIOCEP and the International Workers' Sport Federation, and in Belgium through Fédération Belge de Gymnastique (1865), Fédération Belge Catholique de Gymnastique (1872) and Fédération Belge Socialiste de Gymnastique (1904), also affiliated to the same respective bodies as the Czechs. This tripartite structure, which France also shared, meant that Catholics had to face not just the older challenge from anti-clericalism but new ones from organized labour and potential ones from the Right in the form of fascist ambitions to 'militarize' the body. In Belgium the Catholics faced a threat from the socialist sports groups who organized the Third Workers' Sports Olympics at Antwerp in 1937. [37] It is hardly surprising, therefore, that Belgian Catholics alongside their traditional allegiance to France should develop a new interest in a state like Czechoslovakia which, despite obvious differences, shared so many of the same features.

## Conclusions

Physical culture and ideology were becoming increasingly interconnected. During the interwar period the fascists saturated sport with their own ideology and both the democratic left and the Communists did the same. The Vatican began to take a much closer interest in all forms of socio-cultural activity, including gymnastics and sports, with the foundation of the various forms of Catholic Action in the 1920s. Gymnastics was part of this wider international movement which not only sought to defend the narrow interests of the Church but to oppose 'the evils of modern society'. However, despite the internationalism of the Church itself and of Catholic Action, the main concern remained that of internal consolidation. The threat from the secular so-called 'liberal' clubs and from the socialists remained the main problem for the Catholics and international relations were secondary. Even when an overt challenge to Catholicism arose in Spain in 1936 with the Church-backed military revolt against the socialist government, there was little or no discussion in the specialist Catholic gymnastic press. There was plenty of moral and religious comment and abstract rhetoric about the meaning of sports for the Church and the Church for sports. But concerning the international political situation, there was relatively little comment. Neither Belgian Catholics nor the umbrella federation, the UIOCEP, took the opportunity to condemn fascist sport as, for example, the socialists did when their federations were disbanded. Further research is required to clarify the wider Catholic international reaction, but within Belgium the official gymnastic press avoided these issues. Instead of taking a clear position on the actual situation, the Belgians preferred to present the international movement in vague terms of the universal fraternity of Catholic youth. In both the Flemish and French versions of the Belgian gymnastic journal in the 1930s, *Ons Bondsblad* and *Le Signal*, the front page of each issue continued to show a young gymnast in action next to a signpost pointing to different UIOCEP member countries. But this figure, kneeling above a map of Belgium, arms outstretched to the south, reminded readers of the traditional link with French Catholics, which had remained a constant feature of Belgian policy from the visit to Rome in 1908 to the outbreak of the Second World War.

## References

1. 1908, p. 114–5, published in both French and Dutch, *Belgica*, no. 14. It was translated from the *Giornale d'italia*.
2. Tolleneer, Jan (1990) Gymnastics and religion in Belgium (1892–1914). *International Journal of the History of Sport*, (3), 335–47.
3. La XIIe fête fédérale belge à Tournai, *Belgica*, no. 9, 1903, p. 87
4. Ibid.
5. Hoberman, John (1995) Toward a Theory of Olympic Internationalism. *Journal of Sport History*, (22), 1–27.
6. De Katholieke Turners te Rome/Les Gymnastes Catholiques à Rome, *Belgica*, no. 14, (1908), pp. 111–12.
7. Vergadering van het Bestendig Bestuur gehouden te Brussel den 31 October 1909/Réunion de la Commission Permanente tenue à Bruxelles le 31 octobre 1909, *Belgica*, no. 10, 1909, p. 123.
8. Dubreuil, Bernard (1987) La fédération catholique et la République (1898–1914), in Pierre Arnaud (ed.), *Les athlètes de la république: gymnastique, sport et idéologie républicaine 1870/1914*, Toulouse, pp. 205–21.
9. De Meyer, Guy (1986) *Nicolaas Jan Cupérus (1842–1928) en de ontwikkeling van de turnbeweging*, Leuven.
10. *Belgica*, no. 17, 1911, pp. 69–70.
11. Holt, Richard (1981) *Sport and society in modern France*, London.
12. Hellemans, Staf (1990) *Strijd om de moderniteit: sociale bewegingen en versuiling in Europa sinds 1800*, Leuven.
13. Arnaud, Pierre (1989) Diviser et unir. Sociétés sportives et nationalismes en France (1870–1914). *Sport/Histoire*, (4), 31–47.
14. *Belgica*, 1911, pp. 95–7.
15. Tolleneer, Jan (1996) The Dual Meaning of 'Fatherland' and Catholic Gymnasts in Belgium, 1892–1914, in J.A. Mangan (ed.) *Tribal identities. Nationalism, Europe and Sport*, London, pp. 94–107.

16. Renson, Roland (1994) Corpus alienum. Naschoolse sport in het katholiek onderwijs, in Mark D'hoker, Roland Renson and Jan Tolleneer (eds), *Voor lichaam en geest. Katholieken, lichamelijke opvoeding en sport in de 19de en 20ste eeuw*, Leuven, pp. 99-121.
17. *Belgica*, no. 4, 1920, pp. 2–3.
18. Renson, Roland (1995) *La VIIième Olympiade Anvers 1920. Les jeux ressuscités*, Bruxelles.
19. Renson, *op. cit.*, p. 28.
20. Ibid.
21. Luyckx, Theo and Platel, Marc (1985) *Politieke geschiedenis van België 1: van 1789 tot 1944*, Antwerpen, pp. 283–323.
22. *Belgica*, no. 9, 1921, p. 3.
23. *Belgica*, no. 6, 1921, p. 2–3.
24. *Belgica*, no. 1, 1922, pp. 10–11.
25. *Belgica*, no. 5, 1927, p. 3.
26. *Belgica*, no. 4, 1928, pp. 10–11.
27. *Belgica*, no. 5, 1928, p. 31.
28. Historical overview in *Ons Bondsblad*, no. 3, 1933, pp. 5–7.
29. *Belgica*, no. 4, 1920, pp. 1–2.
30. *Ons Bondsblad*, no. 11, 1938, pp. 5–6.
31. *Belgica*, no. 8,. 1922, pp,. 22–3.
32. *Belgica*, no. 9, 1924, pp. 8–9.
33. *Belgica*, no. 5, 1925, pp. 12–13.
34. Tolleneer, Jan (1992) Gymnastics in Belgium during the interwar period. The Catholic way. *Canadian Journal of History of Sport* (2), 1–16.
35. *Ons Bondsblad*, no. 5, 1938, pp. 3–4.
36. *Belgica*, no. 4, 1928, pp. 3; 10–11.
37. Tolleneer, Jan and Box, Eric (1986–87) An alternative sport festival. The third Workers' Olympics Antwerp 1937. *Stadion. Internationale Zeitschrift fü Geschichte des Sports*, 183–90.

# Chapter 11

# Between revolutionary demands and diplomatic necessity

## The uneasy relationship between Soviet sport and worker and bourgeois sport in Europe from 1920 to 1937

*André Gounot*

## Introduction

Between 1921 and 1937, Soviet sport was closely linked to the international communist movement and was represented by Red Sport International (RSI) in sporting events. Set up in Moscow in 1921 as an auxiliary organization of the Communist International (Comintern), the RSI was supported by its national sections and groups of sympathizers based mainly in central and western Europe and in Scandinavia. However, its largest national section was, by far, that of the Soviet Union.

The RSI's statutes required that all national sections applied decisions taken by the RSI congresses, which were attended by the representatives of the communist workers' sports movements of various countries. One is therefore led to believe that the RSI, along with the worker sports organizations that were affiliated to it, could have had quite an effect on international sports relations in the USSR, relations which cannot be said to have been influenced solely by Soviet foreign policy at the time. But it must also be borne in mind that, during the 1920s, the international communist movement became increasingly dependent on the specific interests of the USSR, and that it is more likely that the RSI contributed to this development. Could the RSI, which was initially central to the revolutionary sports movement, then have evolved into a type of international Soviet sports bureau?

An examination of the relationship between the RSI and Soviet sport will clearly show the potential importance of an international organization as being one of the factors which determine the state of a country's international sports relations, alongside other considerations, such as the nature of its political regime or the diplomatic relations it has with other countries. This examination will also reveal the potential and the limitations of Soviet policy with regard to European sport during the interwar period.

This chapter will attempt to shed some light on the foundations and the intentions of this policy by examining above all to what extent sport was conceived as being a means of support for the revolutionary aims propagated by the international communist movement, and to what extent it was required to satisfy the national and diplomatic interests of the USSR. As soon as the USSR's international sports relations had to perform both these functions at the same time, contradictions and disputes arose; the ambiguous relationship between Soviet sport and bourgeois sport is as much evidence of this as the tense relationship between the RSI and its socialist equivalent, the Lucerne Sports International (LSI).

The well-documented sports events between Germany and the USSR also provide an opportunity to consider the knock-on effect that the international competitions in which the Soviets participated had on the functions which they had been assigned.

Research has been especially helped by the recent opening of the Comintern Archives in Moscow, and from the access that this has provided to the collection of 'Sportintern' documents. [1] With nearly 60 000 documents from the RSI Bureau, this collection houses Europe's richest selection of material on the communist sports movement during the interwar period. The Russian Federation Archives (formerly the 'October Revolution Archives') have provided another rich source, especially with regard to documents from the international commission of Russia's – then later the Soviet Union's – Supreme Council of Physical Culture. [2]

## Training 'athletes of the Revolution': the creation of Red Sport International

The summer of 1920 saw the first attempt to link Soviet sport to the worker sports organizations which had been set up at the end of the 19th and the beginning of the 20th centuries in various European countries as auxiliary organizations. Soviet sport was then subjected to all the contingencies that entailed from a state of war; it was practised almost exclusively within the framework of Vsevobuch. This was an organization founded in 1918 to provide pre-military service training courses, the main aim of which was to supply the Red Army with physically fit soldiers. [3]

While the Second Comintern Congress was being held in Moscow (23 July–7 August 1920), the Red Army was marching on Warsaw. This was partly why this Congress was marked by the delegates' hope that the wave of revolution would continue in Europe. With this idea in mind, Nikolai Podvoïski, director of Vsevobuch, suggested setting up 'an international gymnastics and workers' sports organisation, responsible for disseminating the experiences of the Russian proletariat throughout the world and for training, with the help of these experiences, a sufficiently large reserve of revolutionary soldiers to be used in decisive conflicts'. [4] According to the document from which this quotation was taken, this project was never pursued, owing to the delegates to whom Podvoïski suggested the idea having so few links with sport. Evidence of Podvoïski's initiative, which was not discussed in the minutes of the Congress of the Communiste Internationale, is shown in two letters from the German communist Kurt Leinhardt to Podvoïski. [5] But in any case, the project did not stand much chance of succeeding. This was because the idea of exporting the Russian model of Vsevobuch via an international organization, an idea which supposed workers' sport undergoing a certain degree of militarization, was in complete contradiction with the pacifist tradition and the reformist nature of the worker sports movement in Europe. [6] Indeed, during a congress held on the 12 and 13 September 1920 in Lucerne, the worker sports movement set up an international organization which was to become very close in ideology to the social democratic and socialist parties: the Union internationale d'éducation physique et sportive du Travail (international workers' sports and physical education union). (This union succeeded the Association Socialiste Internationale de l'Education Physique (the International Socialist Association of Physical Education) which was set up in 1913 in Ghent. It ceased to be active after war broke out.) [7] It was later to become better known as l'Internationale Sportive de Lucerne (Lucerne Sport International or LSI).

The LSI declared itself to be neutral with regard to the different political and ideological tendencies within the workers' movement, and adopted a programme of a distinctly reformist nature. No reference was made to the political upheavals in Russia at the Lucerne congress, and the issue of the integration of Soviet sport was not raised. The congress took place as though the worker sports movement had remained indifferent to the victory of the October Revolution and the revolutionary conflicts which had occurred in several European countries just after the First World War; it was as if they were ignorant of the crisis that the international socialist movement was still going through, a crisis which had been provoked by the attitude of the socialist parties to the war and which resulted in the founding of the Comintern in March 1919.

The communists, who were convinced that reformism had failed on all levels and that capitalism could only be vanquished by revolution, considered that the LSI was scarcely equal to the political duties which, in their opinion, all the working classes were bound to perform. The congresses of the Comintern, the Communist Youth International and the Red Trade Union International, all held in June and July 1921 in Moscow in the presence of delegates who were interested in the sports issues, provided the opportunity to reconsider the matter of creating a sports organization with a revolutionary slant, at a time when the communist movement had to deal with an appreciable change in Europe's political situation.

Indeed, after the defeat of the Red Army in Poland, followed by the total failure of the Communist Party's revolutionary plotting in Germany, the Comintern was forced to admit that the postwar period of revolution had come to an end. With the progress of the revolution proving to be slower than expected, the Comintern called upon its sections to devote themselves henceforth to winning over the working-class majority in the long-term, instead of concentrating their efforts on the more immediately revolutionary conflicts. This new strategy can be summarized by the Third Congress's slogan: 'To the People!' [8, 9]

It was with a view to helping to win over the masses that the International Association of Red Sports and Gymnastics Associations, more commonly known as the Red Sport International (RSI) was created on 23 July 1921, after a series of meetings about sports issues that had been initiated and organized by Podvoïski, and attended by 13 people from 8 different countries (Russia, Germany, France, Italy, Hungary, Czechoslovakia, Sweden and the Netherlands). [10] The delegates went to Moscow to take part in the official conferences, which explains why most of them played no role in the sports movements of their countries. It should also be added that the Comintern apparatus did not play any part in the setting up of the RSI. [11] Based in Moscow, the main task of the RSI was to direct all communist activity and to define communist strategy within reformist worker sports organizations with a view to converting them into revolutionary organizations which united the 'physical vanguard of the proletariat'. [12, 13]

Initially, the RSI was very different from the usual type of international sports body which groups together several national federations and which organizes international competitions; it was first and foremost an agitation and propaganda bureau which served the Comintern. It was also unusual in that it had no branch outside of Soviet Russia – the communist sports federation of Czechoslovakia, founded in May 1921, did not officially become a member until October 1922. [14] The worker sports federations of France and Norway followed, becoming branches of the RSI in 1923 and 1924 respectively.

In any case, Soviet sport had many other concerns in 1921, besides taking part in events with foreign countries' sports organizations. [15] In an exhausted country that was braving a serious famine following years of civil war and military intervention, sport was only slowly resumed. [16] Even in the case of football, the most popular sport, it was not until 1922 that the first official competitions were held, and it was only later that year that the first international match took place between a Soviet football team (made up of Muscovites) and a Finnish worker sports federation team (a branch of the LSI). [17, 18, 19]

The founding of the RSI corresponded in part to Soviet sport's desire to establish preliminary relations with European worker sport, so as to exchange ideas concerning technical issues, and to secure practical support. [20, 21] All in all, however, the creation of the RSI was not so much the reflection of sporting ambition as of the political and ideological interest of Soviet Russia. During this period, these interests were entirely directed towards the world revolution which had to result, in the short- or long-term, in the creation of other socialist states. This was thought to be the only means of guaranteeing the survival of Soviet Russia. The leaders of the Bolshevik Party, particularly Lenin, believed that without the support of socialist partner states, Russia would sooner or later be subjugated by the capitalist world.

Convinced that this was the case, Soviet sports officials resolved, on an international level, to collaborate only with communist representatives of workers' sport, i.e. those who were heading the struggle against bourgeois sport and, more particularly, against the reformist leanings of worker sport within the wider context of the revolutionary class struggle. Significantly, the delegates of the RSI's third congress were welcomed to Moscow in 1924 with the slogan 'Every worker athlete must be a soldier of the world revolution'. [22]

This idea that sport activities had to serve exclusively revolutionary aims was associated with a refusal to have any contact with the official sports federations of other countries, especially with the International Olympic Committee (IOC). Furthermore, the members of worker sports organizations would have had difficulty coming to terms with the idea of Soviet Russia taking part in official international competitions, which were seen as instruments of chauvinism, expressing the spirit of rivalry, individualism and the obsession with breaking records – in short, symptoms of a decadent capitalist system. Consequently, the administrators of Soviet sport were not very interested in the way in which the IOC behaved in relation to the 'Russian question', which was dealt with in Rome at the 1923 session of the Committee: Should the Olympic movement integrate Soviet sport or rather sports organizations made up of Russian emigrants? Ultimately, the Committee avoided giving a clear answer to this delicate question; no Russian organization was invited to take part in the 1924 Olympic Games in Paris. [23] But it was clear that had the Soviets been invited, they would have refused to participate. In January 1924, at a meeting of the RSI's Executive Committee attended by the most important representatives of Soviet sport, as well as a delegate from the Comintern, it was decided to issue a press statement, declaring that:

> The sports organisations of the USSR are in no way associated with the bourgeois sports organisations and are in no way represented on the International Olympic Committee. In declaring himself to be a representative of Russia in this institution, Prince Urusov is appropriating a position without authority [. . .] The headquarters of the international proletarian sports union are in Moscow, and it is within this organisation alone that the USSR's sports organisations may have their representatives. [24]

It should, however, be pointed out that the issuing of this press statement was in part a reaction to animosity within the worker sports movement that had been provoked by events in which Russians and bourgeois sports organizations had participated the year before. [25, 26] These events, which were later disapproved of by the Supreme Council of Physical Culture (which had not, however, done anything to prevent them in 1923), were a reflection of the somewhat anarchic state of Soviet sport at the beginning of the 1920s.

## The quest for a coherent policy on sport

During the first half of the 1920s, the growth of sport in Russia was marked by organizational rivalry and contention over popular notions of sport, and debates were held over the subject of physical education and the decisions taken regarding its role and its organizational framework. [27, 28, 29] Vsevobuch and the Komsomol (the Communist youth movement) organized sports events; the Hygienists and the Proletkultists, on the other hand, declared themselves in favour of abandoning the principle of competition and put forward a set of radically new physical education models, seeking to allow socialist ideas to be expressed through body movement and physical performance. [30, 31] In addition to this, the measures taken with regard to physical education and sport varied from region to region, and the institutional framework in which sport was played was the subject of much discussion and dispute, particularly between Vsevobuch, the Komsomol and the trade unions.

Disagreements continued until summer 1925 when the Communist Party intervened to establish the extent and nature of the responsibilities of the various organizations involved in sporting matters, and to make it clear that it would always have the final word. [32, 33] It was decided that the Supreme Council of Physical Culture – set up in June 1923 as a central sports authority for Russia's Central Executive Committee – should be maintained. The Council's main task was to coordinate sports events organized by various organizations and to identify ideas about sport which should be applied in all countries through their local organs. It was made up of one representative each from the People's Commissariats (Defence, Education, Health, Employment and Internal Affairs), plus one from the Komsomol Central Committee, the Trade Union Central Council, and the Moscow City Soviet, [34] and was attached to the RSI. Soviet interests were therefore protected in this organization, not by the delegates of a sports federation – those in power had refused to accept the setting up of such a federation in Russia for fear of sport growing too independently – but by representatives of the State apparatus.

From the outset the Supreme Council of Physical Culture emphasized the value of competitive sport in the education of brave, energetic and resolute socialist citizens. This was a response to certain provincial governments' 'aberrations', one of which had been to forbid football, believing it to be a relic of 'bourgeois practices'. [35, 36]

Once the policy on sport became more defined in the USSR – which saw no contradiction between communist ideology and competitive sport – the issue of the nature and function of Soviet sport's international relations became clear. First and foremost, its most important function was to keep up communist propaganda so as to give worker sport in Europe a more revolutionary aspect and to encourage the identification of the European proletariat with the USSR.

The first instance of this type of political propaganda being used dates back to August–September 1923, when a Moscow football team toured Scandinavia and then later Germany. The German communists thought that representatives of the country of the victorious October Revolution – with exemplary workers who, furthermore, had proven sporting talent – could only have a positive effect on propaganda conducted against the reformist leadership of the Arbeiter-Turn- und Sportbund (ATSB), the Workers' Gymnastics and Sports Union. [37] However, the Soviet leaders had based the selection of their team on sports criteria only, thinking that in order to carry out revolutionary propaganda, they had only to demonstrate the high standard of Soviet sport. It was especially important to show that Soviet workers were given enough opportunity to become good at a sport, and to counterbalance anti-communist propaganda which concentrated on the USSR's poverty and economic problems. [38] However, the members of the team showed such a lack of proletarian and political awareness during their stay that the communist opposition leaders within the ATSB found themselves in a very difficult position.

How was it possible to continue to glorify Soviet sport when its representatives discredited it by their behaviour, although in September 1924, the executive committee of the RSI noted, not without bitterness, that 'the Russian football team has been discredited in Germany since 1923' [39, 40], thus strengthening the social-democrats' anti-Bolshevik arguments? A commission to the Comintern was set up on the initiative of the RSI to examine 'the incidents which occurred during the Russian team's tour of Germany' [41, 42] – which also illustrates that, within the communist movement, it was becoming clear just how important it would be in future for Soviet athletes on the international stage to be better prepared in order to meet political expectations. Consequently, with the federal celebrations of the Czechoslovak branch of the LSI in Karlsbad in the summer of 1924 in mind, the Russian delegation had to be sure to 'receive the most detailed instructions', according to the executive committee of the RSI. [43] It should be added that this delegation, which left Moscow too late, did not appear at the Karlsbad celebrations. [44] This is an example of the serious lack of organization of Soviet sport, which frequently had a negative effect on communist propagandist activity in Europe.

## The relationship with bourgeois sport

A second function of the USSR's participation in international events – which seems almost incompatible with the above role – became apparent in the middle of the 1920s: to help establish the USSR's foreign policy by creating official sports links with certain countries. Neighbouring countries took priority (see Riordan, this volume). Thus, for example, in order to symbolize the friendly relations established with Turkey, six football matches against Turkish teams were held between 1924 and 1925. [45] In these matches, the Soviet teams did not play against worker sports clubs, which did not exist in Turkey, but against teams from the bourgeois sports movement, and even against the national team. Other introductory events with the bourgeois organizations of Eastern countries were to follow. A 'Spartakiad of the East' was even planned in Baku (Azerbaijan), in which Turkey, Afghanistan, Persia, Palestine, Morocco and China would participate. [46, 47] However, this Spartakiad did not take place, no doubt because of financial and organizational problems, as well as the fact that sport was still in the early stages of development in most of the countries mentioned. [48]

These attempts to form links with bourgeois sport in certain countries were in complete contrast with the RSI's condemning of all official contact with bourgeois sports foundations at the beginning of 1924. [49, 50] It was therefore hardly surprising to see that the abandoning of this principle by the Soviet branch of the RSI was not only a source of controversy within the LSI, [51] but also a move that was unequivocally criticized by certain leaders of the RSI, most notably by Bruno Lieske, who was at the time chairman of the West Bureau of the RSI in Berlin. Acting on Lieske's initiative, the leadership of the communist opposition within the German worker sports movement expressed its disagreement in a 'Resolution against the tendencies to render Soviet sport more bourgeois'. [52] (The tendencies to render Soviet sport more bourgeois were also severely criticized by Podvoïski, on behalf of the organization bureau of the executive committee of the Comintern). [53] This resolution first declared itself to be against the use of rational training to improve performance, which was increasingly widespread in the USSR. But above all, it condemned any competition with bourgeois associations, refuting the argument that it was in the interest of the country's diplomatic relations:

> The leadership of the communist factions also declares itself to be against the attempts to justify events with bourgeois counter-revolutionaries for reasons of diplomatic necessity [. . .] An international workers' organisation can only voluntarily serve the interests of diplomacy, which frequently requires the use of bourgeois methods, when it no longer intends to maintain a good reputation among workers of different countries. [54]

However, the authors were later forced to withdraw their resolution, following the intervention of the German Communist Party's policy bureau, which claimed that its criticism was excessive. [55] But this did not prevent the issue of sports events with bourgeois teams being discussed at length within the RSI. [56, 57] The opinion of the German representatives was contrasted with that of a group of leaders of the Russian branch, who pleaded in favour of Russian athletes participating generally in bourgeois sports events. Believing that such an opinion would have a damaging effect on its policies and its image, the RSI interceded with the Central Committee of the Russian Communist Party. [58]

The resolution that the RSI's expanded executive committee adopted in 1926 over the relationship with bourgeois sport was very much a compromise between the European branches and the Soviet branch. In order to eliminate prior differences in opinion and interests, the RSI lost no time in suggesting to the worker athletes that each part of the resolution should be considered as a tactical element of a fundamentally revolutionary strategy, which corresponded to the interest of the entire working class. No allusion was made to the impact of Soviet diplomacy. This resolution, [59] which was particularly important since it outlined the framework within which Soviet sport was to evolve in the long-term on an international bias, contained, amongst others, the following points:

- In the countries which did not have worker sports movements, events between branches of the RSI and the bourgeois sports associations of these countries had, on the whole, to be authorized, since they could be useful for spreading revolutionary propaganda and encouraging the creation of workers' sports clubs. In the case of eastern countries such as Turkey and Persia, 'where the bourgeoisie was still playing a clearly revolutionary role', these events had to be considered as an aspect of the anti-imperialist struggle.
- In countries which had strong worker sports organizations, events with bourgeois sports associations were to be avoided out of respect for the interests and beliefs of the worker athletes.

• However, exceptions could be made within Soviet sport (they had to be authorized by the Presidium of the RSI, who, prior to any decision, would ask the
opinion of the communist parties of the countries concerned [60]), which
were in the best position to spread effective revolutionary propaganda. The
best sports results could 'enhance the standing of the first worker state, thus
reinforcing the proletarian sports movement in capitalist countries'.

The last point is without doubt the most interesting: the notion that capitalism
must be – and indeed would be in the short- or long-term – 'beaten in the stadiums', [61] was emerging for the first time in the form of an official resolution. This
idea not only illustrated how the prestige of competitive sport was being enhanced
in Soviet society; it also seemed to announce a support policy on high-level sport.
Until the 1930s, however, there was no State policy on sport which emphasized the
systematic production of exceptional athletes. Although the Communist Party
was in favour of competitive sport, it reproached the leaders of the sports movement in 1929 for being more interested in the setting of new records than in
encouraging the masses to play sport. [62, 63] Before 1929, which was when the
Communist Party took effective control of the sports movement, the objectives
pursued by the Supreme Council of Physical Culture (which became the Supreme
Council of Physical Culture of the Soviet Union in April 1930) were not exactly
the same in all respects as for those supported by the Party. [64] As far as the 1920s
are concerned, it is therefore difficult to ascertain the extent to which ideas
expressed in the RSI's resolutions under the dominant influence of Soviet representatives corresponded to a policy that had been sanctioned by the Communist
Party.

However, what is clear is the fact that from the mid-1920s onwards, the idea of
using international competitions as a means of enhancing national prestige and
demonstrating the achievements of the socialist system started to influence, at
least in part, sports policy and the development of sport in the USSR. This tendency, which was diametrically opposed to the ideas that the Hygienists and the
Proletkultists had promoted, must be considered in connection with the theory of
'socialism in one country', which Stalin started to support in October 1924, and
with Russian neo-nationalism, which the Communist Party started to propagate in
accordance with this theory. During the first half of the 1920s, the prospect of a
world-wide revolution had become increasingly distant. Stalin realized this and
proposed that socialism should be established in the USSR without waiting for the
communist parties to take power in other countries. [65].

In order to give substance to this idea, and then to prepare the Soviet people for
the huge efforts that the edification of socialism was going to require, the country's
independence and strength had to be stressed, as well as the courage and stoicism
of its people. The theory of 'socialism in one country' nurtured patriotic feelings
that the doctrine of proletarian internationalism had never been able to erase, and
legitimized them, which also served to render the populace more accepting of the
Communist Party. Within this framework of a return to more nationalist and

patriotic views, sport was beginning to be seen as a potential symbol of the strength and dynamism of the USSR.

The theory of 'socialism in one country' also meant the continuation and the sharpening of an international policy focused on maintaining diplomatic relations by the signing of a number of treaties with capitalist countries with a view to guaranteeing the safety of Soviet Russia. If this theory was not yet an official doctrine in 1925, it formed the basis of the politics of the Soviet Union's Communist Party and the Comintern. Moreover, this period saw the progressive deterioration of the Communist International into an instrument of Soviet foreign policy, [66] a development that had repercussions for the International's auxiliary organizations.

The Soviet interest in securing a great deal of latitude concerning international sports relations was therefore linked to sport being considered an asset of foreign policy and as an object of prestige and national identity, as well as continuing to have the values with which it was instilled in the international class struggle.

However, the contacts with bourgeois sport in Europe were to remain very limited. Among the reasons for this was the fact that the USSR was not a member of any official international sports federation, and certain countries' governments refused to issue visas to Soviet athletes. [67] It is also conceivable that, shouldered with the responsibility of having to enhance the USSR's prestige, events organized with bourgeois sports organizations were only of interest when Soviet athletes stood a good chance of winning, and in the 1920s these chances were not very realistic in the majority of sports. In addition, complying with the RSI's resolution of May 1926, the USSR was careful not to thwart the interests of the worker sports federations which played a relatively important role in their own countries. Germany's example is the most significant: not one event between a Soviet team and a German bourgeois team was planned throughout the 1920s and 1930s. However, in 1922, the USSR and Germany had signed the Treaty of Rapallo, which opened up diplomatic relations and set up a basic mutual aid arrangement between two countries that had hitherto been isolated: Germany because it had lost the war and the Soviet Union because it was a socialist country. The Treaty of Rapallo was confirmed in April 1926 and was extended by the conclusion of a 'treaty of neutrality and friendship'. However, given the importance of the German worker sports movement (in terms of numbers, the German worker sports movement was by far the largest in Europe, with over one million members), the USSR gave up using sport as an additional pawn in diplomatic relations with Germany. [68] On the contrary, it was thought that Soviet sports competitions with German workers' sports clubs would help communist propaganda and would consequently challenge the ruling system in Germany. It could be concluded that, in this particular case, sport was on the wrong side of Soviet foreign policy, for which a good relationship with Germany was a particularly important part of its defence strategy. [69] But in fact Soviet foreign policy was pursued on two different fronts: on the one hand it supported revolutionary movements and their subversive activities in capitalist countries through the Comintern, and on the other through official diplomatic channels. [70, 71] In spite of the signing of treaties between the

USSR and Germany's Weimar Republic, intense ideological opposition and suspicion remained as the international communist movement attempted to make Germany the first recipient of its revolutionary message. Sports events between Germany and the USSR were an aspect of the unofficial channel of Soviet foreign policy, and illustrated the ambiguous relations between the two countries very clearly. [72, 73] Furthermore, it was symptomatic that German–Soviet workers' sports events had been prevented from taking place on several occasions, following the German embassy's refusal to issue Soviet athletes with visas. [74]

## Relations with the Lucerne Sport International (1925–1927)

The unlikelihood of a world revolution together with the theory of 'socialism in one country' were also behind the Comintern's change of tactics in 1925, a change which once again involved it seeking to narrow the gap between itself and the socialist movement. Red Sport International immediately applied the new directives and announced its proposals to merge with the LSI, with which it had resumed contact. The negotiations between the RSI and the LSI were to have important consequences for Soviet sport's international relations. Indeed, at its Paris–Pantin congress in November 1925, the LSI officially decided to allow events to be held between its branches and Soviet sport – provided they were not exploited by any party for political purposes. [75]

This decision greatly increased the number of Soviet teams which competed abroad: in 1925, only 7 Soviet delegations went abroad to compete in 21 events, but in 1926, 21 delegations went abroad to compete in 56 events. And although 1927 saw no great increase in terms of numbers of Soviet delegations going abroad (24 delegations for 51 events), the number of delegations from other countries going to compete in events in the USSR quadrupled compared to previous years (20 delegations for 36 events). [76] The greatest number of events was staged against German worker sport teams, after the signing in August 1926 of a special contract between the Arbeiter Turn- und Sportbund and the Supreme Council of Physical Culture governing sports events.

Immediately after the LSI congress in Paris, the RSI attempted to draw up a set of criteria for selecting Soviet athletes, firmly believing that 'commandos of Soviet athletes sent abroad play an important political role in increasing the popularity of the Soviet Union.' [77] (In German language documents, the expression 'Sportkommando' is often used. The use of the military term 'Kommando' by the RSI is characteristic of the way in which international sports relations were seen as an aspect of subversive activity within the context of the revolutionary struggle.) As a result, according to the RSI secretary Fritz Reußner, only those with a clear awareness of the class struggle and a sufficiently broad knowledge of politics should be sent. The members of the team would be noted for their absolute respect of collective interests, their discipline and their obedience of the delegation leader's orders. [78] Reußner referred to certain practices in the past which had discredited Soviet sport and the RSI in the eyes of worker athletes and which had to be prevented from recurring in the future at all costs. [79, 80]

These concerns are more easily understandable when one considers the fact that the RSI itself was investing much of its efforts in increasing the popularity of the Soviet Union, which it always portrayed in the journals and circulars it sent to its branches [81, 82] as an ideal country where all the proletariat's hopes were in the process of being fulfilled. This glorification of the USSR was extremely important for the communist movement: it was a means of setting up strong links between the working classes of capitalist countries and the USSR, which was considered a bastion of communism, permanently threatened by the capitalist world. At the same time, it also confirmed that in wanting to set up political systems analogous to that of the USSR in their own countries, the communist parties were pursuing just aims. Ensuring at all cost that the behaviour and assertions of Soviet athletes abroad did not conflict with the idealist image of Soviet society or the USSR's physical culture perspective that sport could be used to enlist the populace into helping the USSR, this was in harmony not only with the interests of Soviet foreign policy, but also with those of the RSI and the entire communist movement.

However, as far as sports events with Germany were concerned, there was great discrepancy between the propagandist will of the German communists and the success of these competitions, during which numerous problems arose. On several occasions, the Soviet teams did not respect the dates of the events or left earlier than expected, and on others they were conspicuously absent from the receptions held in their honour or they caught people off their guard by making material demands which must have seemed excessive to the German workers. The somewhat unsupportive behaviour of the Russian guests, which was in stark contrast with the enthusiasm with which they were welcomed by the worker athletes, often sparked off dissatisfaction and protest, not only from the social-democrats, but also from the communists. [83, 84, 85, 86, 87] It was remarked in a letter from the leaders of the communist opposition within the ATSB to the Supreme Council of Physical Culture [88] in August 1927, that so far the Russian delegations had all shown a certain lack of tact, and so should be discreetly surveyed by a German associate in the future.

It is evident that the Russian sports delegations were often not up to their political mission – but it should be remembered that they were made up of ordinary athletes, not diplomats. It was above all thanks to the sporting achievements of the USSR's teams, admired by both the public and the press, that their tours were partly successful, in spite of their lack of tact. However, their good reputation on the sports front was somewhat diminished after an extremely aggressive football match between a Soviet team and a Dresden workers team during a tour of Germany in July 1927. This match was commented on at length by the bourgeois sports press which concluded that, contrary to claims, there was no difference between worker and bourgeois football; the worker press, however, could only contemplate the damage that had been done. [89] Another negative point was scored after the first (and only) defeat during this tour (1–3 in a match played at

Dresden against the national team of the worker sports federation of Austria, a branch of the LSI): the leaders of the Soviet team proved themselves to be very bad losers, complaining about the lack of rest that the team had had before the match, and insinuating that the Austrian team was partly made up of professional players – allegations which offended the Austrian social-democrats as much as the Germans. [90] In fact, despite warnings from the RSI against activities or behaviour which might be detrimental to the propagandist effect, [91] at some events it seemed as though the Soviet delegation (which was not, despite appearances, made up of 'counter-revolutionaries') was doing everything it could to provoke criticism of Soviet sport.

Another problem lay in the political significance that the communist movement attributed to events that involved Soviet athletes. According to the agreement reached by the LSI and the RSI, these competitions were not to be used as political vehicles. However, the German Communist Party and its press often portrayed them not only as a symbol of the union between the German proletariat and the USSR, but also as an instrument to rally the masses to the revolutionary movement's cause. The anti-reformist statements which accompanied these portrayals were also sometimes representative of the views of Soviet delegation leaders, which led to serious disagreements with those in charge of the football section of the German gymnastics and worker sports union. [92]

Instead of helping to bridge the gap between the RSI and the LSI, the way in which sports events took place between branches of the LSI and Soviet sports teams only served as another reason for the leadership of the LSI to give up the idea of coming to an understanding with the RSI. In any case, however, the leadership of the LSI had always considered that it would be impossible for a genuine understanding, let alone a merger with the communists, to come about until Soviet sport had broken all links with bourgeois sport [93] – something that the organizers of Soviet sport were not ready to do. It was proving difficult both to use sport as an instrument of diplomacy and to have the international worker sports movement as an ally.

The LSI officially declared its affinity with the Socialist Worker International at its congress in Helsinki in August 1927; furthermore, in order to better communicate this new stance, it changed its name in January 1928 to the Socialist Worker Sports International (SWSI). After the Helsinki congress, sports relations with the RSI and Soviet sport ceased to be looked upon favourably by the leaders of the LSI, which prohibited its branches from taking part in the Spartakiad in 1928 in Moscow. It went on to outlaw all contact with branches of the RSI at its Prague congress of October 1929. [94]

## The USSR in the international network of communist sport

Following yet another tactical turnaround in 1928, the Comintern stated that social-democracy was the main enemy in the class struggle and declared support for the theory of 'social-fascism'. This theory, which prevailed until 1934, gave the Socialist Worker Sports Federation another reason not to go back on its decision to cease sports relations with the Soviet Union. However, this did not mean that Soviet sport was once again to be isolated. Indeed, after relations between the SWSI and the RSI became more and more confrontational, as did those between the socialists and the communists within several national branches of the SWSI, schisms formed and new branches of the RSI were created. This occurred between 1928 and 1931 in the worker sport movements of Germany, German Sudetenland, Switzerland, Great Britain and Finland, while the pro-communist worker sport organization of Alsace-Lorraine was excluded from the SWSI and became a member of the RSI. In Sweden, a branch of the RSI was created in 1927. There were also RSI branches in Norway, Czechoslovakia and France.

Soviet sport was therefore in a position to have strong links with worker sport in central and western Europe and Scandinavia, even if it was often the case that planned events could not take place because the Soviet athletes were refused visas.

As well as events involving Soviet athletes abroad, worker athletes visited the USSR, Finnish, Norwegian and German teams competing there in 1923–4. [95] Following a well-supervised visit, the worker athletes' mission gave a positive image of the host country: 'On returning from the Soviet Union, every group of sports-men should spread the news of Soviet accomplishments.' [96] Of course, all visitors had to be politically sound, which was not always the case. This led, in June 1932, to the Berlin bureau of the RSI reminding people that the members of the delegations sent to the USSR had to be selected according to political criteria by the leaders of the respective workers' sports organizations. [97]

The first major international sports event on Soviet soil, the Spartakiad, was staged in Moscow in August 1928, at the same time as the Comintern's sixth congress. The games were above all intended to demonstrate how far the USSR had progressed in the field of physical culture and to counterbalance bourgeois sport, particularly the Olympic Games held that same year in Amsterdam, by showing the revolutionary nature of Soviet physical culture and by gathering together a large number of worker athletes from foreign countries. [98,99] However, international participation remained relatively weak: 542 men and 70 women from 12 countries as opposed to 3000 men and 879 women from the USSR. [100]

A full cultural and tourism programme was provided for the worker athletes during their stay. In reports written by the participants that were circulated among the German worker athletes, they described visiting eight factories from different industrial sectors, a prison for 'criminals and counter-revolutionaries', two hospitals, a workers' hostel, and a business school; they describe an excursion to Kostroma ('invited by the Kostroma proletariat'), and a large popular festival on the banks of the Moscow River held in honour of those taking part in the Spartakiad. [101] They also had an interview with the chairman of Leningrad's trade union council. The picture painted by these reports is similar to that painted by the Austrian participants, [102] that is, of a happy people living in an almost perfect society, driven by powerful collectivist and internationalist feelings together with a strong identification with the political system. Even the report on the prison is a testimony to the humanism which seemed to reign in Russia. These accounts of the worker athletes' stay implied that all the impressions recounted were formed in a more or less unrehearsed context, and that all the Soviet people's displays of sympathy and solidarity were totally spontaneous; they therefore served as an excellent propaganda tool for the USSR. They gave an image which blatantly contradicted the realities of daily life marked by 'accelerated industrialization' and the Stalinist dictatorship, [103, 104] but which remained effective in the communist movement. The complacency with which the communist movement of the western world recorded Stalin's great purges is a sufficient indication of the extent of the communist imagination which saw the USSR as the ideal country and all the decisions and actions of the Communist Party's apparatus as necessary and good. Part of this imagination was based on the accounts of the worker delegations invited to stay in the Soviet Union; the staging of international sports events in the USSR should therefore not be underestimated, if only because they led to foreign athletes visiting the country and later giving written and oral accounts of their experiences which subtly confirmed the picture of the USSR that was being painted by the communist press. In fact, in Germany, 'information evenings' were held on a regular basis following worker athletes' visit to Russia. The speakers used a text written by leaders of the Communist Party.

From the bourgeois press [105] the Spartakiad was attended by a number of special envoys and was one of the rare occasions for Soviet sport to reveal itself to a public that was not limited to the worker sport movement. Indeed, worker sport remained a separate entity: the bourgeois press was generally unaware of developments within it, being more interested in the Olympic Games, in the prowess of athletes from their own country or in major international football matches.

The Soviet Union, which remained attached to the RSI, had to come to terms with a major decrease in the number of opportunities available for using sport as a means of promoting the nation. At the same time, the competitive strength of its athletes was improving, which meant that worker sports clubs were increasingly less able to provide the opposition needed to make Soviet sport world-class. The only way to do this was to compete against the best, and it became a growing tendency among the executives of the USSR's Supreme Council of Physical Culture to respond favourably to proposals from bourgeois sports organizations to pit their strength against Soviet sport, without giving too much consideration to the ideological implications. However, these tendencies were a source of concern within the RSI Bureau. [106]

Because the USSR was not closely tied in with bourgeois sport, the scope for using sport as a diplomatic weapon was also greatly limited. Talks held with the Italian Football Federation in 1931 with a view to organizing a match between the USSR and Italy failed owing to a veto from the Fédération Internationale de Football-Association (FIFA). [107] These talks were congruent with the Soviet interest in maintaining good relations with Italy under Mussolini; they were in total contradiction with the interests of the international worker sports movement and the RSI. However, when the interests of Soviet foreign policy were at stake, it was obvious that the only option available to the RSI was either to remain silent or to justify the links between Soviet sport and bourgeois sport by using pseudo-revolutionary arguments – even when these links were with bourgeois sports associations of authoritarian or fascist states, such as Turkey or Italy.

The RSI had become dependent on Soviet foreign policy in the same way as the Comintern: this was further illustrated in 1934 when the altering of Soviet diplomacy was followed by a significant change in the RSI's policy on sport.

## 1934: a change of direction

Until the end of 1933, Stalin thought that the USSR was safe from German attack since the Treaty of Rapallo of 1922, which he had upheld three months after Hitler was appointed Chancellor, was still valid. But the situation changed after a non-aggression pact was signed between Germany and Poland on 26 January 1924. Anticipating that the pact could signal the preparation of a German attack against the USSR, Soviet diplomacy started to change direction, and this was characterized by attempts to establish links with the democratic countries of western Europe with a view to forming an anti-Hitler coalition.

This change of direction also corresponded to an overall change in the tactics of the Comintern, which adopted a more moderate policy. The 'social-fascism' theory was rejected, and the Comintern appealed to its branches to form an alliance with the socialists to fight fascism. Later, it asked the communist parties to form an alliance with the progressive bourgeois parties to form 'popular fronts'. [108, 109]

The RSI drew up a plan of action to merge with the SWSI which it sent to its former main rival in September 1934. This policy of reconciliation with the SWSI was followed by a policy of conciliation with the bourgeois sports movement. It was trying, with the reformist sports organizations and the anti-fascist elements of bourgeois sport, to create a huge popular sports movement.

As early as the summer of 1934, even before the 'popular fronts of athletes' policy had been adopted, the RSI abandoned its reservations over relations between Soviet sport and bourgeois sport in European countries. In 1932 and 1933, it had once again expressed its disagreement over the termination of events between Soviet teams and the French, Czechoslovak and Polish bourgeois sports associations. [110, 111] In 1934, the RSI accepted the termination of events with teams representing bourgeois sport. This even included breaking links with professional football clubs in countries which, after the crushing of the German and Austrian worker sports federations by the fascists, were home to the largest worker sports movement in Europe: Czechoslovakia, France and Norway.

In 1934, competitions with top bourgeois teams were held in France, Norway and Sweden and, in Czechoslovakia, boxing and athletics events held between national teams ended in a victory for the USSR. [112] The following year saw an increase in the number of events involving bourgeois sport. [113]

In his report on events held abroad in 1934, Nikolai Antipov, chairman of the Supreme Council of Physical Culture until the end of 1934, [114] expressed his delight in the appreciation that the bourgeois press showed of Soviet athletes' performances. He went on to stress that given the political importance of these international sports events, defeat should be avoided at all costs.

> We should pay great attention to these events abroad. We should view them as great social and political events, and think carefully about each and every one of our actions in each specific context, always bearing in mind that we are representing the great Soviet Union and that it is on our behaviour and success that the entire country is judged by the workers and intellectuals of the capitalist countries. [115]

A few months later, an article in *Pravda* entitled 'The USSR must be an exemplary country for physical culture' indicated that the maxim 'catch up with and better the capitalist countries' sporting performances' was in the process of becoming reality. The article then went on to mention the international success achieved by Soviet athletes and their holding of unofficial world records, and ended: 'We have been working, but we must work more energetically to ensure that Soviet athletes become the best athletes in the world, so that in the years to come the USSR will be the country which holds the most world records.' [116]

Vasily Mantsev, who succeeded Antipov as chairman of the Supreme Council of Physical Culture, was certain that this was within reach. (Both Antipov and Mantsev fell victim to the great purges of 1936–8). [117] At the Congress of the Federation of Young Communists of the Soviet Union in 1936, he emphasized that in 1935–6, 163 new records were set, 19 of which were world records. This, he said, was 'thanks to the attention given to physical culture by our government, our Bolshevik Party, and by the sports movement's best friend: Stalin – the people's guide. We will be a power in the field of physical culture.' [118]

Indeed, by the mid-1930s – much more so than in the 1920s – the State was taking charge of the sports movement, which had lost all autonomy; in June 1936, the Supreme Council of Physical Culture was replaced by the Committee of Physical Culture and Sport attached to the Council of People's Commissars 'with the aim of improving the work carried out in physical culture and strengthening the State's control over physical culture and sport'. [119]

In 1936, therefore, the notion that sport was an activity which should serve as a means of preparing the workers for world revolution was very distant; sport was seen as something which enhanced national prestige, an idea which was quite widespread in capitalist countries. As far as the USSR was concerned, this sports-driven nationalism had a specific ideological function: sporting victories had to demonstrate the superiority of the socialist system.

However, the USSR did not make an appearance on the international sports stage until after the Second World War. It did start to forge links with various international sports federations, particularly with FIFA, from 1935 onwards, but did not join them. [120, 121] Above all, a practical compromise had to be reached which would enable the USSR to take part in sports events organized by the international sports federations without it becoming an official member. [122] A note, most probably written in 1936, from Karpov, Director of the International Department, to Zhelikov, Chairman of the Committee of Physical Culture and Sport, is particularly revealing. Having expressed his regret that the USSR was relatively isolated in relation to international sport, Karpov indicated that the USSR could never, however, join FIFA since it was 'run by anti-Soviet fascists'. According to Karpov, it followed that Soviet sport had to 'sign an agreement with FIFA which would allow them to play against the best teams in the world without their making a commitment to the heads of FIFA'. [123]

It would have been inappropriate for Soviet sport to be a member of a seemingly fascist organization within the context of the anti-fascist struggle, a central point in the Comintern's policies until the signing of the Hitler–Stalin pact in August 1939; neither was Soviet sport able to break away completely from the worker sport movement – at least not officially. The RSI was disbanded in the spring of 1937 by the Presidium of the Comintern, [124] partly so that preparations could be made to integrate Soviet sport into international bourgeois sport. However, this resolution was kept secret, and steps were taken to give the impression that the RSI was still in existence so as not to disillusion the worker sports movements of capitalist countries. [125] Acting on a decision taken by the political bureau of the Communist Party of the Soviet Union, [126] the USSR even took part in the SWSI's Third Worker Olympiad in Antwerp in 1937; an illustration that there had been some reconciliation between the SWSI and the RSI. But the SWSI flatly refused to merge with the RSI – the latter's main objective up until it was disbanded – mainly because of the state of relations between Soviet sport and bourgeois sport.

With its fairly discreet links with bourgeois sport and its concern over overtly withdrawing from worker sport, the USSR's international sports policy of 1934–9 was one of indecision. However, the country's sports ideology meant that Soviet athletes were destined to take part in the highly competitive Olympic Games, but because of the Second World War and postwar relations with the West they would not be able to do so until 1952 in Helsinki. [127]

## Conclusions

Three phases are discernible in the development of Soviet sport's international relations before the Second World War. The first (1920–4) was marked by attempts to form a world-wide revolutionary sports movement, by ceasing to maintain official relations with the bourgeois sports movements, and by keeping Soviet sport relatively isolated. The second phase (1925–34) saw a proliferation in international relations, maintained above all by the European worker sports movement (in 1926 and 1927, these relations were mainly with branches of the LSI, then later – when the 'social-fascism' theory was prevalent, i.e. between 1928 and 1934 – almost exclusively with branches of the RSI), but also by abandoning the rule of maintaining relations only with worker sport. This rule was replaced by the firm belief that sport could – and had to – serve the national interests of the USSR. However, relations with bourgeois sport remained very limited. The third phase (1934–9) saw Soviet sport becoming progressively more and more open with respect to bourgeois sport and ceasing to see the existence of an international sports organization as a pawn in the revolutionary class struggle.

These stages correspond to the major changes in Soviet foreign policy. Having initially pinned all its hopes on revolutions taking place in other countries, it tended towards the 'construction of socialism in one country' in 1924–5, while at the same time continuing to support the subversive activities of communist movements in capitalist countries. In 1934, as the fascist threat increased, the USSR began seeking to form alliances with democratic countries in western Europe; in the same year it was admitted into the League of Nations. This new tendency resulted in the communist movement adopting a conciliatory policy regarding the socialist worker movement and the progressive bourgeois parties, and enabled Soviet sport to adopt the appearance of a more open policy – just as it had in 1925. The long-term objectives, however, were to pit their strengths against the best athletes of bourgeois sport and to strive to set new records with the intention of proving the superior nature of the socialist system through sports victories, and to turn sport into an essential element of Soviet national identity.

The RSI was disbanded when it was seen to be increasingly harmful to the interests of Soviet diplomacy. At the time, these interests were best served by a relaxed relationship with bourgeois sport rather than by maintaining an organization which continued to be seen in the sporting world as being strictly opposed to bourgeois sport. This once again illustrated the subordination of the RSI to Soviet interests, which, as has already been shown, were not always the same as those of the communist worker sports movement of other countries.

If, by virtue of the structures of the international communist movement which had been set up during the 1920s, the Soviet branch of the RSI had authority that it would have been pointless to question, Soviet sport's membership of the RSI severely limited the field of action of international sports policy in the USSR. Events with bourgeois sports organizations could only be held within a very limited context. All in all, it was difficult for Soviet sport to be at the helm of a revolutionary sports movement and at the same time become an efficient instrument of diplomacy as well as an important means of promoting the country as a nation. Conversely, attempts to make sport carry out these various functions – which were to a large extent contradictory – greatly harmed the image and the influence of the RSI.

The entrance of Soviet athletes into the competition arena probably had very little political effect. Admittedly, the gradual improvement in the standard of Soviet sport had been noticed and described by the bourgeois sports press. However, journalists were not always content with simply assessing the athletes' sporting performances: they sometimes made critical allusions to the Soviet system, questioned the amateurism of the athletes or focused on the ideological contradictions of Soviet sport. As for the many reports which *did* concentrate on what was happening on the sports field, thus reflecting the widespread view that sport was an apolitical area, historiographic methods do not enable us to determine to what extent they unconsciously enhanced the image of the USSR. But it is unlikely that they had this effect, especially when one considers that, after the Second World War, the USSR became the world's leading sports nation – which was a recognition of its ambitious policy on sport, clearly formulated since the 1930s – and that, however, even the most spectacular sporting triumphs do not seem to have led to any significant changes in the ideas that people in western countries had of the USSR and the communist system.

However ambitious a country's policy on sport, that policy can hardly influence a nation's image. The way in which the athletic performances of a country are perceived and described depends on the ideas that are associated with the country, as well as on ideological tendencies and political interests. Consequently, the Soviet Union's sporting triumphs could be presented as symptoms of a dictatorship which favoured inhumane training methods just as much as they could be seen as evidence of the superiority of a socialist system which differed from others insofar as it enabled its people to play sport. The performances as such can change neither the reality nor the imaginary; they are a symbol that can be interpreted in a number of different ways. However, they do lend themselves particularly well to political propaganda.

Soviet sport's international relations did indeed form an integral part of the communist movement's propaganda operation during the 1920s and 1930s. The USSR's international sports policy, together with that of the RSI, was marked by an overwhelming determination to use sport as a means of enhancing the USSR's image in the western world and to belie the prejudices that people had concerning Bolshevism. However, this did not prevent there being certain counter-effects resulting from the Soviet delegations' somewhat clumsy behaviour. The reports in the communist press and the worker athletes' accounts of their stays in the USSR were doubtless taken full advantage of; but this use of sport as an instrument of propaganda could only be of limited use, given that almost the only people who could be influenced by it were from a worker milieu that was already more or less linked to the communist movement. All in all, the influence of the emergence of Soviet sport in Europe during the interwar years should be situated within the international communist movement, which could interpret the performances of Soviet athletes as proof of its admiration of the USSR, and present them as such.

## Sources

The Comintern Archives at the Russian centre for the conservation and study of contemporary history documents, Moscow, collection 'Sportinern' (537).

The Russian Federation Archives (RFA), Moscow, collection 'The Supreme Council of Physical Culture, International Relations' (75 76/2).

Stiftung Archiv der Parteien und Massenorganisationen der DDR im Bundesarchiv, Berlin, collection 'Kommunistische Partei Deutschlands – Zentralkomitee' (SAPMO-Barch), Ry/12/710.

## References

1. The Sportintern (537) collection in the Comintern Archives at the Russian centre for the conservation and study of contemporary history documents, Moscow.
2. The Supreme Council of Physical Culture, International Relations collection (75 76/2) in the Russian Federation Archives (RFA), Moscow. The documents on sports events between Germany and the USSR can be found in the Stiftung Archiv der Parteien und Massenorganisationen der DDR im Bundesarchiv Archives in Berlin as part of the Kommmunistische Partei Deutschlands – Zentralkomitee collections (SAPMO-Barch, Ry/12/710).
3. Cf. Riordan, James (1977) *Sport in Soviet Society. Development of Sport and Physical Education in Russia and the USSR*, Cambridge University Press, Cambridge/London/New York, pp. 68–75; 84–5, for information about this organization.
4. RFA, 75 76/2/28, Tätigkeitsbericht der Roten Sportinternationale und seines Exekutivkomitees, s.d. [1926].
5. Cf. the Russian centre for the conservation and study of contemporary history documents, 537 I 73 and 537 II 26.
6. Steinberg, David (1979) Sport under Red Flags! The relations between the Red Sport International and the Socialist Workers' Sport International 1920–1939. Madison. Thesis.
7. Gounot, André, *Sport réformiste ou sport révolutionnaire? Les débuts des Internationales sportives ouvrières*, in Arnaud, Pierre (1994) (eds), *Les origines du sport ouvrier en Europe*, l'Harmattan, Paris, pp. 219–46.
8. Frank, Pierre (ed.) (1979) *Histoire de l'Internationale Communiste*, vol. I, La Brèche, Paris, pp. 153–90.
9. Kriegel, Annie (1977) La IIIe Internationale, in Droz, Jacques (ed.) *Histoire générale du socialisme*, Vol. III de 1919 à 1925, PUF, Paris, pp. 73–118.
10. Cf. the Russian centre for the conservation and study of contemporary history documents, 537 I 2, for the list of people who attended the congress during which the RSI was set up.
11. Cf. correspondence between the RSI and the Comintern, August–October 1921 in the Russian centre for the conservation and study of contemporary history documents, 537 I 71.
12. The Russian centre for the conservation and study of contemporary history documents, 537 I 1 (minutes from the sessions of Sportintern's first Conference, 19–30 July 1921).
13. Ibid., 537 I 2 (manifestos, theses, and the list of delegates at the first conference).
14. *Proletariersport. Organ für proletarisch-physische Kultur* (the official organ of the RSI, published from 1923 to 1927), (1923), (1), pp. 10–11.
15. RFA, 75 76/2/28. Tätigkeitsbericht der Roten Sportinternationale und seines Exekutivkomitees, s.d. [1926], but was in such a mess that at the founding congress of the RSI, Podvoïski spoke of the 'catastrophic state of sport in Russia'.
16. Cf. The Russian centre for the conservation and study of contemporary history documents, 537 I 1.

17. *Sport* (organ of the Worker's Sports Federation. French branch of the RSI) (6) (1933),
18. Hentilä, Seppo (1991) Die finnische Arbeitersportbewegung und ihre Beziehungen zu Deutschland bis 1933, in Luh, Andreas and Beckers, Edgar *Umbruch und Kontinuität im Sport – Reflexionen im Umfeld der Sportgeschichte. Festschrift für Horst Ueberhorst*, Universitätvlg, Dr. N. Brockmeyer, p. 373.
19. Skorning, Lothar (1987) Das erste deutsch-sowjetische Sporttreffen 1923 – ein Höhepunkt der Berliner Sportgeschichte. *Körpererziehung* **37** (10), p. 414.
20. The Russian centre for the conservation and study of contemporary history documents 537 I 1 (minutes from the sessions of the Sportintern's first conference, 19–30 July 1921).
21. RFA, 75 76/2/28, Tätigkeitsbericht der Roten Sportinternationale und seines Exekutivkomitess, s.d. [1926].
22. *Proletariesport* (1), (1925), p. 3.
23. Cf. Ueberhorst, Horst (1971) *Von Athen bis München. Die modernen Olympischen Spiele, der olympische Gedanke, der deutsche Beitrag*, 2nd edn, Vlg. Bartels & Wernitz, Munich/Berlin/Frankfurt a. M., p. 26.
24. The Russian centre for the conservation and study of contemporary history documents, 537 I 79, minutes from the meeting of the executive committee of the RSI, 30 January 1924 in Moscow.
25. Ibid.
26. Arbeiter- Turn- und Sportbund (1924) *14. Bundestag in Cassell 1924*, Leipzig, pp. 12–37.
27. Morton Henry W. (1963) *Medaillen nach Plan. Der Sowjetsport*, Vlg, Wissenschaft und Politik, Cologne, pp. 148–68.
28. Riordan, *Sport in Soviet Society*, *op. cit.*, pp. 82–119.
29. *Proletariersport* (4) (1924).
30. Riordan, *Sport in Soviet Society*, *op. cit.*, pp.. 95–105.
31. Cantelon, Hart (1988) The Leninist/Proletkult'tist Cultural Debates: Implications for Sport Among the Soviet Working Class, in Cantelon, Hart and Hollands, Robert, *Leisure, Sport and Working-Class Cultures: Theory and History*, Garamond Press, Toronto: Ontario, pp. 77–97.
32. The Russian centre for the conservation and study of contemporary history documents, 537 I 105, Aufgaben der Partei auf dem Gebiet der Körperkultur. Resolution des ZK der KPR.
33. Morton, *Medaillen nach Plan*, *op. cit.*, p. 161.
34. Morton, *Medaillen nach Plan*, *op. cit.*, p. 160.
35. *Proletariersport*, (2) (1924), pp. 21–22.
36. *Proletariersport*, (4), (1924), p. 61.
37. Cf. Simon, Hans (1963) Der Kampf der Opposition im Arbeiter- Turn- und Sportbund gegen die Reformisten und um die Gewinnung der Mitglieder in der revolutionären nachkriegskrise 1919–1923. Leipzig. Thesis. p. 150.
38. The Russian centre for the conservation and study of contemporary history documents, 537 I 75, a letter from the Comintern's commission to the executive of the RSI, Moscow, 15 November 1923.
39. Cf. The Russian centre for the conservation and study of contemporary history documents, 537 I 79, minutes of the meeting of the executive committee of the RSI, 10 September 1924.
40. Cf. Arbeiter- Turn- und Sportbund, *14 Bundestag in Cassell 1924. op. cit.*, pp. 12–37: during this congress, the behaviour of the Soviet delegation was severely criticized by the social-democrats.

41. The Russian centre for the conservation and study of contemporary history documents, 537 I 75, a letter from the RSI to the Comintern, Moscow, 17 October 1923.
42. The Russian centre for the conservation and study of contemporary history documents, 537 I 75, a letter from the commission of the Comintern to the executive of the RSI Moscow, 15 November 1923.
43. The Russian centre for the conservation and study of contemporary history documents, 537 I 79, the minutes of the meeting of the executive committee of the RSI, 1 August 1924.
44. The Russian centre for the conservation and study of contemporary history documents, 537 I 79, the minutes of a meeting of the executive committee of the RSI, 20 August 1924.
45. *Proletariersport*, (11) (1926), p. 180.
46. Ibid., (1) (1926), pp. 2–3.
47. RFA, 75 76/2/28, Tätigkeitsbericht der Roten Sportinternationale und seines Exekutivkomitees, s.d. [1926], p. 41.
48. The Russian centre for the conservation and study of contemporary history documents, 537 I 54, Thesen über die Arbeit der RSI im Osten und in den Kolonien, angenommen auf der Erweiterten Exekutive der RSI im Mai 1926, for details of the relationship between the RSI and Soviet sport and the countries of the East.
49. Cf. The Russian centre for the conservation and study of contemporary history documents, 537 I 79, the minutes of the meeting of the executive committee of the RSI, 30 January 1924 in Moscow.
50. *Proletariersport* (4) (1924), p. 63.
51. Arbeiter-Turn-Zeitung (an organ of the workers' gymnastics and sports Union of Germany), 9 June 1926 (a report of the meeting of the LSI Bureau from 25 to 27 May 1926 in Amsterdam).
52. SABMO-Barch, RY/12/710/6, Resolution gegen die Verbürgerlichungstendenzen im russischen Sport, s.d. [1925].
53. Cf. The Russian centre for the conservation and study of contemporary history documents, 537 I 102, Denkschrift der Kommission des Orgbüros des EKKI über die Richtung der int. A- und Bauern-Sport- und Turnbewegung, 26.II.1925.
54. SABMO-Barch, RY/12/710/6, Resolution gegen die Verbürgerlichungstendenzen im russischen Sport, s.d. [1925].
55. Cf. SAMBO-Barch, RY/12/710/7, f. 16–22, minutes from communist faction leadership meetings, 29 May 1925 and 11 June 1925.
56. Cf. The Russian centre for the conservation and study of contemporary history documents, 537 I 104, Bruno Lieske's letter of resignation, August 1925.
57. SABMO-Barch, RY/12/710/5, Aus dem Protokoll von der Sitzung des Internationalen Büros der Luzerner Sportinternationale am 25. und 26. Mai 1926 in Amsterdam.
58. The Russian centre for the conservation and study of contemporary history documents, 537 I 75, Einige Bemerkungen zu den Gutachten des Genossen Wollenberger über die Teilnahme der russischen Arbeitersportler an Veranstaltungen der bürgerlichen Sportorganisationen, s.d. [1926]
59. *Proletariersport* (5) (1926), pp. 66–7.
60. The Russian centre for the conservation and study of contemporary history documents, 537 I 125, Gutachten über die Teilnahme der russischen Arbeitersportler an Veranstaltungen der bürgerlichen Sportorganisationen, s.d. [1926].

61. Cf. *Proletariersport* (3) (1926), p. 36.
62. Riordan, *Sport in Soviet Society*, *op. cit.*, p. 93.
63. Ruffman, Karl-Heinz, (1980) *Sport und Körperkultur in der Sowjetunion*, DTV, München, p. 51.
64. Cf. Riordan, *Sport in Soviet Society*, *op. cit.*, p. 118.
65. Deutscher, Issac (1990) *Stalin, Eine politische Biographie*, Dietz Vlg., Berlin, pp. 366–82, 500–8.
66. Cf. Triska, Jan F. and Finley, David D. (1968) *Soviet Foreign Policy*, Macmillan, London, pp. 2–7.
67. Cf. RFA, 75 76/2/35, Fritz Reußner: Unsere internationalen Sportspiele, s.d. [end of 1925].
68. Cf. *Proletariersport* (4) (1926), p. 55.
69. Cf. Allard, Sven, (1974) *Stalin und Hitler. Die sowjetrussische Außenpolitik 1930–1941*, Francke Vlg., Bern/München, pp 7–11.
70. Cf. Triska and Finley, *Soviet Foreign Policy*, *op. cit.*, p. 5
71. Deutscher, *Stalin*, *op. cit.*, p. 501.
72. Cf. Hartl, Hans and Marx, Werner (1967) *Fünfzig Jahre sowjetische Deutschlandpolitik*, Harald Boldt Vlg./, Boppard am Rhein.
73. Carr, Edward H. (1954) *Berlin–Moskau. Deutschland und Rußland zwischen den beiden Weltkriegen*, Deutsche Vlg. Anstalt, Stuttgart.
74. Cf. Skorning, Lothar (1967) Chronik der deutsch-sowjetischen Sportbeziehungen bis 1937. *Theorie und Praxis der Körperkultur* (16) (1967), pp. 885–900.
75. Internationaler Sozialistischer Verband für Arbeitersport und Körperkultur, *Bericht über den 3. Kongreß zu Paris–Pantin. 31. Oktober, 1. und 2. November 1925*, s.l., s.d. [1926]
76. *Internationaler Arbeitersport. Zeitschrift für Fragen der internationalen revolutionären Arbeitersportbewegung* (an organ of the RSI from 1930 to 1933), October 1932, p. 213.
77. RFA, 75 76/2/35, Fritz Reußner. Unsere internationalen Sportspiele, s.d. [end of 1925].
78. RFA, 75 76/2/35, Fritz Reußner: Unsere internationalen Sportspiele.
79. RFA, 75 76/2/28, Tätigkeitsbericht der Roten Sportinternationale und seines Exekutivkomitees, s.d. [1926]/.
80. The Russian centre for the conservation and study of contemporary history documents, 537 I 125, Gutachten über die Teilnahme der russischen Arbeitersportler an Veranstaltungen der bürgerlichen Sportorganisationen, s.d. [1926].
81. The Russian centre for the conservation and study of contemporary history documents, 537 I 175, An alle Sektionen der Roten Sportinternationale und sympathisierende Organisationen (a circular from the Secretariat of the RSI, September 1929).
82. The Russian centre for the conservation and study of contemporary history documents, 537 I 75 Circular addressed to all the branches and all the organisations which are sympathetic to the RSI, s.d. [1929].
83. SABPMO BArch, Ry/12/710/6, W. Sänger an die K.P.D., Polbüro, Berlin, den 19. Juli 1927.
84. SABPMO BArch, Ry/12/710/6, Abschrift aus einem Briefe vom Genossen H. Richter, Jena über den Kreistag der Arbeiter-Athleten in Weimar am 8. und 9. Januar 1927.
85. SABPMO BArch, Ry/12/710/6, Bericht über den Verlauf des Russenringens. Stuttgart, den 15. Dezember 26.

86. SABPMO BArch, Ry/12/710/5, Zentralkomitee der KPD an das Sekretariat der roten Sportinternationale Moskau. Berlin, den 5. November 1926.

87. Arbeiter- Turn- und Sportbund (1927) Sparte Fußball, *Die Fußballspiele der Ländermannschaften der Union der Sozialistischen Sowjet-Republiken in Deutschland, Juli 1927*, Leipzig.

88. SABPMO BArch, Ry/12/710/6, 92–93.

89. *Die Russenspiele, op. cit.*, p. 51–4.

90. Ibid., p. 75–6.

91. RFA, 75 76/2/28, Tätigkeitsbericht der Roten Sportinternationale und seines Exekutivkomitees, s.d. [1926].

92. Cf. SABPMO, BArch, Ry/12/710/6, Protokoll über die Verhandlungen der deutschen Bundesfußballeitung im D.S.V. – Heim in Dresden am 16. Juli 1927.

93. Cf. *Arbeiter-Turn-Zeitung*, 9 June 1926 (report on the meeting of the International Bureau of the LSI in Amsterdam).

94. Cf. Dierker, Herbert (1990) *Arbeitersport im Spannungsfeld der Zwanziger Jahre. Sportpolitik und Alltagserfahrungen auf internationaler, deutscher und Berliner Ebene*, Klartext, Essen, pp. 46–7.

95. *Proletariersport*, (5)(1924), p. 84.

96. RFA, 75 76/2/35, Fritz Reußner: Unsere internationalen Sportspiele.

97. RFA, 75 76/2/118, Sekretariat der RSI an den Obersten Rat für physische Kultur, Berlin, den 7. Juni 1932.

98. *Internationaler Arbeitersport*, (December) (1927), p. 14.

99. RFA, 75 76/2/82, An alle Arbeitersportorganisationen! An alle Arbeitersportler und Sportlerinnen! An alle Werktätigen!, s.d. [1927].

100. Sporthistorisches Kabinett des Fachbereichs Sportwissenschaft der Universität Leipzig, documents from the German Committee of the Spartakiade, Tatsachen von der Spartakiade 1928, s.d. [1928].

101. Sporthistorisches Kabinett des Fachbereichs Sportwissenschaft der Universität Leipzig, documents from the German committee of the Spartakiade.

102. *66 österreichische Arbeitersportler berichten über die Sowjetunion. Bericht der österreichischen Besucher der Moskauer Spartakiade 1928*, Wien, 1929.

103. Peter, Antonio and Maier, Robert, (1991) *Die Sowjetunion im Zeichen des Stalinismus*, Vlg. Wissenschaft und Gesellschaft, Köln.

104. Bonwetsch, Bernd (1993) Der Stalinismus der dreißiger Jahre. Zur Deformation einer Gesellschaft, in Arbeitsbereich DDR-Geschichte im Mannheimer Zentrum für Europäische Sozialforschung der Universität Mannheim, *Jahrbuch für historische Kommunismusforschung*, Akademie Vlg., Berlin, pp. 110–36.

105. Cf. Ruffman, *Sport und Körperkultur in der Sowjetunion, op. cit.*, pp. 57–8.

106. RFA, 75 76/2/132, letters from the Copenhagen Bureau of the RSI to the Moscow Bureau, 28 September and 15 November 1933.

107. *Internationaler Sportspressedienst* (Sozialistische Arbeiter-Sportinternationale) (6) (1932) 2 February.

108. Firsow, Fridrich, Igorewitsch (1990) Stalin und die Komintern, in Institut für Geschichte der Arbeiterbewegung, *Die Komintern und Stalin. Sowjetische Historiker zur Geschichte der Kommunistischen Internationale*, Dietz Vlg., Berlin, p. 111.

109. Fischer, Alexander, (1991), Kollektive Sicherheit und imperialistischer Krieg. Sowjetische Außenpolitik im Vorfeld des Hitler-Stalin-Paktes, in Antonio and Maier, *Die Sowjetunion im Zeichen des Stalinismus, op. cit.*, p. 87.

110. RFA, 75 76/2/118, letters from the Secretariat of the RSI (Berlin) to the Supreme Council of Physical Culture, 13 and 20 January 1932.

111. RFA, 75 76/2/132, letters from the RSI Bureau to the Supreme Council of Physical Culture, 28 September and 15 November 1933.
112. *Internationale Sportrundschau. Zeitschrift für Theorie und Körperkultur* (official organ of the RSI, published between 1933 and 1936), 1935 (February), pp. 71–3.
113. Ibid., (October), p. 414–15.
114. Ibid., (February), p. 84.
115. Ibid., (February), pp. 71–3.
116. Quoted in *Internationale Sportrundschau*, 1935 (July), pp. 257–9.
117. Riordan, *Sport in Soviet Society*, *op. cit.*, p. 124.
118. *Internationale Sportrundschau*, 1936 (May) pp. 144–5.
119. The Russian centre for the conservation and study of contemporary history documents, 17/3/978, session of the political bureau of the Communist Party of the Soviet Union, 22 June 1936.
120. RFA, 75 76/2/176 (correspondence with FIFA).
121. RFA, 75 76/2/186 (a box containing documents from various international sports federations collected between January and June 1937).
122. The Russian centre for the conservation and study of contemporary history documents, 537 I 219, C. Aksamit: Zur gegenwärtigen Lage der Sportbewegung und der Perspektiven ihrer weiteren Entwicklung, s.d. [1936].
123. RFA, 75 76/2/176.
124. The Russian centre for the conservation and study of contemporary history documents, 537 I 219, Translation from German, 11-4-37: the decision concerning the transformation of the secretariat of the RSI into an auxiliary organ of the Comintern for sport.
125. Ibid.
126. The Russian centre for the conservation and study of contemporary history documents, 17/3/987, a session of the political bureau of the Communist Party of the Soviet Union, 11 May 1937.
127. Riordan, *Sports in Soviet Society*, *op. cit.*, pp. 120–52.

# Chapter 12

# Interwar sport and interwar relations: some conclusions

*Richard Holt*

This topic falls naturally into two parts: firstly, there is the way liberal democracies like France, Great Britain and the United States came to terms with the reality of modern sport as a mass phenomenon and chose – or chose not – to respond to its manipulation by illiberal states of various kinds; conversely, there is a second group of authoritarian or totalitarian states, adopting sporting forms derived from liberal democracy – autonomous federations, constitutions, even elections – and appropriating sport for an ultra-nationalist project; or in the case of the Soviet Union and 'Red Sport' for an ostensibly internationalist purpose. For the communists this involved a blanket denunciation of western sport as 'bourgeois', 'nationalist', 'imperialist' and 'militarist'; the fascist regimes, on the other hand, clearly thought democratic sport had lost its way, falling victim to commercialism and individualism instead of preparing the youth of the nation for collective sacrifice through bodily discipline.

The 'apolitical' character of sport, which was often claimed by those involved, was largely a myth. French gymnastics was anti-German and divided between a secular and a Catholic organization. In Britain sport was closely linked with the Empire, especially cricket and Rugby, and in the hands of a privileged elite of gentlemen amateurs. However, the fact that sport was inevitably embedded in the political values and practices of its host country does not mean there was a formal or official relationship between sport and the State. This distinction is of prime importance for understanding the role of sport in international relations. British sport, for example, had informal links with government ministries through personal acquaintances – contacts that were used effectively by the Foreign Office to persuade the British Olympic Association in 1936 to withdraw its bid for the 1940 Olympics. However, there was no British government ministry to deal with sport; there was no formal interference from the Foreign Office or, before the First World War, from the Quai d'Orsay.

The First World War, however, saw the extension of government activity into a vast range of 'private' matters; this was the first 'total war' in which the State expanded its activity to control not just military but economic and social arrangements of various kinds. What happened after the war? Did the liberal democracies begin to use sport for the enhancement of national prestige? There is a well-established idea that in 'liberal' states sport was 'neutral', occupying a distinct area away from politics, while in authoritarian or totalitarian states of the Right and the Left sport became a vehicle for state diplomacy and control. However, Arnaud's account of the internationalization of sport from the turn of the century alongside his detailed account of the sports policy of the French State between the wars effectively dispels this myth. It was not the fascist states which first grasped the significance of sport for international relations. Precursors of fascism, like the monarchical nationalist Charles Maurras had seen the possibility of using an event like the Olympic Games to promote national virility and competition from the outset. The First World War profoundly aggravated the principle of state competition in sport, which had already been apparent in London in 1908 and even more evident at Stockholm in 1912 -- so much so that thought of French failure at the projected Berlin Games of 1916 stimulated vigorous debate about how to save national honour against a hereditary enemy; and the Germans, as Kruger has shown, shared similar worries about letting down the race in front of their own people.

Four years of slaughter on the Western Front had raised the stakes too high to permit athletic contests soon afterwards. The French simply could not risk losing in front of the Germans in 1920 or even in 1924 when the other Central Powers were allowed to compete in the Paris Olympics. Contrary to received opinion, it was the liberal states, notably Britain, France and Belgium, rather than fascist Italy or Nazi Germany which first explicitly politicized international sporting contacts. France had emerged victorious from the Great War but with huge losses of resources and population. The fears of a declining population and a weak economy that had haunted France before the war coexisted with the triumphant mood of national assertion immediately after it at the Treaty of Versailles. The French State was keen that success in sport should show how France had triumphed over disaster. Sporting heroes like Carpentier in boxing or the Pelissier brothers in cycling had to carry the weight of national expectations of glory and for the first time the government showed a clear awareness of the value of such sporting propaganda.

Nor was it only the French who were gripped by this intense postwar politicizing of sport. The British, for whom 'fair play' and 'non-interference' were supposedly an article of faith, in fact took a lead banning the Germans and their allies from international sport. Not content with blocking their participation in the Antwerp Olympics, the British even insisted that all nations, which as neutrals had played sport with Germany or her allies during the war, should be isolated. However, as Holt indicated in setting the context for his discussion of the sporting relations of Britain and Germany in the mid-1930s, this boycott of the Central Powers was not *government* policy, although it clearly had government sympathy. Polley has made it clear that the foreign office only formally accepted an invitation to the Antwerp Games by accident – an official on the point of retirement replied positively to a formal invitation instead of referring it directly to the British Olympic Committee as was the standard practice. [1] France, it seems, was earlier than Britain in intervening in sport at the level of the State and Britain had no equivalent of the sports propaganda Service des Oeuvres Françaises à L'Etranger (SOFE), which in 1920 took over the 'Section du Tourisme et du Sport' that had been created in the French Foreign Ministry. The British, trapped by an administrative error, had to provide some support for a British contingent to Antwerp but refused to subsidize their team unlike the French who provided 200 000 francs to ensure their country would be properly represented. The head of the Foreign Office simply wrote 'Olympic Games are an international farce, no action' on an appeal from the British Olympic Committee for support for the Antwerp Games. [2] No doubt the British government supported the ban on Germany but unlike France it did not instigate a boycott or manoeuvre to exclude the Germans from the Paris Games. Arnaud's research in the hitherto untouched SOFE sports archives reveals a fascinating new picture. For the British the role of sport in post-war international relations was the result of the activities of the Football Association itself and not the Foreign Office. Men whose brothers or sons, friends and colleagues, had been killed or wounded in the war were simply not willing to put personal feelings to one side as soon as the war was over.

During the 1920s there was little or no British government interest in the sporting politics of other states. Even fascist Italy with its vast new sport and leisure programme evoked no formal response until public attention was stimulated by the Italian challenge to England's pre-eminence in world soccer. The British government missed an opportunity to promote good relations with Italy through sport just when they needed them, i.e. during the delicate diplomatic negotiations to form the Stresa front against the new threat from Nazi Germany.

Similarly, when a game was arranged against Germany at the end of 1935, the British government was caught unprepared. The match had been agreed without consulting the Foreign Office, although the German sports authorities were in essence part of the Nazi administration. The British government became involved only when there was a threat to public order from those opposed to the match in the trade unions and on the Left. Significantly, the Home Secretary refused to stop the match and he was supported in this by the Foreign Office, which did not want to cause unnecessary offence to Germany. Internal government documents and comment in the national press both strongly supported the idea of non-intervention and 'apolitical' sport. Hence the paradox that the British government intervened to ensure non-intervention; this was the *de facto* position established in late 1935 which also applied to the Berlin Games. The British government did not want a boycott of the Games, although the possible value of the threat of one was briefly discussed. The England–Germany match of December 1935 had been a dress rehearsal for such a move and it had failed. Britain had too strong a tradition of amateurism and too pressing reasons for not wishing to alienate Germany. The British wanted normality in relations with Germany in so far as this was possible with a regime such as Hitler's. However, the British position of state 'purity' was not consistent; the Foreign Office, for example, moved swiftly on rumours of a French boycott in May 1936 to express their disapproval; they also urged the British Olympic Committee to withdraw a bid to hold the 1940 Games in London for diplomatic and strategic reasons concerning Japan.

But these moments of exertion were exceptional. The British government for the most part did not need to take a position over the Berlin Games because, unlike the United States, Britain had neither strong Jewish nor black pressure groups agitating against the abuse of sport by the Nazi state. However, as Guttmann shows, in the United States the situation was rather different, especially in terms of the activism of pressure groups on the American Olympic Committee to investigate Nazi practice. Of the major nations involved in the Games, it was only in the United States that participation was genuinely in doubt. Guttmann neatly shows the complexity of such alignments. For it was true and not surprising that Jews and Communists outside of sport and inclined to prejudge the German case were active in the boycott campaign in the USA and Canada. But it was also true – and shocking – that the leaders of the International Olympic Committee and the International Amateur Athletic Federation like Baillet Latour and Edström were clearly not prepared to condemn anti-Semitism root and branch. The American case shows the importance of a key individual in the international politics of sport. For it was mainly the desperate commitment of Avery Brundage to send a team that ensured the narrowest of votes against further investigations of the political conditions of sport in Germany (after Brundage's initial 'inspection'). Without Brundage the decision of Jahncke, one of the three American members of the IOC, to condemn participants in a public letter to the *New York Times*, might have had more effect.

However, politics are rarely simple, especially the pressure group politics of sport. For black American organizations were split over involvement and not themselves entirely free of anti-Semitism. Ideologically, the American objection centred on the issue of 'access' – the Olympics had to be open to all, including German Jews. The Germans had to appear to support an ideal of open competition and meritocracy to satisfy American as well as Olympic values. Before the Nazis came to power they denounced racial mixing in sport and wanted a 'whites only' Olympics. Hence the surprise of Lewald and Diem when Hitler abruptly saw his chance for a huge national propaganda exercise and supported the Berlin Games. Opportunism proved more important than a strict adherence to ideology. Racism was temporarily suspended; even Hitler's snub of Jesse Owens turns out to be a myth. This, as Kruger shows in a wide-ranging survey of German sport between the wars, made the Nazis particularly difficult to deal with. For they paid lip service to the ideals of international sport when it suited them and courted good relations with major athletic powers.

Nevertheless, the Nazi manipulation of sport was built upon an existing tradition of politicized sport within Germany. In fact, the very idea of 'sport' was itself ideologically charged. The indigenous gymnastic '*Turner*' tradition, closely identified with the Wilhelmine state, denounced sport as foreign, individualistic and decadent. *Turnen* were themselves, of course, internally split with a strong rival to the nationalist Deutsche Turnerschaft in the socialist Arbeiter Turnbund. This tradition of politicized physical culture continued during and after the war as the German military and the State increasingly came to see the advantages of sport, with Carl Diem and Theodore Lewald providing broadly conservative and nationalist continuity from the Wilhelmine period through Weimar and into the Third Reich.

The advent of Hitler in 1933 dramatized the conflict between the declining 'Turner' tradition and the growth of athletic sports. Naturally the *Turners* hoped their indigenous 'blood and earth' values would be taken over by the Nazis whose propaganda had hitherto been sympathetic to the ideal of physical discipline for military service and dubious about the cult of records associated with the Olympics, despite the fact Germany did very well at Amsterdam in 1928. What seems to have proved decisive in Nazi thinking was not simply the popularity of sport but the extent to which Italy had revealed how it could be a powerful source of international prestige. Mutual surveillance of status was very much a part of the flow of sporting influence between states – especially fascist ones run by egotistical dictators. Mussolini backed the Italian football team which was having great success – and went on to win the World Cup hosted in Rome in 1934 – and supported the Italian Olympic team that came second in the medal table in Los Angeles. Germany could not afford to listen to the isolationist 'purity' of the *Turnen* and instead the Nazis enthusiastically took up sport, rapidly increasing the number of international meetings and continued in this vein after the Berlin Olympics and even into the war itself.

Here Kruger's work fits nicely into Teja's analysis of the evolution of fascist sports policy in Italy, which in many respects provided a working model for the Germans and later for Franco. After Mussolini seized power in 1922 the Gentile educational reforms of the following year gave increased importance to the role of physical education in schools as part of a wider militarizing of Italian society to create the young fascist citizen-soldier of the future. In these early years physical culture seemed to have triumphed over sport, which patriarchal fascist policy backed up by Catholicism feared might encourage women to resist the imposition of a submissive maternal role. In 1928 the Carta dello Sport marked a change of direction towards an appreciation of the role of sport in international relations which was in turn part of a wider fascist constitutional revolution, which disbanded parallel sports organizations and concentrated overall control in the CONI, ostensibly the Italian Olympic body but in reality the tool of the fascist State run by party bureaucracy.

There followed a process of 'sportification' by which fascist physical education was increasingly infiltrated by competitive individual and team sports culminating in the enormous importance given to football (called *calcio* to minimize the British connection and stress its ancient origins as an Italian game). The Fascist Party identified the Olympics as a major forum to display the new energy of the fascist State. As part of this drive for physical dominance the fascists were very anxious to beat England at football, especially after their victory in the World Cup in 1934. The clash of these two countries in the Battle of Highbury in 1934 forges a link with Holt's paper, pointing up the striking differences between the liberal and fascist approach to sport. The British government stayed out of the sporting sphere whilst Mussolini operated in exactly the opposite fashion, openly advocating sport as 'the expression of fascist dynamism'. His personal feelings and the party line swiftly changed to limited contact with friendly powers after the imposition of League of Nations sanctions over the invasion of Abyssinia. This politicized promotion of international sport was accompanied by extensive exploitation of the new technology of radio and use of the press-organs that were likewise pressed into service to justify the later policy of sporting 'self-sufficiency'.

Fascist Italy not only influenced German sport, arguably it had a greater and certainly more prolonged impact on Spain. British sports came to Spain via the aristocracy and established an exclusive image in the period before the First World War. Alphonse XIII took an active interest and supported Spain's candidature for the Olympics in 1924. With the overthrow of the monarch and the inauguration of the Republic in 1931, Spain's politics polarized, the government shifting to the Left, opposing Spain's participation in the Berlin Olympics of 1936 and supporting an international socialist proposal for a People's Olympics in Barcelona; this attracted a very large entry but was ruined when that Civil War broke out on 18 July 1936 – a day before the Games were due to begin. The Civil War paralysed civilian social life and when Franco emerged victorious he signed a decree in February 1941, which handed over the running of Spanish sport to the National Sports Delegation of the Traditionalist Falange and of the JONS (National Syndicate of Offensive Juntas). This body tried to put in place a corporate Mussolini style sports policy but was consistently denied resources – the Spanish Right would not put enough money or energy into sport to produce results – and failed to make any international impact, especially at the Olympics.

They had great success, however, in the other half of the sports project derived from Mussolini's Italy: the drive to create a world-class football team. Not an international team but a club side that would take advantage of the new opportunities for international football in the post Second World War era. Real Madrid represented Franco's Spain superbly, taking Europe by storm, recruiting some of the greatest players of the age like Kopa and di Stefano, who were for the first time seen across Europe on television in their 'royal' all-white strips. Every schoolboy knew Real Madrid, a new kind of phenomenon – the state-run commercial club whose income from sales could be topped up by the state to ensure the best performance. The European Cup, where Real Madrid had had its greatest triumphs, winning the first five titles, included the famous 7–3 victory over Eintracht Frankfurt in Glasgow in 1960 that many consider to be the greatest club game ever played. But, as the Franco camp discovered, soccer could also become a focus for rival 'national' claims within the state, especially with the rise to world prominence of Barcelona and its intimate attachment to the cause of Catalan nationalism and of Bilbao to the Basque cause. Football emerged as a major form of cultural resistance to the regime as well as a source of international and ideological support for it.

If Spanish sport was for much of the century the prisoner of Spanish internal politics, so the wider international movements that affected sports between the wars were similarly internally divided and dominated by national interests. If Spain was the successor of an interwar sports politics of the Right, Russia, which made up the core of the new Soviet Union, pioneered a leftist international approach. Yet both in the end followed a similar line, seeking to maximize the propaganda value of international sport for the good of the State. The most striking indication of the interwar internationalization of sport, in fact, comes from the new communist system. Here the contribution of Riordan and Gounot together provide a valuable and complementary insight into the problem of sport as a national and an international movement; sport as diplomacy and sport as ideology. Riordan sets sport in the wider context of the evolution of the Soviet regime from a revolutionary internationalist force to a more inward looking self-protecting State structure. Here is the classic view of the evolution of the USSR from Bolshevik insurrection to 'Socialism in one country', from the popular front against fascism to the opportunistic pact with Hitler on the eve of war which brought the Soviets briefly into the Nazi ambit and promoted sporting relations as Hitler invaded Poland and declared war on liberal democracies.

Gounot has taken advantage of the new access to former Soviet archives to fill out this picture, especially insofar as it relates to the setting up of an international communist sporting movement: the Red Sport International (RSI). Neither Riordan nor Gounot are mainly concerned with going over again in detail how the wave of insurrection in Europe at the end of the war divided the worker sports movement not the social-democratic element based in Lucerne and the Communists in Moscow operating through the Comintern. Gounot gives particular attention to the extent to which the Red Sport International acted independently of the power structure of the Soviet Union itself. Was this body a distinctive part of the Comintern or little more than an extension of Soviet foreign and sports policy? Although the RSI was set up as an auxiliary body to the Comintern in 1921 with the task of bringing together the communist sports movements mainly in other European states, it was in reality strongly influenced by the Soviet Union from the start.

The Soviet Union itself was obviously by far and away the largest member of the RSI. As the declared purpose of the Soviet Union was to foster the class struggle throughout the world and this too was the object of other Comintern bodies, it was easy for the Soviet Union to pass off its particular 'national' interests as part of a wider ideological struggle. Worker sport elsewhere in Europe was a minority phenomenon trying to challenge 'bourgeois' sport and the role of the Church. But in the Soviet Union sport found itself in the first workers' state with quite different needs and priorities. Despite the view of the RSI and Comintern that sports encounters should be restricted to workers, both Gounot and Riordan stress how the Soviets were ready to accommodate non-communist teams from neighbouring states where the bourgeoisie was seen to be useful or play a progressive anticolonial role. Hence the USSR played a 'bourgeois' team from Turkey simply because the Soviet Union had signed a treaty with Turkey in 1925. This placed the

Red Sport International in a tricky ideological position exposing its contradictions as an ostensibly international body but depending almost entirely on support from Moscow. Despite the Treaty of Rapallo between the two outsiders of post-Versailles Europe, there had been few significant sporting contacts. That Red sport was really a creature of Soviet diplomacy became crystal clear with the creation of the popular front against fascism. Here the international body meekly followed the national needs of the Soviet Union following to the letter the abrupt shift in Soviet foreign policy that came in 1934. The final proof of Soviet manipulation of the RSI came in 1937 with its closure by the Soviet government when anti-bourgeois agitation was deemed no longer useful to Soviet foreign policy.

If Communist sport was in reality an arm of Soviet foreign policy, there were other international developments less obviously determined by the needs of individual states. The Worker Sport International was, of course, backed up by the strong Weimar socialist party but it had a significant French and Belgian element with a Workers' Olympiad in Antwerp in 1937. However, it was the Catholics who probably came closest to providing an international framework of sport despite fascist hostility towards separate Catholic structures. This topic, the full international dimensions of which still await their historian, was explored in the Belgian context by Tolleneer. The Catholic gymnastics movement was begun in 1894 and grew initially out of the need to combat the role of the liberal state-supported Fédération Belge de Gymnastique, and in 1904 a Belgian socialist sports organization was also set up. Catholic gymnastics was largely urban as it was in the larger cities that the challenge from the liberals and from the socialists in the recruitment of the young was strongest. Similar bodies sprang up in France and in central Europe, notably the Orel movement in Czechoslovakia. Orel arose out of the need for a Catholic nationalist gymnastic movement to challenge the role of the more famous Sokols, which promoted a paramilitary Czech nationalism from the secular perspective. Belgian Catholic interest in Orel was striking and offers an unusual perspective on the increasing internationalization of sport, including gymnastics.

As part of an effort to coordinate these different Catholic gymnastic bodies and to organize international festivals – some of which were very large indeed – the Federation Internationale Catholique de l'Education Physique (FICEP) was set up in 1913. Belgian Catholic gymnasts had participated before then in various international initiatives, the largest of which was the huge festival in Rome in 1908 to celebrate the fiftieth anniversary of the ordination of Pius X as a priest. It was appropriate that Belgian Catholics should have been prominent in making international contacts for it was their rival body led by Cupérus, the pioneer of Belgian gymnastics, who had taken the lead in forming the secular Fédération Européenne de Gymnastique – anther potential research topic. Belgian Catholics wanted to show that they could be similarly active on the international scene and the Catholic Church in any case was by nature supranational. Apart from Belgium and Czechoslovakia, France was important in FICEP as well as the Netherlands, Italy and Austria. In Germany Die Deutsche Jugendkraft was set up by the Catholics under the Weimar Republic and was strongly involved in physical exercise.

However, after the Nazi take-over and the process of 'integration', inevitably this body was closed down and its functions assumed by the totalitarian state sports movement. The fortunes of this 'Catholic International' seem a promising topic for future research.

In 'Towards a Theory of Olympic Internationalism', Hoberman has recently located international sport in the context of *fin de siècle* utopian internationalism. [3] He stresses the ideological roots of sport – and of Olympism in particular – in a shared ideal of male heroism, which involved idealized visions of the athletic male body from Greek legend through medieval chivalry to the present. There was, as he notes, a widespread male mythology of the chivalric warrior fighting for his country in the trenches or on the track, dear to the Right but shared also by many liberal amateurs. [4,5 ] This bound together much international sport, the study of which, as he says, has been neglected. In particular, this made cooperation between the IOC and the Nazis much easier. Carl Diem, as Guttmann notes, and arguably de Coubertin too, despite their scholarship and cosmopolitan sporting interests, were steeped in a kind of conservative nationalism expressed in the idea of the purity and beauty of sport. It was this that some leftists, as Riordan and Gounot observe, denounced as 'bourgeois' or 'militarist and imperialist' sport. However, they had abruptly to revise that view in the face of the evident purposes behind Nazi sport, making common cause with the democratic states until the volte-face of 1939, which revealed that their own 'alternative' proletarian vision was much the same as the fascist agenda. For, if most liberal athletes adopted the rhetoric of nationalism and sacrifice to some extent, the heroic masculinities of British and French athletes turned out to be a lot less threatening than the fascist variety. The common physical and emotional processes of sport turned out to be less important than its specific national traditions and diplomatic context.

## References

1. Polley, Martin (1991) *The Foreign Office and International Sport 1918–1948*. St David's College, University of Wales, Ph.D. thesis, May 1991, chap. 2.
2. Polley, *op. cit.* The Foreign Office and International Sport, p. 41 (citing FO 371/3647/196763, Minute of 10 May 1920).
3. Hoberman, John (1995) Towards a Theory of Olympic Internationalism. *Journal of Sport History*, 22, (1) Spring, 1–37.
4. For example, (1995) Duty unto Death: English Masculinity and Militarism in the Age of the New Imperialism, in J.A. Mangan (ed.), *Tribal Identities: Nationalism, Europe, Sport*, (London: Cass), pp. 10–38.
5. Holt, R., Mangan, J.A. and Lanfranchi, P. (eds) (1996) *European Heroes: Myth, Identity, Sport* (London: Cass).

# Index